*Culture and
Political Economy
in Western Sicily*

STUDIES IN SOCIAL DISCONTINUITY

Under the Consulting Editorship of:

CHARLES TILLY   EDWARD SHORTER
University of Michigan   *University of Toronto*

William A. Christian, Jr. Person and God in a Spanish Valley

Joel Samaha. Law and Order in Historical Perspective: The Case of Elizabethan Essex

John W. Cole and Eric R. Wolf. The Hidden Frontier: Ecology and Ethnicity in an Alpine Valley

Immanuel Wallerstein. The Modern World-System: Capitalist Agriculture and the Origins of the European World-Economy in the Sixteenth Century

John R. Gillis. Youth and History: Tradition and Change in European Age Relations 1770 – Present

D. E. H. Russell. Rebellion, Revolution, and Armed Force: A Comparative Study of Fifteen Countries with Special Emphasis on Cuba and South Africa

Kristian Hvidt. Flight to America: The Social Background of 300,000 Danish Emigrants

James Lang. Conquest and Commerce: Spain and England in the Americas

Stanley H. Brandes. Migration, Kinship, and Community: Tradition and Transition in a Spanish Village

Daniel Chirot. Social Change in a Peripheral Society: The Creation of a Balkan Colony

Jane Schneider and Peter Schneider. Culture and Political Economy in Western Sicily

In preparation

Michael Schwartz. Radical Protest and Social Structure: The Southern Farmers' Alliance and Cotton Tenancy, 1880-1890

Dirk Hoerder. Crowd Action in Revolutionary Massachusetts, 1765-1780

Culture and Political Economy in Western Sicily

Jane Schneider

City University of New York
New York, New York

Peter Schneider

Fordham University
New York, New York

ACADEMIC PRESS   New York   San Francisco   London

A Subsidiary of Harcourt Brace Jovanovich, Publishers

For Ben and Julia

ACADEMIC PRESS, INC.
111 Fifth Avenue, New York, New York 10003

United Kingdom Edition published by
ACADEMIC PRESS, INC. (LONDON) LTD.
24/28 Oval Road, London NW1

Library of Congress Cataloging in Publication Data

Schneider, Jane.
    Culture and political economy in western Sicily.

    (Studies in social discontinuity series)
    Bibliography: p.
    Includes index.
    1.   Sicily—Economic conditions.   2.   Sicily—Social
conditions.   3.   Sicily—Social life and customs.
I.   Schneider, Peter,   Date   joint author.   II.   Ti-
tle.   III.   Series: Studies in social discontinuity.
HC307.S5S33   1975   309.1′458′209   76-18286
ISBN 0–12–627850–4

PRINTED IN THE UNITED STATES OF AMERICA

Contents

v

PART II
Sicily in a Postindustrial World-System

Preface

For many centuries Sicily, particularly western Sicily, exported wheat to foreign cities and imported manufactured goods; it served as a bread basket for expanding metropolies in Italy and Spain. In the nineteenth century, however, on the great plains of the United States and elsewhere, technological change revolutionized wheat production with the result that Sicilian wheat ceased to be competitive in foreign markets. Since 1900, in place of wheat Sicily has exported people—millions of migrants in search of work in foreign economies. The nineteenth century, 1860, also marked the unification of Italy, and Sicily's incorporation into a national state. Partly in response to the imminent presence of state institutions and partly in response to the decline of wheat, local cliques—or mafias—formed to protect the interests of those who controlled the large estates on which wheat was produced in rotation with pasturage: principally rentiers, brokers, and those who owned livestock.

This book is about the relationship between the early colonial period (during which Sicily exported wheat and animal products) and a later neocolonial period (during which manpower is the principal energy loss). It traces the rise and development of mafia to these conditions. In addition, it analyzes cultural codes which are especially salient to contemporary social organization—codes which celebrate honor, cleverness, and friendship. We seek the origins of these codes in early adaptations of the Sicilian people to externally generated political and economic forces, and suggest that similar codes may have played similar roles in other pre-nineteenth-century colonial regions. In other words, like emigration and mafia, culture is held to be the product of determinant historical processes—processes of dominance, subordination, and local reactions to dominance in relations between Sicily and more powerful populations, going back hundreds of years.

The emphasis that we place on Sicily's early and continuing dependency vis à vis outsiders will be familiar to those who have already encountered Immanuel Wallerstein's *The Modern World-System* (1974). Wallerstein uses the concepts "core" and "periphery" to describe relationships between the various regions of Europe as they developed from the mid-fifteenth century. In particular, his analysis of Poland—which was also a wheat-exporting peripheral region—helped us to clarify our own understanding of western Sicily. Yet we did not have the benefit of his work until 1974, and were led to a similar "world-system" perspective by a somewhat different route, namely as a consequence of anthropological field work conducted in western Sicily from 1965 to 1967 and again during the summers of 1968 and 1971.

We did not begin our field work with that perspective. Our initial intent was to examine the structures through which peasant communities are articulated with the nation–state. Yet we soon discovered the importance of labor migration and the ways in which it connected our field site not only to the state, but to an international labor market as well. Almost everyone we met told us of their emigrant relatives in Australia, Argentina, Venezuela, Canada, Chicago, Brooklyn, and in all the countries of western Europe. For many, ties to *Brookolino* were as significant as ties to Rome.

We also soon discovered the importance of the past. The history of western Sicily is etched in the eroded and deforested mountains, in the architecture of the hillside towns, in the barren quality of uninhabited valleys once dominated by large estates, and in the proverbs and parables of the people. Above all, it was the people who impressed upon us their poignant sense of their own place in space and time, and the forces of history which had brought them there. This was manifest in the parish priest who talked about "our late noblemen and their charitable works"; in the reminiscence of a contemporary baron who traced the vicissitudes of his family's vast holdings; and in the Communist peasant who explained at length the consequences of such holdings for peasant land tenure. Indeed, the people themselves insisted that we put the island's predicament in a world geopolitical and historical perspective. They were truly our collaborators and not our subjects.

Acknowledgments

We are grateful for the support of several institutions and many individuals. We received financial assistance from the University of Michigan Project for the Study of Social Networks in the Mediterranean Area; the Ford Foundation Foreign Area Fellowship Program (a grant to Jane Schneider); the City University of New York Urban Studies Program; the Fordham University Faculty Research Council (a grant to Peter Schneider); and the City University of New York Faculty Research Award Program (a grant to Jane Schneider).

Eric Wolf's early encouragement, his visit to us in the field, his own work, and his criticism of ours were indispensable to the project from beginning to end. Wolf must also be counted among those teachers at the University of Michigan in the early 1960s who effectively resisted the narrowing of intellectual horizons which accompanied the growing disciplinary specialization in social science. Pursuing degrees outside of anthropology (Jane Schneider in political theory, Peter Schneider in social psychology), yet drawn to the research strategy of ethnography and the study of peasant society, we were the beneficiaries of this resistance. Others who contributed breadth to our intellectual perspective were James Meisel in political science, Amos Hawley and Morris Janowitz in sociology, Daniel Katz in social psychology, and Marshall Sahlins in anthropology.

People whose good advice and guidance helped prepare us for field work and for Sicily were Jeremy Boissevain, Constance Cronin, Leonard Moss, William Schorger, and Tullio Tentori. Annabella Rossi was especially kind to us on several occasions in Rome. In Sicily, first and foremost there was Pasquale Marchese, publisher, connoisseur and collector of books, and a cherished friend to many students of the island. He was an invaluable source of knowledge, introductions, good fellowship, and level-headed advice and his contribution to our work has been enormous, We are grateful to Professor Gabrielo Morello of ISIDA, and Professors Carmelo Schifani and Antonino Simetti of the Faculty of Agriculture of the University of Palermo, who put the libraries and other resources of their institutions at our disposal. We also remember with pleasure our visits with Professor Giuseppe Montalbano of the University of Palermo, and Danilo Dolci and his co-workers at the *Centro Studi* in Trapetto.

Anton Blok of the University of Nijmegen, The Netherlands, was already engaged in field work in Sicily when we arrived there in 1965. We met him during our first days in Palermo (at Marchese's of course), and shortly afterward settled to do our work in a town not far from his. We were often together during the succeeding year and a half, talking about our mutual interests. It is difficult to express our gratitude and respect for his collegial friendship. Blok also read and carefully criticized an early manuscript of this book.

As consulting editor for the "Studies in Social Discontinuity Series," Charles Tilly provided a detailed analysis of the manuscript which was the inspiration and guide for its final revision. Rod Aya and F. G. Bailey also read it and made many useful comments. Colleagues who read our work and contributed many suggestions were Jeremy Beckett, Ernestine Friedl, Edward Hansen, Shirley Lindenbaum, Mervyn Meggitt, Joyce Riegelhaupt, Roger Sanjek, and Sydel Silverman. Laura Nicolosi accompanied us to Sicily during the summer of 1971 as a research assistant. Nicola Scafidi of Palermo offered several of his excellent photographs as illustrations, including the photo that appears on the book jacket. Robert Glasse also helped reproduce photographs and taught us an effective method of notation for transcribing geneaologies. And, although we have never met them, we wish to acknowledge our debt to Denis Mack Smith for his valuable two-volume history of Sicily (1968a; 1968b), and to E. J. Hobsbawm whose book, *Primitive Rebels* (1959), first stimulated our interest in the region.

To protect the privacy of the many Sicilians who let us participate in their lives we have used pseudonyms for the towns and people of the immediate region in which we worked. We have also altered some details of the illustrative examples to make it difficult to identify the individuals involved. Everywhere in Sicily we were struck by the generosity, warmth, and hospitality of the good people who live there. Were it not for our respect for their privacy, we would thank them by name.

chapter 1

Introduction

As the industrial revolution transformed world markets in the nineteenth century, it altered the economic division of labor between populations throughout the world and intensified relations of dominance and subordination among them. Peripheral regions like western Sicily, which is the subject of this book, brought their own many-faceted social existence to this rapidly changing geopolitical environment. Competing local interest groups confronted the new forces, drawing on their resources and power within the region, and in some cases on their long-standing connections to external centers of power and influence as well. In western Sicily, the emergent field contained two events of great significance—a shift in the island's major export from wheat to unskilled labor, and the rise of mafia. Both contributed to persistent economic underdevelopment.

Scholars and others concerned with underdevelopment often link it to the presumably reactionary and traditional qualities of peasant culture. In our view, such cultural determinism is incorrect, yet it is seductive. One does indeed find that people continue to appeal to many age-old ideas about proper behavior and the nature of reality. In the course of anthropological study in a west Sicilian agricultural community we identified three cultural codes as particularly interesting and salient. The code of family honor (*onore*) asserts the primacy of the nuclear family in society and establishes women as symbols of familial worth. The code of friendship (*amicizia*) and hospitality helps solidify the omnipresent coalitions and cliques through which business affairs and other ventures are conducted. *Furberia,* the code of cleverness or astuteness, focuses on the individual and his immediate family, and helps legitimate the idea that almost anything goes in defense of one's personal interests. "Better a devil with a pocket full of money than a fool with five cents" is a well-known Sicilian proverb.

All of these codes have in one way or another been associated with the rise of mafia; all have been blamed for the failure of agrarian and industrial reform programs which, had they been successful, would have stemmed the migration of unskilled labor. Local as well as foreign observers frequently attribute the island's economic difficulties to the codes in question, noting, for example, that preoccupation with family honor undermines the kind of trust that is necessary to collective organization for long-term gain, while friendship and cleverness rationalize foul play and corruption. We see these codes, however, in another light. We intend that this volume should provide a clear case for a different understanding of the role of culture in change, and that it should do this by demonstrating (1) that exogenous colonial and neo-colonial forces have had an overwhelming impact on Sicily, not only in the recent past but also over centuries, and (2) that the cultural codes at issue were instruments of adaptation to these secular forces, and not simply residua of a "traditional" preindustrial past.

WORLD FORCES OF THE PRESENT

Few people today doubt that the world is integrated through relationships of great inequality among different regions. Through a geographical division of labor, some regions or areas specialize in the export of unskilled labor, foodstuffs, or raw materials. Other areas receive labor and primary products and export manufactured goods as well as food. The latter areas are economically most developed. Great gaps in power and living standard divide the two types, as they divide social classes within each. How to reduce these inequalities or, from the point of view of the rich and powerful, how to maintain them against the opposition they inevitably create is the engrossing political issue of our time.

To overcome underdevelopment means to cease exchanging labor and primary products at a loss, in return for other people's manufactures. This may require doing without or substituting for imported commodities or services, at least temporarily. It may mean that primary producers will seriously attempt to control their own commerce, to "extort" a greater return on the export of critical resources. Because powerholders of the industrial societies often resist such challenges to the world division of labor, development almost always presupposes a degree of deliberate closure in which, through economic policy and militant ideology—perhaps also through military action—the underdeveloped society severs ties with certain international labor or commodity markets. Such closure usually requires strong central government and "socialist" restrictions on the private sector, particularly that portion of it—the landowners and mine owners—which earlier profited from the export of primary products. The government of a society that is open to foreign influence is extremely weak in relation to this sector (see Seers 1970).

In the light of such considerations, we have found it useful to distinguish between processes of *modernization* and processes of *development,* both of which involve growth and change, but of a quite different sort.[1] Societies that modernize in the absence of economic development are vulnerable to the ideologies and life-styles of industrial metropolitan centers, as well as to their manufactures and capital. But it is unlikely that modernizing societies will undergo any effective increase in their own productive capacity which would place them in serious competition with the more advanced centers upon which they are dependent. A modernizing society may experience rapid and marked social change, but it does not control or direct it.

A developing society, by contrast, attempts to withdraw, at least partially, from the influence of advanced metropolitan centers in order to create a more diversified economy and exert greater control over its own natural and human resources. Successful development leads to increased productive capacity and an improved rate of

[1] These concepts were first elaborated in an article we wrote together with Edward Hansen (Schneider, Schneider, and Hansen 1972). They were influenced by, and closely parallel, the works of Frank (1969), Geertz (1968), Seers (1970), and Stein and Stein (1970). We are aware that, as we outline them here, the expansion of multinational corporations, with its accompanying decentralization of industrial production, renders them in some respects obsolete.

foreign exchange. However, since the process of development involves an initial period of retrenchment in an attempt to accumulate capital and end the dominance of foreign imports, it may be slow to yield advances in such conventional growth indexes as standard of living, percentage of the population engaged in nonagricultural pursuits, and gross production. On the other hand, a modernizing society, its privileged classes in particular, may demonstrate dramatic change in these factors. Such change, however, is highly responsive to changing market conditions and recession in the dominant foreign centers. Modernization is the fruit of contact between rich regions and poor regions; although it may be to the mutual advantage of certain interests in both, it maintains the basic relation of superordination and subordination between them.

Consistent with the distinction between modernization and development is a parallel distinction between types of political leadership group—in modernizing societies a *dependence elite* has a vested interest in continued subordination to foreign powerholders; in developing (or would-be developing) societies a *development elite* advocates severing connections, or altering connections, with international markets in the interests of economic diversification and greater autonomy. Although the interests and goals of dependence and development elites are antithetical, both types of elite may exist in the same place at the same time, competing for control over political institutions and popular support. Given the realities of economic and political power in the twentieth century, however, the advantage usually lies with the dependence elite. In particular, a development elite is unlikely to succeed where a dominant foreign power mobilizes economic or military sanctions against it; where no transportation infrastructure exists to move food quickly and efficiently from the hinterland into indigenous (rather than foreign) cities; and where the internal class structure reflects strong support for the export of primary products (Keyfitz 1965). Development impulses are most unlikely where indigenous intellectuals, professionals, and businessmen are loyal clients of propertied classes which in turn have a vested interest in the perpetuation of dependency. Under these conditions some sectors of the propertyless masses, even those who have been displaced by industrial imperialism, may find continued dependency a more plausible option than futile attempts at development (that is, if they find any options at all in the situation).

Applying to Sicily the distinction between dependence and development elites, one is struck by the virtual absence of development elite formation over the past 150 years, a period during which changes in the world economy have shaken most societies to the core.

Rather, successive regional political leaders have been content to perpetuate, or unable to stop, the drain of basic energy resources from
the island. Since about the turn of the century one of Sicily's most
important exportable resources has been unskilled labor. From the
late 1800s until the early 1920s, thousands of Sicilians left to seek work
in America; since World War II thousands more have gone to
northern Europe. Emigration remittances, sent home by these migrant
workers, make possible an increasingly modern way of life:
motorcycles and automobiles, appliances and store-bought clothing,
television sets, radios, and high school diplomas, new roads, new
stores, new office buildings, even new kinds of food. But this new
standard of living is costly in two ways. First, there are the sacrifices
inevitably associated with emigration—families and communities
deprived of a large proportion of their young men, and young men
who must travel long distances and live for long periods away from
their families and communities. Second, the new life-style is based
upon the widespread consumption of other people's manufactures.
Through it all, Sicily remains incapable of expanding employment
opportunities in industry or agriculture at home. And, to the extent
that the Sicilian economy is based upon remittance monies, the island
is vulnerable in a particular way: A serious recession in northern
Europe will manifest itself in the layoff of "guest laborers," whose
return home will coincide with the breakdown of the remittance
system and widespread unemployment in the service occupations that
depend upon that system (house construction, retail sales, etc.). With
no autonomy and little leverage in export markets, many Sicilians
realistically fear that their new living standard, so recently acquired at
such great sacrifice, is in danger of collapse.[2]

THE MYTH OF TRADITION

How did Sicily become vulnerable in this way? The answer lies
partly in the incredible power generated by foreign metropolitan
centers since the industrial transformation, which brought about new
technologies of communication, transportation, and production, mak-

[2] Economists might object that we apply to regions criteria that are appropriate
for much larger and more complex units only—nation-states or even supranational consortia. We are not here attempting to describe the conditions for heavy industrial
development, however, but rather the process by which a geographically localized
society might establish a somewhat more equitable position for itself vis-à-vis external
dominants. Regions, no less than nations, may be units of development in this sense.

ing it ever more difficult for Sicilian producers to compete in world markets. But the answer also lies in the interplay of social groups and their vested interests which occurred in Sicily in the nineteenth and early twentieth centuries. These groups, the product of a much earlier and longer colonial history, were not traditional—if traditional means stable, enduring, precapitalist, noncompetitive, primary, ascriptive, and the like. Because the word *traditional* usually conveys these meanings it is misleading here; for Sicily was part of vast systems of economic specialization and exchange at least as far back as the Roman Empire. Throughout most of this history the island, and particularly its western region, exported grain and imported cloth and clothing manufactured abroad. Sicily has long been involved in world trade, and the effects of this involvement do great violence to common assumptions about pre-nineteenth-century agrarian—so-called traditional—societies.

In a recent book that goes a long way toward establishing this important point, Immanuel Wallerstein analyzed the emergence of the capitalist world-system in the sixteenth century and forcefully documented its geographic division of labor (1974). He draws our attention to the gross inequalities that emerged between areas that exported primary products and those that exported manufactures. The core of the system was in Europe, first Mediterranean, then northwestern Europe. The populations of Asia and Africa remained external to it, in world-systems or enclaves of their own, but western Europe's periphery, or colonial hinterland, embraced Spanish America and eastern Europe. Even though such a vast and complex system was not world*wide*, Wallerstein suggests we call it a "world-system." Indeed, he uses this concept for any economic entity that transcends the boundaries of particular regional and national societies and integrates a variety of disparate activities over many parts of the globe (see also Verlinden 1970).

Within the European world-system of the sixteenth century, the interdependence of the various parts was no less crucial than it is today, such that then, as now, the development of some areas and the underdevelopment or "de-development" of others went hand in hand (Frank 1969). The system then, as now, rewarded skilled labor and capital accumulation but everywhere exploited unskilled labor. Also then, as now, exploited regions often attempted to resist, their protest aimed at economic closure and autonomy. Such resistance to the hegemony of industrial centers could sometimes result in genuine development, so that some peripheral areas became core areas and others—once industrial—declined. In general, however, as Wallerstein emphasizes, the tendency of the world-system was to maintain an established division of labor, with its geographic maldistribution of tasks and rewards, over long periods of time.

Once one recognizes the existence of such world-systems as early as the sixteenth century (and earlier), it becomes impossible to lump all preindustrial social groups under the single heading "traditional." Generally useful labels like "feudal lord," "landed aristocracy," "rising bourgeoisie," and "peasantry" tell us little about important variations from region to region and offer an insufficient guide to the specific interests of these groups at any given place and time.

Sicily is a case in point. Exporting wheat under several past empires, it still bears the imprint of its colonial history. Especially in the west of the island, specialization in wheat led to great latifundia, large estates, on which wheat was raised in rotation with natural pastures. This export-oriented monocrop economy, with its associated patterns of land tenure and settlement, was accompanied by the rise of certain social groups. These included a market-oriented dependence elite composed of great latifundist lords, for the most part descendants of the colonial adventurers who migrated to Sicily from northern Italy and Spain; a feeble noncommercial, nonindustrial urban bourgeoisie made up primarily of lawyers and clergymen who were followers of the latifundist lords and equally committed to foreign trade in wheat; peasants who farmed land under contracts of day labor, tenancy and especially sharecropping; pastoralists, under pressure from the spread of wheat over the land, but able to respond with violence and banditry; and finally the most significant group, rural entrepreneurs who would ultimately supplant the feudal lords. Very different from the urban bourgeois entrepreneurs of industrializing northern Europe, these were the estate superintendents, chief herders, carters, and others who played key roles in the organization of the latifundia. At home in the countryside as well as in the towns and cities, this group had as its major base of operations the *massaria,* the social and administrative headquarters of the large estate. Here the pastoral and agrarian economies of the latifundium were articulated. Because of their close relationship to the *massaria* and its associated complex of activities, rural entrepreneurs had contacts which the rest of the population, whether rich or poor, did not have. These contacts provided the protection, hospitality, and sustenance without which travel and commerce in the countryside would have been difficult, if not impossible.

Their strategic relationship to the *massaria* complex and their geographic mobility enabled Sicily's rural entrepreneurs to organize and control the initial movement of commodities into export markets.

They, too, supported the specialization in wheat associated with pastoralism. In other words, rural entrepreneurs were a decisive obstacle to the rise of a development elite oriented toward diversification of agriculture and regional autonomy. But nothing in the concept "traditional" would account for either their influence or their conservatism since both were derived from activities that tied them to a world economy. Without foreign demand for Sicilian wheat and animal products the *massaria* would not have existed, and it would not have provided a vehicle for the accumulation of capital by rural entrepreneurs.

Part II of this book examines in detail the role of the rural entrepreneurs in the unification of Italy in 1860, and Sicily's first encounter with postindustrial imperialism. After 1860, the newly formed state was controlled by various segments of the north Italian industrial bourgeoisie. This class had to mobilize the resources of the nation in the service of north Italian industrial growth and in the process it had to come to grips with regional powerholders. In the resulting configuration of forces, Sicilian rural entrepreneurs emerged as a powerful vested interest—a force to be reckoned with and not displaced.

The encounter with postindustrial imperialism was disastrous for other social groups. Population grew rapidly, just as peasants' and herdsmen's rights to land were being expropriated. The period saw many uprisings and rebellions. But it also saw rural entrepreneurs crush this resistance through the use of force and allocation of patronage. Given the hard bargain they were able to drive with external powerholders, and given their middle position between landlords and peasants, rural entrepreneurs were ideally suited to *verticalize* the regional society, such that conflict, structured along lines of great patron–client chains led by bosses, was greater within than across class lines.

The result was continued peripheral status in the world-system, always qualified by that measure of autonomy which could be won from bargaining with outsiders. Frustrated peasant rebellion and entrenched dependency paved the way for Sicily to specialize in a new export commodity; hundreds of thousands of unemployed and underemployed laborers who would migrate in search of work.

THE RISE OF MAFIA

That the rural entrepreneurs of Sicily were a powerful vested interest is demonstrated most clearly by the rise of mafia, a phenomenon which crystallized over the nineteenth century in the western part of the island where a grain-exporting colonial economy had long been dominant and rural entrepreneurs were numerous and successful. Here entrepreneurs were both favored and pressured by the industrial development of northern Italy and the associated expansion of nationwide state institutions. They were favored because the state, needing their support, supplied them with protection and patronage, which in turn sustained their power on the local level. But they were also under pressure because the unification and industrialization of Italy threatened to render them obsolete. Mafia originated as an organizational and ideological response to these conditions, of power on the one hand and pending obsolescence on the other. By neutralizing the police and the judiciary it protected a wide range of business interests that depended for profit, at least partly, on illegal acts including the use, threat, or implied threat of violence. Most, if not all, of the first mafiosi were rural entrepreneurs.

This book is not primarily about mafia, although an explanation of its origins and distribution is inevitably an important part of our discussion. Our readers are also urged to explore Anton Blok's recent book on a Sicilian mafia which treats the subject in considerably greater detail. Blok's understanding of mafia is similar to ours; indeed, we conducted research in the same part of western Sicily and have been much influenced by him. There is, however, a difference in emphasis between his work and ours. For Blok, mafiosi are primarily peasant entrepreneurs-cum-political middlemen or power brokers. They bridge and exploit the gap between local and national levels of the government, controlling "paths linking the infrastructure of the village to the superstructure of the larger society [1974: 7]." They are also armed and can use physical violence with impunity. According to Blok, it was the prior isolation and marginality of Sicily which led armed entrepreneurs to assume a number of statelike functions, on the basis of which they were later powerful enough to block or arrest the penetration of Sicily by modern state institutions. Above all, their initial power derived from the fact that they policed a rebellious and bandit-ridden countryside on behalf of the landed class.

Blok's peasant entrepreneurs are the same as our rural entrepreneurs, with the distinction that we found a more pastoral than peasant bias in their backgrounds. In addition, our work treats these figures as businessmen whose political activities are secondary and, like the politicking of businessmen everywhere, designed to protect vested economic interests. Blok, in contrast, stresses their political role. In other words, he finds mafia somewhat comparable to a state. Like a state it controls the means of violence for a given territory, keeps law and order in the countryside, and skims off protection money as if it were collecting taxes. Yet unlike a state, as Charles Tilly notes in his preface to Blok's book, mafiosi have no visibility and are accountable to no one (1974: xix). The present treatment compares mafia to private enterprise, rather than to government (see Chapter 9). Its low visibility and nonaccountability thus fall into place, for these are characteristic of the private sector. What is unusual is that as private entrepreneurs mafiosi organize their own instruments of coercion, independent of and apart from the state's. Since this is illegal, they must invest heavily in strategies that will save them from arrest and conviction.

Blok's thesis that peasant entrepreneurs were so powerful to begin with because Sicily was isolated and had a weak central government interestingly reflects the primacy of the political framework in his thinking. In economic terms, the weakness of the central authority in pre-nineteenth-century Sicily was the consequence not of isolation—of "relative local and regional self-sufficiency"—but of engagement, because the region was the bread basket of an integrated world economy. Viewed in this way, pre-nineteenth-century Sicily gave rise to powerful (rural) entrepreneurs because such figures were critical to the emergence of international capitalism.

BROKER CAPITALISM

In order to shield their activities from the surveillance of the state, mafiosi exploited the cultural codes mentioned at the beginning of this chapter. The codes of honor, friendship, and cleverness are in fact fused in the mafia-linked ideology of *omertà,* according to which justice is a private, not a public, matter, and a man of honor will handle his own affairs without recourse to legally constituted authority. Because mafia has this ideological aspect, people are sometimes tempted to view it as the product of age-old cultural patterns peculiar to western Sicily. But this explanation (which Blok also would not accept) runs counter to Sicily's centuries-long history as an exporter of foodstuffs and her pivotal position in worldwide trade networks. Although in its origins mafia was specific to a particular geographical area, many aspects of the phenomenon had parallels in other parts of the world that were subjected to similar historical forces.

To facilitate the comparison, we shall introduce a new concept. The rural entrepreneurs characteristic of Sicily—its western region in particular—are the backbone of an economy we call *broker capitalism*. Broker capitalism differs from merchant, industrial, and finance capitalism in several important ways. Among these categories there is an implicit order, although they are not mutually exclusive and usually coexist. From broker to finance capitalism, the number of capitalists decreases while their power to accumulate surplus and make critical decisions vastly increases. Compared with the merchants, industrialists, and financiers of the metropolis, broker capitalists control only marginal assets, their most significant resource being their networks of personal contacts. This is not to say that metropolitan capitalists operate without such networks (or even that they utilize them less), but only that for them this asset is relatively less critical when compared with the ships, warehouses, factories, and banks they own. Because broker capitalists do not own assets of this sort, they do not make decisions that affect millions of people. Nevertheless, in the local arena they are a viable, full-fledged market force, with the capacity to promote or obstruct change within parameters set by the world-system.[3]

Broker capitalism flourishes at the periphery because core interests are unable, or do not choose, to monopolize and administer the local level activities connected with the production, marketing, and export of primary products. For this reason, it promotes short-term speculative investment, reflecting the uncertainties in which ultimate control over markets lies in the hands of unpredictable foreigners. It selects for those who are able—by structural position or personality—to seize opportunities, to engage in ad hoc creative planning, mobilizing friends and friends of friends to live, as it were, by their wits. "Better a devil than a fool." Finally, broker capitalism advances by means of short-term, fluid, egocentric coalitions, reinforced by friendship ties, rather than by the long-term corporate associations which organize commerce, industry, and finance in the metropolis. Friendship and *furberia* are broker capitalist codes.

One of the questions this book addresses is why broker capitalism seems pronounced in some underdeveloped areas and not in

---

[3] The concept "broker capitalist" subsumes the concepts "broker," "middleman," "mediator." Often these terms have been used to characterize men who link local to supralocal political structures (see Blok 1969b: 369). Although this usage does not preclude earning profits, we wanted a concept that emphasized profitmaking. For reasons discussed by Goubert (1967: 174–175), the concept "rural bourgeoisie" is inappropriate. Broker capitalists, like all entrepreneurs, organize themselves politically when it suits them. Under these conditions, the concept embraces a political as well as an economic meaning.

others. We think that populations which became colonial outposts for metropolitan centers in the Spanish Empire—in Sicily and southern Italy, Latin America (including Brazil under Portugal), and to some extent in the Philippines—reveal historical careers strongly influenced by its presence.[4] They, too, provide examples of failed peasant rebellions, coupled with strong vertical political structures based on patronage, *caciquismo,* or bossism, and violence. The reason for these similarities lies in the structure of the world-system forged by Spain in the sixteenth century and altered in subsequent centuries by the emerging hegemony of the North Atlantic core.

In many ways Spain's was an accidental empire with little power in relation to territory claimed. Its emperors were heavily financed by foreign capital: Flemish, south German, north Italian, and especially Genoese. Spain, although it "conquered" northern Italy, could also be considered a front for Italian imperialism, that is, not a true metropolitan core. It would have been difficult in those days to determine whether Spain dominated Italy, or Italy, Spain (Wallerstein 1974: 129, 173). Furthermore, the strength of the Spanish crown, its power within Spain, was intimately tied to a great pastoral enterprise, the *Mesta,* which Castilians organized in the late Middle Ages as they reconquered land from the Moors. This enterprise provided the Castilian kings with a very lucrative export, for in medieval and Renaissance Europe, wool was as oil is today—much in demand and difficult to obtain. Yet raw wool was nonetheless a commodity that could not guarantee its producers the wealth and power of exported manufactures. In addition, the *Mesta* contradicted industrial development and ruined the land for other forms of agriculture. The arid climate of Spain ensured that sheep would "eat men" and that, lacking an agrarian base for industrialism, no development elite would be strong enough to override the influence of wool exporters, close the economy, and shelter indigenous textiles. Even New World silver, so abundant in the late sixteenth century, could not—without closure—finance development. Silver flowed through Spain like sand through a sieve, as it was used to purchase commodities manufactured elsewhere.

What was the result? Unlike core areas before and since, Spain was hardly more industrial than its periphery. According to Elliot, its

---

[4] The Philippines was a part of the Spanish Empire, yet in some respects it resembled other Asian societies by remaining outside of, or external to, sixteenth-century capitalism (see Wallerstein 1974: 335–336). Its parallels with Sicily, although many and fascinating, lie beyond the scope of this volume.

economy was "closer in many ways to that of an East-European State like Poland, exporting basic raw materials and importing luxury products, than to the economies of West-European states [1967: 190]." Braudel provides another forceful image: "Philip II seems to me to have regularly found himself in the position of a 19th century South American government, rich in its production and its mines, or in its plantations, but disarmed all the more vis-à-vis international finance [1966: Vol. I, 464]." In this condition, Spain's principal exports went to more, rather than less, developed areas—a unique circumstance for an empire—and opportunists in her colonies found plenty of scope to serve and profit as brokers.

Wallerstein suggests another Spanish anomaly based on a distinction he makes between precapitalist and capitalist world-systems. The ancient, precapitalist empires extended administrative control to the boundaries of the area within which they claimed resources; they extracted primary products by demanding tribute. In contrast, metropolitan centers of the capitalist world-system limit political control to the nation-states of the core area and dominate their vast periphery economically, through the mechanism of the market. The modern world-system is an economic, not a political, entity. The state is "less the central economic enterprise than the means of assuring certain terms of trade in other (i.e., private) economic transactions [1974: 16]." Because it spends proportionately less for administrative and military personnel, the modern system "accumulates surplus more efficiently." Capitalism, in short, is a much more powerful form of dominance.

Spain forged the last political empire of the West, and it did so simultaneously with the growth of capitalist markets which accompanied the rise of a new core area in North Atlantic Europe. It is because of this fundamental contradiction, which persisted into the eighteenth century, that Spain's lax control mattered most. At the same time that it imposed itself politically and administratively over a vast domain, Spain became vulnerable to infiltration by the merchants, pirates, smugglers, and interlopers of the capitalist marketplace. The more these forces put the crown on the defensive, the more its administrative structure sagged—to the point that all boundary-maintaining regulations were circumvented and brokers got more rewards than did officials. Neither before nor since have broker capitalists fared so well. In the postindustrial colonies of North Atlantic Europe they were subordinate and interstitial. In places like Sicily, by contrast, they helped shape the regional culture and its future.

VILLAMAURA

The plan of our book is chronological. Part I seeks to establish the specialized role of Sicily in historical world-systems, to explain this role, and to examine its consequences for the economy, for the political and social structure, and for the cultural codes of the region. Part II concerns Sicily's confrontation with postindustrial imperialism in the nineteenth and twentieth centuries. We examine the fate of peasants in this encounter, as Sicily moved from exporting wheat to exporting human labor. Part II also contrasts peasants with herdsmen and rural entrepreneurs. The latter, by virtue of their relationship to the *massaria* complex and their particular economic activities, were in a better position than the peasants to resist the pressures of the postindustrial world and partially to turn new inputs to their own advantage. Their resistance ultimately culminated in mafia. Finally in Part II we describe and analyze the consequences of modernization without development and assess both persistence and change in cultural codes. A concluding chapter reaffirms the view that one cannot attribute underdevelopment to culture or character.

The analysis that follows is the product of 2 years (1965–1967) and 2 summers (1968 and 1971) of anthropological fieldwork in a west Sicilian community. It was this fieldwork which raised many questions about Sicily's past. For example, our interest in the origins of cultural codes derived from our observation of these codes in action. Similarly, it was only after we came to know several contemporary rural entrepreneurs that we began to speculate on the importance of similar figures in the late nineteenth century. The analysis of Sicily's confrontation with postindustrial imperialism, contained in Part II, draws on material found in the archives of the town in which we lived. In short, we are breaking with the standard community study format, with its history chapter in one place and its ethnography in another, in the belief that history and ethnography are interdependent elements in a single unified analysis.

The town we lived in is called Villamaura. This pseudonym is borrowed from Emanuele Navarro della Miraglia, a nineteenth-century resident of the town, who used it as a setting for his novel *La Nana* (1963). Villamaura has a population of approximately 7500, about average for settlements of the Sicilian interior, most of which contain 5000–10,000 people, although they might range in population from fewer than 2000 to upward of 50,000. (Villamaura's population peaked at 11,000 in the early twentieth century.) The town is located on a hill about 350 meters above sea level, near the southwest corner of the island, in the province of Agrigento. To the south and west is the coastal lowland zone; to the north and east, the territories of several mountain towns. In some respects Villamaura combines features of both the inland mountain towns and the coastal communities, although its ecology is most like that of the former. The town was very much a part of the latifundist interior—the zone that produced wheat on vast estates—but there is an admixture of more specialized farming characteristic of the lowland areas in recent decades. A national roadway connects Villamaura with the regional and provincial capitals (Palermo and Agrigento, respectively) and other towns as well, but the road is not in good repair and the trip to either capital takes over 2 hours (as of 1971).

Typical of west Sicilian settlements, Villamaura consists of a large densely settled and quasi-urban nucleus of houses, shops, and public buildings surrounded by a virtually uninhabited countryside. What is called the *comune* embraces both this settlement, where everyone lives, and the surrounding land, into which agricultural laborers, sharecroppers, and small landholders travel every day to earn their livelihood. One exception to this pattern is the herder, whose family lives in town, but who himself must spend most nights at the *massaria* or at an even more rustic shelter in the open countryside.

Villamaura is atypical of west Sicilian agrotowns in at least one respect. It has been administered since 1946 by a fairly stable coalition of left wing parties, dominated by the Communist party. Certain features of the local ecology and pattern of land use suggest why this is so. A relatively large belt of arable valley land around the town encouraged the rise of a proportionately larger group of propertied peasants than is found in most communities of the latifundist interior. We think that this group in turn supported a disproportionately large artisan category. In the nineteenth century, socialism took root among these artisans, and many of their descendants are among the most prominent leaders of the Socialist and Communist parties today in Villamaura. For several reasons we chose Villamaura as the focal point of our research in spite of its atypical political color (every town is atypical in some respect). It was the right size (5000–10,000 people) and located in the latifundist region that we wanted to study. Most important, a Palermitan friend, native to a nearby coastal city, knew the town well and could introduce us to the mayor, the archpriest, and several national political figures from the zone. He suggested, quite correctly it turned out, that these contacts could be of tremendous value to our research, as they would help to establish our legiti-

macy among the Villamauresi. In the midst of these careful calcula-
tions there was also an intangible reason—we were at first sight drawn
to the place and its people and just wanted to live there for awhile. It
turned out to be an excellent vantage point from which to conduct
the study of western Sicily described in the following chapters.

Preindustrial World-Systems

Land Use and Settlement in Historical and Geographical Perspective

The history of Sicily is a history of successive foreign conquerors: Greeks, Phoenecians, Romans, Byzantines, Saracens, Normans, Angevins, Catalans, Lombards, Spaniards, Frenchmen, Englishmen, Italians, Germans, and Americans. Important differences distinguish various periods of domination. During some, the island enjoyed relative autonomy from external centers of power, but most of the time it was very much an economic and sometimes a political appendage of a larger integrated system, exporting grain and animal products and importing manufactured commodities. Looking closely one discovers that the role of colonial appendage was unevenly played throughout Sicily; it was a much more significant feature of the western than of the eastern region. The different forms of relationship to external metropolitan centers explain a good deal about how people settled on the land in Sicily and about how the land was used. For, notwithstanding the natural parameters of the Mediterranean environment, different patterns of land use and settlement characterized different epochs of Sicilian history and also different regions of the island. The purpose of this chapter is to relate these differences in land use and settlement to the predominant roles which Sicily played in empires of the past. The outline with which the chapter begins focuses on the most decisive foreign influences; some of the many conquerors have been dropped for simplification.

SICILY'S ROLES IN HISTORICAL WORLD-SYSTEMS

Greek settlements in Sicily, dating from the eighth century B.C., were relatively independent of Athens. Their agricultural surplus supported the rise of cities on the island which, by the fifth century B.C., were pressing upon and Hellenizing the indigenous Neolithic population. Some of these cities were in western Sicily: Agrigento, Selinunte, Mazara, Segesta, and others. But these cities were established later and farther apart than the cities of the eastern coast and had less impact on the inhabitants of the interior. Syracuse, in the southeast, was by far the most important city, and eventually its rulers claimed tribute from most of the island.

The Greeks were followed by the Romans. Unlike the Greek colonists, who were driven from their homeland in search of land, the Romans came to extract and export an agricultural surplus. By introducing the large estate, or latifundium, by importing tax farmers to administer it and slaves to work it, Rome integrated Sicily into the periphery of its empire. The island, Cato said, was "the Republic's granary, the nurse at whose breast the Roman people is fed [quoted in Finley 1968: 123]." According to Finley, "the base of the Roman tribute system was one-tenth of the wheat and barley crop, paid in kind and shipped straight to Rome. . . . The grain tithe has been estimated at about . . . 825,000 bushels a year." In addition to the tithe, although only under special conditions, Sicilians were forced to sell grain to Rome at prices fixed by the Roman senate, and they were required to obtain a special license before exporting grain to any place other than Italy (Finley 1968: 123). Western Sicily bore the greatest burden. At first the eastern sector of the island remained independent, governed by Hiero, the emperor of Syracuse. Even after Roman rule had been extended to the entire island, more of the eastern cities remained outside the Roman tribute system, and the eastern cities supported the rebellion of Brutus and Cassius after Caesar's death. All of this suggests that the eastern cities were able to control their own local agricultural resources and that this most urbanized region of Sicily retained some degree of autonomy in the face of imperial pressures.

The Arab invasions of the late ninth century initiated another period of relative autonomy which lasted until the late Middle Ages. Arab settlement and control was most intense in western Sicily, but in any event the estimated 300,000 Arabs and Berbers (many of whom were victims of land shortage in North Africa) came to settle and farm the land, not to extract primary products for export to the metropolis. To the contrary, the Arabs vastly improved existing technologies of agricultural production and introduced a variety of new crops which could benefit from irrigation and skilled labor. Many of these new products received better returns than did wheat in external trade. Wheat exports continued, but wheat no longer dominated the economy, as it was supplemented by lemons, oranges, melons, sugar cane, silk, cotton, and rice. In addition, craftsmen in Sicily manufactured silk fabrics for export (de Planhol 1959: 63–64; Goitein 1967: 102). Nor was Sicily governed from abroad as it had been under Rome. After 948, Sicily's Islamic emirs founded their own hereditary dynasty in Palermo, its only link to Egypt being the formal homage paid upon investiture of the island by the caliph (Mack Smith 1968a: 9; Romano 1964: 133–134; Scaturro 1926: Vol. I, 165–166). If Wallerstein's distinction between precapitalist empires and the modern world-system is valid, Sicily's political independence under the Arabs can be taken as a measure of economic autonomy as well. (Today, of course, political independence seems common, economic independence extremely rare.)

This situation—political independence and a diversified agriculture—continued even after the Norman conquest in the late eleventh century. The Normans restored the Latin church at the expense of both Byzantium and Islam and introduced feudal institutions from northern Europe. Yet little changed in terms of Sicily's participation in a world economic system. If anything, the Norman kings enhanced Sicilian autonomy by seizing control of the wheat trade from foreign merchants of Amalfi, who had carried it during the Arab period (Citarella 1967). They also retained many Arab institutions and encouraged Moslem craftsmen, administrators, and peasants to stay. Sicilian exports, including wheat, paid well, and the profits remained in Sicily to underwrite economic development and a flourishing court in Palermo. Indeed, the Norman period is frequently referred to as the island's "golden age."

By the late twelfth century, however, this flourishing kingdom began to lose its independence. By the end of the fourteenth century,

Sicily, especially western Sicily, had once again become a colonial dependency, specializing in the production of wheat and wool to meet the needs of distant metropolies. Europe now had a number of competing core areas, each of which manufactured woolen cloth. Initially concentrated in northern France and the Low Countries, subsequently scattered throughout France and Germany, and eventually developed most fully in England, woolen cloth manufacture was the medieval industry par excellence. It was an important European export toward markets in the Near and Far East, from which Europe habitually imported manufactures, and it was, as a consequence, a critical means of capital accumulation (Bautier 1971: 107–118; Bloch 1962: 70). On the basis of accumulated capital, centers of cloth manufacture were in a position to exert hegemony over an expanding periphery.

     In the latter part of the thirteenth century, Mediterranean cities, rich from playing a commercial role in East–West trade, as well as from dyeing and finishing northern cloth for export, launched their own textile industries. The most advanced of these were in northern Italy, especially Florence, and in the Catalan region of Spain, especially Barcelona. The Lombards of northern Italy and the Catalans of eastern Spain challenged each other for control of Sicily, with the result that the island was torn apart by civil war throughout the fourteenth and into the fifteenth centuries. From within, the struggle was like a fierce and protracted vendetta between two great baronial groups, a Catalan faction consisting of noble adventurers, newly arrived from Spain, and a Latin faction consisting of Sicilian descendants of the Norman conquerors. Aragonese sovereigns backed the Catalan faction, while the pope and French Angevin sovereigns supported the Latins. Throughout this stormy period there were frequent military campaigns in which the Aragonese kept the upper hand. Each campaign would be followed by a redistribution of some feudal tenures, as the victorious sovereigns confiscated the properties of rebels and traitors and awarded them to loyal vassals. There were also some strategic marriages whereby the daughters and dowries of Latin families passed into Catalan hands.

     The fortunes of one Catalan family, prominent in and around Villamaura, illustrate the process. Raymond Peralta, an admiral in the Catalan navy, defended the Aragonese crown against a revolt of the Latin barons in 1337; for his efforts he received a county made up of several fiefs confiscated from the conspirators. In 1340, Peralta was granted the land and castle of Alcamo in western Sicily, together with surrounding villages. His first son, William, inherited these properties and also married the Latin duchess of Sclafani. He thus became count of one territory, baron of another, and duke of yet a third. Raymond's second son, "Little Raymond," received a fief that was confiscated from a rebel Latin family, but since his son died a young man without heirs, this property passed to his already rich count–baron–duke uncle, William Peralta. The son of this William, called "Big William," thus held land all over western Sicily. Needless to say he married well, taking as his bride Eleanor of Aragon, whose father had married a Latin heiress and whose dowry consisted of several additional territories (Scaturro 1926: Vol. I, 394–583).

By the end of the fourteenth century, families such as the Peraltas were powerful enough to block successors to the throne. Between 1378 and 1392, two Latins and two Catalans, one of whom was the son of Big William Peralta, formed a vicarate to rule Sicily in the absence of a sovereign, each king of his own domain. The vicarate came to an end when three of its principals negotiated a secret alliance with an Aragonese pretender to the throne. The fourth vicar, member of an established Latin family, the Chiaramonte, refused to enter the alliance and held out for something which resembled Sicilian nationalism. Significantly, the most important Chairamonte holdings were in southeastern Sicily, the "Greek" territory once controlled by Syracuse and its emperor, Hiero. The Chiaramonte family also owned an imposing palace in the center of Palermo, where it vied with the Aragonese for the throne of Sicily.

With the dissolution of the vicarate and the arrival of a new sovereign, Catalans accused the Chiaramonte family of inciting the peasants of western Sicily to rebel against their masters. In the early fifteenth century Bernardo Cabrera, a Catalan newcomer, led a military campaign against them, at the close of which he succeeded to their holdings in the southeast, thus advancing Catalan hegemony in eastern Sicily. (The Chiaramonte palace in Palermo eventually became the seat of the Spanish Inquisition in Sicily.) Now only the northeast remained a haven for Angevin and papal interests and the stronghold of a predominantly Latin ruling class. Finally, in 1412, the crown of Sicily was assumed by the house of Castile as Aragon and Castile were united in the famous marriage of Ferdinand and Isabella. Sicily was no longer an independent monarchy; it was now governed by Spain indirectly through a viceroy. For awhile, however, it remained a preeminently Catalan, rather than Spanish, colony; Spanish newcomers to the aristocracy continued to come from Catalonia and not Castile (Koenigsberger 1969: 51).

What did Catalonia want from its colony, Sicily? Primarily wheat and an outlet for its cloth goods (Vilar 1962: Vol. I, 413–414). Yet the

Catalans also encouraged the expansion of pastoral enterprises, and this was crucial for the shape of things to come. Wool pelts and cheese became significant exports in this period and whole stretches of countryside, especially in the west, were dedicated to raising sheep (Bautier 1971: 204; Jones 1966: 386, 393–394; Petino 1946–1947: 64–68; Ziino 1911: 26).

By the middle of the fifteenth century, that is by the beginning of what historians call the "long" sixteenth century (1450–1650), Sicily was constrained to cultivate more and more wheat. Changes external to the island underlay this shift. In the fourteenth and early fifteenth centuries, Catalonia faced eastward toward the Mediterranean; the Tyrrhenian Sea became, in Vilar's words, a "Catalan lake [1962: Vol. I, 414]." This was true even after the crowns of Aragon and Castile were united. Eventually, however, Aragon and Catalonia, together with central and southern Spain, turned away from the Mediterranean in the direction of Atlantic expansion. By the end of the fifteenth century, Catalonia sent cloth to the Spanish interior in exchange for wool and wheat (Vilar 1962: Vol. I, 543–544).

This did not mean autonomy for Sicily (still nominally a vice royalty of Spain), for north Italian interests stepped quickly into the breach. Nor was this a contradiction. Spain was united at the expense of Catalan industry, and Barcelona no longer threatened Italian cities like Florence. Moreover, although the Spanish Empire claimed large parts of Italy, including the state of Milan, Genoese capital helped finance it (Braudel 1966: Vol. I, 405–406; Elliot 1968: 59–60; Vicens Vives 1969: 335–336, 382–384). Merchants from Genoa carried the Sicilian trade as the island imported textiles from Florence and Venice and continued to export wheat. Sicily moved from a Catalan into a Spanish–Genoese sphere of influence (Jones 1966: 387). In Villamaura the new magnate family came from Bologna.

The island's value in the eyes of foreigners also changed as they demanded fewer animals and animal products in relation to wheat: wheat to provision the Spanish army and navy and to feed the growing cities of Renaissance Italy. Once again, as under Rome, Sicily specialized in cereal production, mostly in hard wheat (grano duro) well suited for long sea voyages. By the early sixteenth century, according to Mack Smith, the island exported about 2 million bushels of this wheat in a good year, which is more than twice as much per year as had been extracted by Rome (1968a: 191). Bianchini, an Italian historian, estimated that producers smuggled out an equivalent amount to avoid an export tax levied by Spain (Romano 1964: 214), and according to Jones, in favorable years one-third of the Sicilian wheat crop was surplus (1966: 384; see also Parry 1967). The accompanying

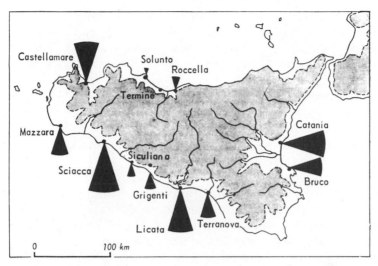

Map 1. Sicily. Location of grain storage warehouses in the sixteenth century. [Source: Figure 49 "The Sicilian *caricatori* in 1532" (p. 580) from *The Mediterranean and the Mediterranean World in the Age of Philip II,* Volume I, by Fernand Braudel (Harper & Row, 1972).]

return to monoculture involved most of the island. The distribution of grain storage warehouses, however, indicated that production was far and away heaviest in the west (see Map 1).

The emphasis on wheat, evident from the mid-fifteenth century and pronounced in the sixteenth century, was closely related to the major demographic and economic trends of the period. The Mediterranean population nearly doubled in these years and grew especially rapidly in cities (Braudel 1966: Vol. I, 368–369). Population growth meant increased demand for food, which in turn led to restricting the domain of animals. All over Europe, grazing land was reduced to cultivation, and cotton and linen supplemented wool in textile manufacturing (Braudel 1966: Vol. I, 540–541; Slicher van Bath 1963: 243–254; Vilar 1962: Vol. I, 568). Only in northern Europe, and specifically in England, where sheep required relatively less land, did a woolen cloth industry continue to expand. Mediterranean manufacturers now concentrated on silk cloth. The latter, of course, was imported into Sicily in exchange for wheat. Mack Smith reports that in 1622 Sicilians spent on imported textiles an amount comparable to the government's total budget (1968a: 188–189).

After the period 1620–1640—a turning point in European history—external pressures on the Sicilian economy relaxed somewhat, as the emergence of a new core area in northern Europe undermined the north Italian city-states and Spain. This breathing spell was short, however. By the early eighteenth century Sicily was a viceroyalty of the Bourbon crown at Naples, which was in turn a satellite of Bourbon France. Through the eighteenth century, the island once again specialized in producing wheat and imported manufactures from northern, as well as southern, Europe (Arnolfini 1962: 130–131). As we will see in Chapter 3, the population of Sicily grew considerably during this period. This placed the Neapolitan crown in an increasingly difficult position, for the drain of wheat to export markets caused high prices, famine, and rioting at home.

The rise of North Atlantic Europe to supplant Spain and Italy as the core of European capitalism also undercut the position of eastern Sicily as the last vestige of insular autonomy. Strong and independent under the Greeks, recalcitrant under the Romans, the eastern provinces of Messina, Catania, and Syracuse were the last to be overrun by the Catalans. Throughout the period of Spanish and north Italian dominance, the northeastern province of Messina swung in the orbit of France. With this additional leverage, its role was to produce and export silk, a crop which is both more labor intensive and more profitable than wheat.

The grain trade was carried on by foreign merchants, but it was the local merchants of Messina who won from the Spanish government the right to monopolize the export trade in silk. They even vied with Palermo to host the viceroyal court and have Messina become capital of the island. Yet by its tax policies the Spanish government discouraged the efforts of local merchants to capitalize the production of silk cloth in Sicily. Sicily's primary role as a grain producer was tied to her secondary role as a market for Italian cloth. In the 1670s, following an increase in the export tax for silk, northeastern Sicily rebelled against Spain. The rebellion was crushed, and mulberry groves up and down the coast were destroyed. Silk producers emigrated, and the population of Messina fell sharply, down to 33,000 from the 120,000 it had reached in the sixteenth century (Mack Smith 1968a: 233). At last the city was vulnerable to Palermo and the grain interests represented there. Meanwhile, by the early eighteenth century France had developed luxury commodities which outstripped those of Italy, and Sicilian grain barons were competing with each other in the conspicuous consumption of French silks.

To summarize our progress to this point, the history of Sicily up to the eighteenth century reveals two major themes. The first is that Sicily alternated between periods of relative independence and servitude. Independence was marked during the Greek period, before the Punic wars, and again under Arab and Norman rule. The island was most dependent, subordinate to external centers of control, under the Romans, the Catalans, and the north Italians, and eventually as a peripheral part of a world-system the center of which was northern Europe. Throughout these dominations Sicily specialized as a producer of primary resources—animal products and, above all, wheat. Foreign merchants exported her golden wheat and they, together with their financial backers in cities like Florence and Genoa, enjoyed the lion's share of the proceeds. Sicily's agricultural resources were not her own.

The second theme which emerges from this historical outline has to do with differences in space rather than time: Western Sicily was always more dependent, more exploited by outsiders than was eastern Sicily. The east retained its integrity longer against the onslaught of colonial pressures and did not collapse before external demands until the late seventeenth century. The alternation in time between dependency and autonomy, and differences between the eastern and western regions of the island, are central to an understanding of Sicily's agrarian economy, discussed in the following section.

THE RELATIONSHIP OF ANIMALS TO AGRICULTURE IN SICILY

Sicilian agriculture was (and is) characteristically Mediterranean. It combined wheat cultivation with such labor-intensive vine and tree crops as grapes, nuts, and olives, and with fruits, citrus fruits, and vegetables that require small-scale irrigation. The fourth essential ingredient was livestock: cattle, sheep, goats, mules, donkeys, and a few horses. These animals were a crucial adjunct to agriculture, not only as draft animals and for the products they supplied, but also for their manure. As is typical in arid climates, however, animals also competed with other forms of agriculture because they could not be fed on cultivated forage and confined to meadows and stalls. In the absence of either widespread irrigation or chemical fertilizers, it is difficult or impossible to cultivate forage crops in places like Sicily which have no summer rainfall. Until well into the twentieth century, therefore, such places never saw the rotation system on which European agriculture north of the Alps thrived: a system based on triennial rotations with a nitrogen-fixing crop of legumes planted in the spring. Instead, animals grazed on natural pastures, exploiting high altitudes in the summer and lower altitudes and plains in the winter, following a system of transhumance, or seasonal migration. Natural pastures are less predictable than cultivated forage. In an arid environment, moreover, they are vulnerable to the timing of autumn rains and generally not too rich. A late nineteenth-century Sicilian observer lamented that sheep in Sicily required three times the grazing land of their English counterparts and still gave less wool (Loncao 1899: 43; Jones 1966: 382).

As a consequence of transhumant grazing, land in Sicily could be intensively cultivated only where animals were not permitted to graze. Elsewhere it was cultivated extensively, with animals allowed to graze after the harvest, or it was left to pasturage and not cultivated at all. Over the centuries the eastern and western regions of the island gave rise to two different modes of articulating cultigens with animals. The western mode reveals that the colonial overlords who were so powerful there were interested in promoting livestock as well as wheat.

Statistics on land use were not compiled until 1833, but data from that census indicate that tree crops were more important in the three eastern provinces of Messina, Catania, and Syracuse than in the provinces of the west. In addition, considerably more land was irrigated in the east, where intensive agriculture was for the most part concentrated at low altitudes, along the coast.[1] The eastern coastal zone was thus specialized for luxury crop production and differentiated from the interior by the absence or near absence of grazing flocks and herds.

Western Sicily presented a different picture. Not only was intensive agriculture less developed there, but with the exception of the Conca d'Oro area near Palermo it was not concentrated in any particular zone. Each rural community was surrounded by a belt of tree crops, rarely irrigated and poorly differentiated from surrounding zones of extensive cultivation and grazing. This pattern was nearly as prevalent on the coast as in the interior. Indeed, one of the most remarkable features of the mode of production in western as opposed to eastern Sicily was the overall similarity of land use at different altitudes and the tendency for the coast to be subordinate to the interior.

Wheat, the island's most important crop, was also cultivated dif-

[1] In the eastern provinces of Messina, Catania, and Syracuse, the proportion of irrigated and irrigable land was 1.9%, 1.5%, and 1.8%, respectively. In the western provinces it was: Palermo, 1.5%; Caltanissetta, 0.2%; Agrigento, 0.7%; and Trapani, 0.8% (Scrofani 1962: 127).

ferently in the western and eastern regions. Although in the east wheat was sometimes planted in alternation with grazing, there were places unlike the west where wheat was cultivated more intensively. Thus wheat was grown with irrigation on the eastern Plain of Catania, and in the interior of the province of Syracuse farmers planted it on small holdings in combination with olive and nut groves. In the west, agriculture was less diversified, wheat more often a monocrop. In a parliamentary inquest of 1907–1908, Lorenzoni described wheat as extensively cultivated in two degrees. He labeled "primitive" the system he found at high altitudes and on poor soils. Here, if there were any harvests at all, they occurred every 4–6 years; the intervening years were dedicated to fallow or pasturage. Overgrown land was cleared by fire for cultivation. More common was a system he called the "Roman type," or "attenuated extensive," in which three fields underwent a staggered rotation: 1 year in grain, 1 in fallow, and 1 in pastures (Lorenzoni 1910).

These differences in agriculture between the eastern and western parts of Sicily point to different technologies of animal husbandry. Eastern cattle were raised separately from sheep and goats. In the provinces of Messina and Syracuse they were kept in specially prepared and enclosed, if not cultivated, meadows and were fed in stalls on cultivated forage (by the end of the nineteenth century). Sheep and goats were raised on mountain pastures, many of them vast stretches of communal or ecclesiastical land high in the province of Messina. Flocks tended to be smaller than those in western Sicily and to be dissociated from agriculture. Thus the province of Catania in 1833 had less land in pastures than any other Sicilian province, but its percentage of hectares in wheat was among the highest. Messina, with a high percentage of land in pastures, contributed very little wheat. Everywhere, livestock kept a respectable distance from intensive agriculture, vines, and trees.

Not so in the west. Here cattle were herded together with sheep and goats, and all three were closely bound to the cereal economy. Flocks and herds were larger, cycles of migration longer, and the cycles united coast and interior into a single system of transhumance. The relationship of this system to wheat was symbiotic, for the animals manured the land as they grazed on the wheat stubble after the harvest. The two types of land use were alternating and to some degree interchangeable. Generally, land at high altitudes was devoted more to pasturage and land at low altitudes to wheat, but even this distinction dissolved under market pressures. Depending upon market demand, marginal mountain land was cultivated in wheat or good lowland arable reverted to pasture. Wheat and pasturage reinforced each other, and their joint effect was to undermine production in vine, tree, and vegetable crops.

Sicilian agriculture is known for its latifundia yet little enough attention has been paid to the way in which latifundism emerged. Technically a latifundium is a large estate, although estimates of size vary. Before some of the reforms of the nineteenth century, a single latifundium could integrate several ranch-farm enterprises, each of which easily exceeded 200 hectares. The total estate could have encompassed 1000–2000 hectares. Roman latifundia were said to be so large that a man on horseback could not ride the breadth of one in a single day (Ziino 1911). Pontieri, writing about the late eighteenth century, said the land was covered by "a continuous stretch of fiefs" and this "great mass of property was owned by a very few [1933: 11–13]." Significantly, such immense estates covered a range of altitudes great enough to provide for both winter and summer grazing. Some estates extended from the mountainous interior to the coast, contributing to the integration and functional homogeneity of lowlands and highlands which is so characteristic of western Sicily. In short, large estates had a pastoral substructure.

There were some latifundia in the east, but their presence had a greater impact on the western landscape, where they flourished first in the Roman and then since the Catalan period. In the intervening centuries of Arab–Norman rule, large estates declined. In both periods of latifundium formation, animal husbandry played a major role. Roman latifundists were the first to organize long-distance routes of transhumance, to bring small-scale herding operations under the aegis of the large-scale pastoral enterprise, and to subordinate the coastal lowlands to the pastoral interests of the latifundium, extending their interior estates down to the very beaches. The Greeks had done the opposite by concentrating their efforts in the coastal zone and making little use of the interior (Scrofani 1962: 28).

Under Catalan dominance the Roman strategy was repeated. Greedy for pasturelands, the Catalan lords usurped woodlands and common lands on which peasants had previously pastured their animals. They created illegal "enclosures" (called *difesi*) which, although not fenced off, were utilized as if they were private property. Typically an "enclosure" was left ungrazed for a year or more at a time, after which it provided richer grass for the lords' animals, especially his cattle (Genuardi 1911: 80–84; Loncao 1899: 25–27, 30–31). At the same time that they curtailed the grazing rights of others, Catalan lords expanded their own control over pasturage. Local courts supported their claims to seasonal pasturage on peasant holdings, even though this made it impossible for such holdings to be fenced or cropped continuously. Gradually, peasants lost their capacity to resist the lords' intrusion and even to keep their land (Loncao 1899: 15). Sheep were eating men, as the saying goes.

In both Roman and Catalan times, pastoralism was soon supplemented by the spread of wheat cultivation. Yet wheat did not eclipse the pastoral regime. On the contrary, while pastoralism was indeed squeezed to accommodate the spread of wheat, the export-oriented wheat economy was organized by lords who still retained an interest in animals. Wheat was thus cultivated on estates that were large enough to provide for transhumant grazing. The real casualty of expanding wheat production was not so much pasturage but forest cover and tree crops, in the coastal zone as well as in the interior. Lands described by Arab geographers as "rich in a variety of rare fruits" became "veritable deserts" in the words of Goethe, who observed them in the eighteenth century. In his autobiographical sketch, "Places of My Infancy," Giuseppe di Lampedusa (author of *The Leopard*) recalled "the immeasurable scenery of feudal Sicily,

"The immeasurable scenery of feudal Sicily, desolate, breathless, oppressed by a leaden sun [Lampedusa 1962: 43]."

"The settlement pattern concentrates population in large compact agglomerations, located on mountainsides or hilltops."

desolate, breathless, oppressed by a leaden sun [1962: 43]." His family, on its annual trip from Palermo to its estates of the interior, could not find a shade tree under which to lunch.

COLONIAL PRESSURES AND
SETTLEMENT PATTERNS

As distinctive as the absence or near absence of trees in western and interior Sicily is the absence of habitation, for the settlement pattern concentrates population in large compact agglomerations, located on mountainsides or hilltops, and leaves the vast spaces between almost without people. In 1850 there were 348 communes (a rural commune is a settlement plus its hinterland) in Sicily with an average population of 6000 and an average territorial extension of about 74 square kilometers, two and one-half times greater than the average for Italy. (Rural communes averaged 10 square kilometers in Lombardy, 20 in Piedmont, and 42 in the Neapolitan provinces.) A century later, the Sicilian population had doubled, but there were still only 379 communities, each on the average 67 square kilometers in territory (Milone 1960: 218). (Villamaura is larger than the average; its communal territory is approximately 100 square kilometers.) In the coastal zone of eastern Sicily much of the rural population lives dispersed across the land in hamlets and farmsteads, while in western and interior Sicily over 90% of the people live in agglomerated settlements, on the coast as well as inland.

These settlements vary considerably in population, from about 1500 to over 60,000 (Villamaura, with a population of approximately 11,000 in the early twentieth century and 7500 now, is about average). The settlements are predominantly agricultural, with well more than half of the labor force engaged directly in cultivation; yet each community has a nearly full complement of urban functions—there are professionals, merchants, and artisans, as well as peasants. Each settlement has some two- and three-story houses inhabited by members of an upper stratum, and dense quarters of one-storey peasant dwellings (many no larger than one or two rooms) which in the past included a stall for a mule or donkey. Large and small, the buildings are constructed to present an unbroken facade along mostly narrow streets and courtyards, leaving little room for gardens and trees or for stalls separate from living quarters. Scattered throughout each settlement are several open piazzas, and the churches, monasteries, baronial *palazzi,* and municipal buildings through which the history of a town can be read. Villamaura, for example, descends on the ridge of a hill from the remains of an Arab castle. Immediately around this castle is a network of narrow streets called the *vicoli* (alleyways) of the Saracens. Buried in another quarter at the opposite end of the town is a fourteenth-century church in an architectural style typical of the Catalan period. The main street in the center of town boasts an imposing baroque building, the palace of the Bolognese noblemen who were feudal lords over Villamaura in the Spanish period. In the middle of the facade is still the family crest. One of several churches also dates from the era of Spanish rule, and a few other churches and *palazzi* were constructed under the Bourbons and later in the nineteenth century.

The variety of goods and services available, the physical aspect of the community, its size, and the absence of gardens and barns all give a settlement such as Villamaura an urban appearance, so that one does not want to call it a village. This is particularly so since many of these settlements are located in high places some distance from arable valleys and basin lands. Villamaura is something of an exception to this rule. Although much of the communal territory is far away, the town is located on a small hill in the middle of a rich alluvial basin. In general, however, the remoteness of the settlements from arable land is an additional factor that makes the label "agrotown" more appropriate in western Sicily than "peasant village."

But how can one explain the origin and persistence of the agrotown settlement pattern? Was it malaria in the lowland basins which drove peasants off the land? Was it the location of water, or Turkish pirates, or fear of conquering armies? All of these explanations are possible and have been offered in the past, but we agree with Anton Blok, who argues that the agrotown phenomenon is clearly related to the requirements of a latifundist technology. It is found, he argues, because large landholders claimed vast extensions of the best land for their estates and resisted any peasant counterclaims, with violence if necessary (Blok 1969a). We would argue further that the latifundium and the agrotown were joint consequences of the island's peripheral and subordinate role in the developing world (as was also the case in much of the southern Italian mainland, where agrotowns are equally common). Indeed, one can identify the historical moment when the agrotowns emerged, as well as the forces that created them.

For Sicily, the agrotown arose in the course of the long conflict between Catalan and Latin barons, from the thirteenth to the early fifteenth centuries. During the preceding Arab–Norman period, the west Sicilian countryside had been dotted by villages, or *casali*. When the Norman kings granted these villages as fiefs they were called *feudo-casali*. Many of these settlements were located on good basin land where the *villa*, or administrative center, of the Roman latifundium once stood (and where, in the later Catalan–Spanish period, powerful landholders established their *massarie*). According to a local authority, "we call *casali* those places which the Arabs called *Rahal* and the Romans called *Villae* and then *Curtes* or *Massae* [Ciaccio 1900: 411]." One Arab geographer knew of 300 such settlements in Sicily; another said that there was "an infinity" of them (Milone 1960: 188).

The Arab–Norman villages were seriously weakened in the early thirteenth century when Frederick II—the German emperor who had acquired Sicily through marriage—launched a successful military campaign against the Moslems and deported several thousand of them to his territories in mainland Italy. Latin barons, hungry for land, supported this policy. Frederick decreed the foundation of new villages in order to compensate for the abandonment of the old ones by departing Moslems, but no new villages were in fact founded in the thirteenth century (Di Cristina 1965: App. III; Scaturro 1926: Vol. I, 322). Villages that survived the attack on the Moslems fell in the fourteenth and early fifteenth centuries under the pressure of the Catalan campaign. From records of taxation and military levies we know, for example, that in the fourteenth century there were five inhabited *casali* in the 10,000-hectare communal territory of Villamaura (Scaturro 1926: Vol. I, 342, 347). A consequence of the Catalan campaign in this area was the disappearance of these villages, only one of which survived as the hill town of Villamaura (Scaturro 1926: Vol. I, 477, 582). There and everywhere disappearing villages lent their names to latifundia: Misilfurmi, Rachalmaymuni, Misilbesi, and many others today betray their origin as *casali*.[2]

When the Latin and Catalan barons overran villages in fourteenth-century Sicily, their interest in livestock was paramount. In this regard Sicily conformed to a wider pattern, for the disappearance of villages and village agriculture was tied to the expansion of sheep raising (along with plague and population decline) in many other regions of Europe in the late Middle Ages. Only in Sicily (and in southern Italy), however, did expanding pastoralism literally prepare the ground for expanding wheat cultivation, such that wheat growing was founded on a pastoral base. Elsewhere land use was more specialized. By the sixteenth century in England, for example, disappearing villages and expanded ranches in the north and midlands had been complemented in the south by village-dwelling yeoman farmers who improved agricultural production (Thirsk 1967). In neither region did agrotowns arise. One suspects it was the pastoral substructure of west Sicilian agriculture which made agrotowns so widespread and resistant to change there.

That they were solidly entrenched is illustrated by the fate of settlements founded in the sixteenth and seventeenth centuries. Chartered by the Spanish viceroys, these communities were supposed to improve the yield of uncultivated or poorly cultivated land. Anyone

---

[2] People make much of the survival of Arabic nomenclature in western Sicily. In addition to the prefix *rahal* (or *ragal*), others such as *menzil* and *calat* are often found in contemporary place names. In Arab usage, *calat* designates a settlement of greater importance than a village and it appears today in the names of many towns; for example, Caltanissetta, Calascibetta, and Caltabellotta. *Menzil* and *rahal*, on the other hand, refer to villages and rural suburbs which, with the fifteenth-century reentry of the latifundium, largely disappeared. These prefixes are still used for a few settlements—Misilmeri, Regalbuto, Racalmuto, and others—but they are also commonly found in the names of latifundia.

who financed such a community, and enticed peasants to settle it, was guaranteed enoblement as lord of a populated fief and with this a seat in parliament. Over 100 new communities were founded, most of them between 1570 and 1650, the great majority located in western Sicily (Garufi 1946–1947: Vol. II, 60–61; Rochefort 1961: 42). Initially and superfically, the new communities were villages. In order to recruit settlers, the founders promised extensive use rights on communal domain and offered secure tenures. The generosity of the founders and the details of the contracts varied, reflecting supply and demand in the labor market. In general, these contracts favored the rise of a middle peasantry over a nearly landless, plurally occupied, rural semi-proletariat. Yet, just as the Arab dominance was erased by subsequent events, so this movement toward resettlement of the countryside was limited in its impact on western Sicily. Many new settlements were founded on undesirable land and with inadequate funding (Genuardi 1911: 46–47). None had the capacity to resist renewed pressure which, in the eighteenth century, came from northern Europe as well as the Mediterranean. Indeed, only four colonies were founded after 1700. On the contrary, several new settlements were abandoned, while those that survived became dormitory towns for nearby latifundia. Landlords, with the tacit consent of the central power, reneged on the contracts that were favorable to tenants. Nothing like village agriculture remained (Mack Smith 1968b: 278–279).

CAUSES: THE ROLE OF ENVIRONMENT IN LATIFUNDISM

The latifundia and agrotowns of western Sicily constitute the parameters within which the regional society, polity, and culture have evolved. Their impact on various aspects of life leads one to ask what caused these patterns of land use and settlement to arise. What makes human societies evolve in this, as opposed to that, direction? One answer frequently put forth and in many respects compelling is "environment." We will conclude our review of land use and settlement with an assessment of the role of the natural environment in the evolution of human adaptations in Sicily, as compared with the role of core–periphery relationships in the island's geopolitical environment. In the end we will propose that both types of environment (the natural and the geopolitical) interacted to produce latifundism and the agrotown (see Sahlins and Service 1960).

There is no question that climate and topography have been limiting factors for Sicily. Belonging to a Mediterranean habitat, the island as a whole receives an uneven distribution of rain. There are very heavy rains in the winter months, but from May to October there is almost no rainfall. Sicily's natural vegetation suffers from aridity: Several thousand years ago, tall evergreen oaks began to yield, through a process of irreversible deforestation, to scrub oak, evergreen shrubs, and other degenerate forms of plant life called *maquis* and *garrigue,* which are characterized by small leaf surfaces and the capacity to revive quickly after fire. Regression in plant life brought with it a deterioration of soil conditions through loss of humus and the consequent exposure of limestone (Houston 1964: 79–105). In Sicily, either soils are stony, eroded, and limestone, or they are mostly clay and often impermeable (Milone 1960).

Sicily also shares with the Mediterranean area a mountainous terrain. Of its 26,000 square kilometers, scarcely 3600 are classified as plains; over 93% of the total land area exceeds 500 meters in altitude (Rochefort 1961: 30). High altitudes, shifting rock beds, and landslides are natural obstacles to transportation, communication, and agriculture. In addition, until recently the concentrated winter rainfall and rapidly warming spring, together with an abundance of clay soils in lowland basins and plains, favored the malaria mosquito.

We have already discussed the limitations that climate and topography set for livestock raising. This, perhaps, was the overriding disadvantage of all Mediterranean regions when compared to northern Europe. Before the industrial revolution, animals were the most significant energy resource to set Europe off from the great civilizations of the East. For military purposes, horses were to that epoch what jet planes are to this, and sheep provided the raw material for the only Western manufacture that was widely sought in Eastern markets. The temperate climate of northern Europe made it possible to raise horses, cattle, and sheep without sacrificing cultivated land. Thus, England with its interdependent regional specializations could mount its knights on horseback, provide wool for its spinners and weavers—and feed them all. The arid Mediterranean countries could not easily feed animals as well as people engaged in nonagricultural pursuits because in an arid climate animals and people are sustained by the same land.

The environmental advantages of northern Europe when compared to the Mediterranean offer a clue to the eventual emergence of the North Atlantic industrial core. Were there also different environmental potentialities in the preindustrial Mediterranean and in Sicily?

We note that Sicily as a whole has no vast arable plain to compare with northern Italy's Po valley and that within Sicily itself flatland is unevenly distributed as are good soils. The eastern Plain of Catania, watered by the Simeto River, is the island's largest plain, occupying some 165 square miles. The other major plains—Lentini, Gela, Milazzo—also are located in the east. Flatlands in the west are less extensive and less well watered. Rising above the Plain of Catania stands Mount Etna, a source of volcanic ash that has greatly enriched surrounding soils. To the south of Catania, in the province of Syracuse, much of the land resembles that of western Sicily, but there are plateaus enriched by lava which support intensive agriculture. In south central Sicily, by contrast, a large plateau covering sulfur deposits provides a poor base for cultivation even though altitudes there are relatively low and the land is level (Milone 1960: 30–31).

The rest of western and interior Sicily is mountainous, although mountains rarely exceed 900 meters in altitude. These soils are mostly clay, sometimes mixed with limestone and quite permeable, sometimes packed hard to create great banks of solid rock which jut abruptly out of the earth (Milone 1960: 26). Although there are no clearly definable valleys, basins of relatively low altitude are scattered throughout the interior. Lined with clay, they receive deposits of decomposed calcium and sandstone washed down from surrounding mountains or carried down in tiny underground rivulets and streams. Interacting with the clay lining, these accumulations create a surface which is easily cultivated and rich. Too often in the past, however, the basins were allowed to collect stagnant water and became malarial.

The mountains of northeastern Sicily are higher than the mountains of the west and interior and are organized into patterned ranges separated by rivers that run at right angles to the coast. Topography seems to have protected the forest cover of these mountains, and they alone, in all of Sicily, receive summer rainfall worth measuring (see Map 2). The resulting watersheds have for centuries facilitated irrigation on the coast and represent a significant environmental resource.

We have seen that if ever there were forces for autonomous development in Sicily, their roots were in the northeast, a region with its own merchant bourgeoisie and the wherewithal briefly to challenge Spain. Elsewhere, resistance to external pressure barely got off the ground.

The location of Greek settlements in eastern, rather than western, Sicily probably reflected the greater agricultural potential of the eastern region, as well as its proximity to an important trade route for metals which passed through the Strait of Messina and on to Elba

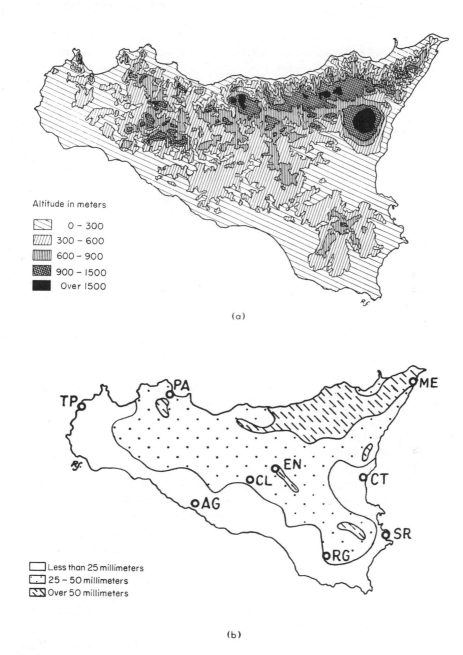

(a)

Altitude in meters

- 0 – 300
- 300 – 600
- 600 – 900
- 900 – 1500
- Over 1500

(b)

Less than 25 millimeters
25 – 50 millimeters
Over 50 millimeters

Map 2. Special topographical and climatological features of northeastern Sicily. (a) Altitude in meters. [Source: Milone 1960:37.] (b) Distribution of winter rainfall. [Source: Milone 1960: 57.]

and Spain (Finley 1968: 17; Pulgram 1958: 108–133). But not all settlements of Greek origin were located in the lowland plains. Some were sustained as much by commercial activity as by a cultivated hinterland. Messina, a seaport almost entirely enclosed by mountains, and Taormina, a bastion of Greek influence, "suspended between rocks and sea on a narrow ledge of Mount Tauro [Touring Club Italiano 1953: 468]," are good examples of this sort of settlement. In any case, there was a reciprocal relationship between autonomous urban development and increased productivity on the land, as wealth accumulated in trade was allocated to agriculture. An outstanding example is the Plain of Catania, which was transformed by drainage and irrigation.

Western Sicily was less urbanized and not so well cultivated under Greek rule. For this reason, perhaps, it was more vulnerable to Roman dominance than was eastern Sicily, and the natural environment deteriorated at the hands of the Romans. Roman latifundia spread against population centers, trees, and irrigated gardens, even in the lowland basins and the coastal zone. The result was increased soil erosion. Furthermore, as water control systems were abandoned and lowland populations declined, malaria became a problem, for malaria does not drive people from the land as much as uninhabited and poorly drained land gives rise to malaria (Maranelli 1946).

But the impact of Roman latifundism was shallow compared to that of its counterpart of the fourteenth–eighteenth centuries. Indeed, the Arabs and Normans reversed its deteriorating effect on the natural environment, if only temporarily. In the second wave of latifundism the deterioration went much further, especially after 1700, when radical deforestation accompanied the spread of wheat cultivation to feed a growing Sicilian as well as foreign population. The confrontation with the exploding capitalist world-system in the nineteenth and twentieth centuries only contributed further to the degradation of the natural environment. Thus, although environment and geography were responsible for the small initial differences that set Sicily off from Italy, and western from eastern Sicily, the divergent adaptations of these regions, their progressive differentiation over centuries at the hand of man, accounted for much more. In western Sicily, pressure to produce wheat for foreign cities depleted the already limited natural resource base of the region. The outcome, which we are about to explore, would have been considerably different if industrial and commercial wealth had been utilized to reclaim marshlands, to terrace hillsides, and to irrigate lowlands and plains.

chapter 3

Political Structure under the Spanish Empire and the Emergence of Broker Capitalism

Sicily's role in historical world-systems explains more than the patterns of land use and settlement characteristic of the island. It also helps to explain the broad outlines of the corresponding political structure, system of social stratification, and cultural codes. This chapter describes the political structure that was a function of the region's specialized role as a source of primary exports under the Spanish Hapsburgs and the Neapolitan Bourbons. The key elements of this structure were (1) a "diarchic" relationship between crown and barons such that the barons more or less kept the upper hand; (2) a feeble bureaucracy easily circumvented by powerful individuals for personal profit; (3) an even more feeble infrastructure of transportation and communication that operated adequately only to place wheat and animal products into foreign markets; and (4) little capacity to provide security in the countryside.

We will argue below that these characteristics were not the result of feudalism or isolation but were symptomatic of colonial status on the periphery of the Spanish Empire, where political controls were continually undermined by economic realities. It is not surprising

41

therefore to find the same elements documented for Latin America and southern (mainland) Italy as well as Sicily. Everywhere they existed, they provided the foundation upon which broker capitalism arose and flourished. Although found in many parts of the world, broker capitalism seems frequently to be an important legacy of Spanish imperialism. Where it flourished, it had a decisive impact on changes that occurred in the nineteenth and early twentieth centuries, and broker capitalism continues to organize the economy today. We will attempt to establish its relationship to the political structure of western Sicily and, where possible, discuss parallel developments in other regions that were peripheral to the Spanish Empire, particularly in Latin America.

DIARCHY, NOT MONARCHY

In the late sixteenth century, a viceroy of Sicily, the count of Olivares, commenting on his own political weakness said, "with the barons you are everything; without them you are nothing." According to the historian Salvatore Romano, the baronage of that period was indeed strong enough to compete with the viceroyal crown, and the island was governed by a "diarchy," not a monarchy (1964: 230–235). Although they were of foreign extraction, mainly Catalan and north Italian, the sixteenth-century grain barons considered themselves Sicilian. Yet, unlike the development-oriented mercantile elite of the northeastern province of Messina, they did not think of rebelling against Spain, mainly because their power in the local arena, roughly equivalent to that of their Spanish governors, made revolt unnecessary. Sicily, says Romano, "was not strong enough to render itself independent . . . , neither was it weak enough to be absorbed into the unity of another nation. Somehow it always got away with special liberties or privileges under different foreign governments [1964: 235–236]."

Koenigsberger made a similar point in his analysis of the Spanish administration of Sicily under Philip II. For Sicily, according to Koenigsberger, Spain had no theory of empire. Its strategy called for viceroys to distribute patronage among feudal lords and reconfirm their special privileges in return for financial support to the empire (1969: 83). Lacking a supervisory capacity, it self-consciously promoted factional strife, scandal, and counterscandal among these great lords in order to keep them in line. The administration of Sicily was a matter of checks, balances, and compromises among nearly equal and autonomous forces; it had no "positive direction from the center." Thus, says

Koenigsberger, it encouraged no genuine political development, but rather an almost total lack of governance (Koenigsberger 1969: 197; 1971: 80–93, 255).

In the sixteenth and seventeenth centuries, the Spanish vice-royalty in Sicily instituted a number of financial and administrative reforms designed to bolster the power of the state against the centrifugal pull of the baronage. Plans were laid for a census, a new land register and standardized weights and measures, while viceroys commissioned the construction of opulent baroque palaces to symbolize the public interest, not only in Palermo but in smaller towns and cities of the realm, too. It is a measure of the inadequacy of these reforms that densely populated slums today crowd the baroque *palazzi* which line an important seventeenth-century street like the Via Maqueda in Palermo, and land and commodities in an interior town like Villamaura are still measured in ancient units, which vary from town to town.

The situation was generally similar in Latin America. One difference is that the Spanish imposed no trade monopolies on Sicily, as they did in their New World colonies. Yet this difference is superficial, partly because it became difficult to enforce these monopolies in Latin America, partly because the Sicilian grain trade was more or less monopolized by north Italian merchants whose interests were in any case closely intertwined with those of Spain. In the New World, as in Sicily, "Spain did not have the administrative energy to create a large bureaucracy. . . . Nor did Spain have the energy to control entirely its own settlers. . . . The settlers were nonetheless dependent on continued Spanish support . . . against intrusions into their trade, and hence their profit margins. Hence, though they were occasionally unhappy with the Crown and its bureaucracy, they did not organize as an autonomous force [Wallerstein 1974: 188]." Again, they did not have to do so. The overburdened Castilian taxpayers supported the colonial system, while the colonists themselves were free to seek their fortunes.

FEUDALISM AND ISOLATION: MISLEADING ISSUES

Because the colonists in Sicily acquired land from the crown as fiefs (which Spain discouraged in the New World) and because they took great stock in feudal titles—baron, count, marquis, and prince—the Sicilian political structure of that time has often been understood (or misunderstood) as an outgrowth of feudalism. After all, is not a weak central government an important characteristic of feudal regimes? Not necessarily. The Normans, who first introduced feudal institutions to Sicily, retained the strong administrative structure of the preceding Arab period, employing many Arab bureaucrats and court eunuchs. Retaining the Arab land register (*catasto*), the Norman kings also kept strong control over the feudal lords. As late as the mid-thirteenth century, the sovereign of Sicily was still the greatest pro-prietor of the realm, in control of much arable land, woodland, and pastures, hunting preserves, palaces, and large herds of animals (Di Salvo 1894; Loncao 1900: 105–107; Mack Smith 1968a: 58; Ziino 1911: 26).

The relative strength of the central power in this early phase of feudalism gave some protection to peasants and preserved the *casali*, or villages, described in Chapter 2, from the land-hungry lords. But then the same forces—those of Catalan and north Italian impe-rialism—which brought about the demise of the villages also un-dermined the foundation of a central power. Scaturro writes that, in addition to the disappearance of villages in the fourteenth and fifteenth centuries, there was a "progressive dissolution of the powers of the state, which little by little were assumed by the most powerful lords [Scaturro 1926: Vol. I, 444]."

It is worth recalling here that the new lords of Sicily sought to extend pastoral, as well as agricultural, enterprises. In the process, the central power lost the pastures and animals it had earlier controlled. Whereas in Spain, Castilian monarchs claimed jurisdiction over routes of transhumance and taxed the movement of animals, Catalan ranchers in Sicily acquired their own pastures and routes of transhu-mance by appropriating ever more land. In Spain, the *Mesta* ce-mented the power of the state in relation to that of the feudal lords. Pastoral husbandry in Sicily was a centrifugal force which helped to disperse power among the lords. These lords acquired new fiefs, carved out of royal domain, together with the power to administer civil and criminal justice over their subjects (Scaturro 1926: Vol. I, 551). Rather than submit to increased taxation, they purchased demesnial towns and cities. By the late fifteenth century, barons owned 160 of the 244 communes in Sicily, their hegemony being most advanced in the western region.[1] In addition, feudal lords increased their control over the export economy as the crown infeudated tax collections on

[1] According to a late eighteenth-century census, the ratio of demesnial to baronial communes was about 1 to 7 in western Sicily, as against 1 to 2 or 3 in the eastern region (Maggiore-Perni 1897: 6–11). This difference indicates that the dissolu-tion of royal authority was more advanced in western than in eastern Sicily; it is entirely consistent with the greater impact of Catalan imperialism in the west.

grain exports, the collection of fees for the use of docks, bridges, and warehouses, and the collection of fees for weighing and measuring. Even the tax that muleteers paid to transport wheat from the royal storehouses was administered *in feudo* (Scaturro 1926: Vol. I, 485; for southern Italy see Winspeare 1883).

In one sense the reversal of relations between the central power and the barons increased the diffusion of feudalism in Sicily. Feudal forms spread as land, towns, cities, offices and sources of revenue, rivers and streams, mills and presses, inns and taverns, roads, mines, and industries were acquired or usurped by feudal lords. Paradoxically, however, the more autonomous and powerful these lords became, the more the processes and resources under their control were divested of feudal content. Feudal tenures presumably belong to the realm and, unlike private property, they are subject to many layers of social usage. The lord enjoys his grant, but the sovereign may reclaim it if the lord fails to meet his obligations, if he leaves no heir, or if his heirs are negligent in relation to the contract. The Sicilian barons, like lords in Europe, soon developed techniques to avoid royal claims on their holdings. During the fourteenth century, the investiture ceremony was greatly reduced and eventually abolished, while a law was passed permitting the inheritance of fiefs in collateral lines to the sixth grade (including women), which made it impossible for an estate to revert to the crown for want of an heir. Another law recognized as legitimate any estate or privileges held by a baron for 30 years or more even if, originally, the estate or privileges had been usurped (Mack Smith 1968a: 94). Conveniently, the land register fell into disuse, to aid these usurpations. In addition, the outright alienation of feudal holdings, portions of them, or buildings on them became possible through special dispensation (and to some extent by law) from the end of the thirteenth century (Orlando 1847: 201–295). In the records, real estate sales may appear modest and infrequent, but not because they were prohibited by the overwhelming weight of feudal usage. We must also keep in mind that marriages, usurpations, and the indebtedness of the realm facilitated the exchange of property through means other than direct market transactions. Sicilian feudalism was pregnant with capitalist relations.[2]

---

[2] Nor did serfdom necessarily preclude relations with markets. In the thirteenth century, England exhibited considerably more serfdom than in either the twelfth or the fourteenth centuries. Yet it was precisely in the thirteenth century that foreign financial and wool interests held England in their sphere of influence (Postan 1966: 581–591; Power 1965). The same can be said for the "second serfdom" in eastern Europe. In these situations, serfdom meant that landlords or bailiffs stood between the peasants and the market, not that the market was absent.

The career of feudalism in Sicily was different from that of feudalism in western Europe. Not only did infeudation advance in Sicily when in Europe it was receding, but it did not retreat in the centuries that followed. So pervasive were feudal forms that even today latifundia are called *feudi* in popular usage. Indeed, older peasants in Villamaura persist in the observance of antiquated *banalités* and rituals: the gift of a hen or eggs to a *padrone* at Easter time, and the practice of greeting a landlord with the subservient phrase "I kiss your hand" (*baccio la mano*). In Sicily, much of the feudal superstructure survived the French Revolution and was not dismantled until the nineteenth century. Like eastern Europe, Sicily stood on the periphery of North Atlantic capitalism, becoming more feudal in some ways as western Europe became less so. Yet to conclude, as is often done, that the island's feeble government was the consequence of an overbearing and overextended feudalism, or a consequence of the isolation often associated with feudalism in Europe, is to miss the point. In Sicily (as in eastern Europe), a feudal superstructure served to organize the production of agricultural surpluses for an integrated world-system in which—far from being isolated and far from being self-sufficient—the island played a critical, if specialized and subordinate, role.

In western Europe, feudal institutions of the early Middle Ages helped to establish European autonomy from the Byzantine and Moslem empires, both far more developed commercially and industrially than was Europe at that time. When feudal Europe retreated into the countryside and choked off urban life and commerce, it was largely the commerce of others, and the loss was in effect Europe's gain. Europeans began gradually to manufacture their own clothing and luxuries and to make their own household goods. They paved the way for this change with a strong military capability and with policies of closure, self-denial, and import substitution. In Sicily, especially western Sicily, feudal institutions of the late Middle Ages (that is, after the thirteenth century) had the reverse effect. They helped to undermine and destroy the island's autonomy vis-à-vis more developed (European) core areas and to ensure that, in the future, urban and commercial life would be a mere adjunct to foreign interests. Imports increased astronomically in proportion to commodities manufactured at home, and the island's military defense was assumed by outsiders— exactly opposite to the consequences of feudalism in Europe. Among the feudal lords of Sicily there was none of the disciplined asceticism which pervaded early European feudalism. Indeed, Sicily's barons must rank among history's most avid consumers.[3]

[3] They also abandoned their estates, their dislike of country life perhaps offering a clue as to why landlords sometimes reside in cities and sometimes not. Dependence

In Latin America, the Spanish government attempted to avoid the centrifugal tendencies which feudalism encouraged in Sicily by instituting a system of land and labor grants. According to this *encomienda* system, agents of the empire controlled Indian land and labor in the colonies and issued licences to colonists to utilize these resources for stipulated periods of time. But the empire lacked the administrative control to prevent colonists from becoming proprietors with unencumbered rights to land and labor. As one authority has suggested, in the end the *encomienda* enhanced the maneuverability of the colonists by providing them with additional means of coercing labor (Wallerstein 1974: 93, n. 91). In Latin America, no less than in Sicily, feudal trappings and foreign luxuries spread rapidly through the landowning classes by means of status rivalry and tied them irrevocably to the world-system which demanded their primary production in exchange. Thus, they had no great interest in the economic diversification and development of their own regions, whose governments they systematically directed to serve their own ends. The landowners were a dependence, not a development, elite, and this—not the titles they acquired or their passionate attachment to "feudalism"—accounts for the resulting erosion of central power (see Stavenhagen 1967).

ROYAL BUREAUCRACIES OUTWITTED

European governments made their first major advances in the centralization of state power during the sixteenth century. These advances rested heavily upon the creation of bureaucratic offices, including the recruitment of a professional army to enforce the policies of the state. Military and other officials, however, were rarely salaried since states did not yet control sufficient resources. Often the official's loyalty was based on "prebendal domain"—the sale of offices, franchises, and concessions by the state. Prebendalism produced the mercenary soldier who was licensed to reward himself from the booty of war. Among civilian officials, the best-known prebendal office was that of tax farmer. Under a prebendal regime, tax collection is a concession which produces an income for the concessionaires of the state. Instead of a salary, the concessionaire receives all the tax returns beyond a predetermined amount which is forwarded to the

---

on foreign markets and investments would, one suspects, draw them into cities, whereas under conditions of withdrawal from markets and investments they might gravitate toward the land.

state. Clearly, the prebendal official has a certain incentive to exercise his office above and beyond the call of duty, and where public and private interests clash, the tax farmer's loyalty to the state may be tenuous. Such tax farmers had (and have) a reputation as entrepreneurs who habitually earned a profit in addition to that stipulated in their concessions, by cheating the state, on the one hand, and extorting excess taxes from the population, on the other.

This private use of public office in the state bureaucracy was more common in peripheral than in core societies. The reasons lie in the preceding distinction between diarchy and monarchy, that is, in the forces that so severely weakened the presence of the central authority in peripheral colonial regions. As Wittfogel (1957: 255–256) and Weber (1968: 33–36) both suggested in their analyses of bureaucracy, entrepreneurial behavior for personal gain characterizes officeholders in the degree that central control and surveillance are lax. Sicilian grain barons were not motivated to rebel against the Spanish crown, but neither were they compelled to sacrifice their own interests for those of the state.

In Sicily, prebendal offices attracted entrepreneurs who were eager not only to earn a steady income in exchange for loyal service but to profit further from "creative officeholding," by whatever means. Koenigsberger tells us that the Castilian monarchy, which adamantly excluded Sicilians from official positions at the court, lamented the great dearth of capable and honest officials in its colony. The island had only one law school, in the eastern city of Catania, and there they said, the training was of poor quality. Sicilian officials were considered eminently corruptible, and there is little reason to doubt that they were, especially considering the structure of regional government. According to Koenigsberger, tax collectors did little more (and could do no less) than engage in "legalized robbery," while "free enterprise" pervaded all administrative levels. Judges, for example, were taken off salary on the ground that their work would proceed more efficiently if they were paid from fees they could charge the litigants. The fees were called *candles,* and it was often said that "he who could light the most candles for the judge to see the truth would win his case . . . [Koenigsberger 1969: 91]." Koenigsberger reports further that the judges neglected criminal for civil cases, in which there were more, and wealthier, litigants and hence greater profit. The prisons were filled with the poor awaiting trial for criminal offenses (1969: 91–92).

The royal bureaucracy's paralysis in the face of local private interests is best seen in the Bourbons' attempt to control the export of wheat in the late eighteenth century. In Sicily, as almost everywhere, population was growing. Just over 1 million in 1700, it climbed to 1.5 million by 1800. Much of this population growth was concentrated in Palermo and other large towns and cities. Palermo grew from an estimated 145,000–200,000 inhabitants in the eighteenth century, making it the second largest city in Italy (after Naples; Pontieri 1961: 35–38). The Neapolitan Bourbons, confronted with this, vacillated between free trade and export controls. On the one hand they feared unemployment, landlessness, and famine, which might produce popular uprisings, especially the inevitable food riot. On the other hand, they were impressed by England's accomplishments under a regime of competition and free trade. As a result, a feeble and halting version of closure characterized their reign, while private interests continued to proliferate, supported by their control over an exportable commodity. The situation was not unlike that of France's *l'ancien régime,* which similarly wavered between free trade and protectionism. It heard arguments from the agriculturally based and liberal-minded physiocrats, eager to improve agriculture through competition. It also faced the politically explosive consequences of scarce and expensive bread. On the eve of the French Revolution, it was very much a government sitting on the fence, uncertain which way to tumble—not an unusual predicament for "old regimes."

According to Bourbon policy, producers were required to sell a third of their crop to the towns in which their lands were located, at prices current immediately following the harvest. The producers responded to this regulation by underestimating the volume of the harvest or by claiming not to know their own production in official reports and hiding portions of the harvest. This prompted the state to survey crops before they were harvested, but like all other forms of state surveillance under the Bourbons, this policy was scarcely effective. The officials who administered the survey either were poor and easily bribed or were themselves speculators in grain—or both. Not only did the producers minimize what they owed to the towns, they created an impression of shortage which drove up prices (Brancato, 1946; Petino, 1946). In the words of one observer, "resisting to the point of famine meant earning 1000 percent [Balsamo 1803: 59–61, 63]."

The policy on exports was equally difficult to administer. According to law, producers were to deposit surplus grain (beyond that consumed locally) in royal warehouses. Twice a year, in December and April, owners of this grain were invited to purchase export licenses for amounts of grain that would threaten neither the estimated requirement of the island, nor an emergency reserve to be left in the royal magazines. It was not difficult, however, to circumvent these regulations. The island's uncharted and unpatrolled coastline provided every natural advantage to clandestine exporters of grain. Secret storehouses were built near hidden coves from which grain was regularly smuggled into European trade. The mule paths and transhumance routes which carried the grain from the interior to the coast could hardly be policed by the state. Moreover, certificates of deposit in royal warehouses were negotiable, and circulated like currency, encouraging speculation. Some of these certificates were counterfeit; the deposits did not actually exist.

An important ingredient in these tactics was collusion between the producers and exporters, and the administrative staff of the royal warehouses (Pontieri 1933: 198). The state attempted to discipline warehouse administrators by rotating them from post to post and subjecting them to rigorous performance standards. These disciplinary measures only inspired more sophisticated frauds, for surveillance was weak and the market was strong. Following the winter of 1784–1785, when shortages created disorders which rocked Palermo, the Viceroy Caracciolo complained of "the extraordinary haste with which everyone was transporting his grain to the royal warehouses in a year when the harvest was sterile [1785: 15–16]." One prince exported 20,000 bushels during a year when the island had to import grain to feed the population of Palermo (Mack Smith 1968b: 275). Faced with such greed, a viceroy could curtail export licenses altogether, but this, lamented Caracciolo, "was like sounding the trumpet in the ears of all, advising them of the shortage of wheat and giving them time to hide it [1785: 21]." Fear of shortage and widespread hoarding were as effective in raising prices as actual shortages, and restrictions on exports did more to create famine than they did to prevent it.

The Latin American parallel is described by Wolf and Hansen in an article on *caudillos* (1967). In Latin America, as in Sicily, the Spanish Empire imposed restrictions it could not enforce. These restrictions were incompatible with the evolving market forces of North Atlantic Europe. Thus, state officials and anyone who dealt with them were motivated to recognize and seize opportunities in the interstices of formal authority, to bend and circumvent rules in their own self-interest. Particularly in the eighteenth century, when Spain still clung to its New World colonies against the irresistible pull of Dutch, French, and English markets, was the contradiction between norm and fact intense. In Latin America, as in Sicily and southern Italy, contraband flourished (Stein and Stein 1970: 101–103), and with the same result: middlemen or brokers who "earned a living by their wits." This was one foundation of broker capitalism, a weak and easily circumvented state machine which encouraged the private use of public resources. Other foundations, a weak infrastructure connecting settlements and a lack of security in the countryside, are discussed in the next two sections.

RELATIONS AMONG SETTLEMENTS

Accompanying the disappearance of villages in fourteenth-century Sicily was the disappearance of regional markets and roads, break-of-bulk points, and centers of refinement and craft production. As a result, the structure of settlements in the latifundist area became less differentiated and less complex. Several routes roughly coinciding with Roman and Arab roads fell into disuse and at least four major towns (Corleone, Piazza Armerina, Salemi, and Sciacca) ceased to function as specialized commercial centers. Proceeds from the annual fair at Sciacca fell sharply (Ciaccio 1900: 53; Scaturro 1926: Vol. II, 19–20), and the fairs of the other three towns were discontinued (Sergio and Perez 1962: vii–ix). Even provincial capitals were abolished in the fifteenth century in favor of local autonomy for the baronial towns (Scaturro 1926: Vol. I, 410). In effect, Sicily, especially western Sicily, abandoned a structure in which villages, towns, and cities were integrated through bureaucratic and commercial hierarchies. The new structure was different: Settlements were each internally stratified but each resembled the others; there was no division of labor and little hierarchical order among settlements; and each settlement was linked to the outside world through grain exports.

The same pattern prevailed in the analogous regions of southern Italy. Pitkin, for example, draws attention to the morphological similarity of settlements in the Mezzogiorno, as contrasted with settlements in northern Italy, where village, town, and city are clearly distinct (1963: 127). The Latin American parallel is also striking. Richard Morse's analysis of settlement patterns in certain Latin American regions agrees with our observations of western Sicily. In common is a relative lack of differentiation among communities such that there is no hierarchy of settlements ranging from cities, to principal towns, to minor towns, to villages. The agrotowns (Morse calls them "colony towns") are functionally similar, although they vary considerably in population size (1962).

Agrotowns, or colony towns, were internally heterogeneous and this in part compensated for the reduced integration among them. In Sicily such towns typically included landowners or their representatives, plus merchants, professionals, shopkeepers, and artisans, as well as peasants. Each community was therefore quite self-contained. People were born, married, and died within its borders and, except for the peasants who commuted daily to their fields, they rarely if ever traveled much beyond the community. We met two very old women in Villamaura who, in the mid-1960s, claimed that they had never left the parish of their birth to cross the main street of the town. Theirs is an extreme example, yet it symbolized the bonds which tied people—women more tightly than men, it is true—to their towns in traditional Sicily. These bonds were strong enough that today one still encounters dialect words and phrases that are unique to particular towns.

Local attachment is also reflected in religious festivals. In the past (as now) each community had its own patron saints and madonnas who were honored by an annual procession. Except for the shrine of the Black Madonna at Tindari on the northeastern coast, and that of Santa Rosalia in Palermo, there were no major pilgrimage centers in Sicily to attract people from afar. Just as there were no market towns, theocratically specialized centers did not exist, and people clung all the more vigorously to their local protectors (Sciascia 1965). In 1929, Chapman found that a newly wed husband might take his wife to some important *festa* in another town during their first year of marriage but this was "the only occasion on which the woman ever [left] her native village [1971: 105]."

INSECURITY IN THE COUNTRYSIDE

The nucleated agrotown was surrounded by an almost uninhabited, barren, and desolate countryside in which travel was extraordinarily difficult and often dangerous. Until the late eighteenth century, there were virtually no carriageable roads in western Sicily and travel was largely by mule, horseback, or sedan chair, along paths of transhumance which were impassible in the torrential rains of winter. If they were lucky, travelers averaged 4 kilometers an hour. To the difficult terrain was added the threat of banditry. This phenomenon was common throughout Europe in the sixteenth century. In peripheral areas like Latin America and Sicily, it was particularly pronounced and lasted longer into the nineteenth and even the twentieth century. Bandits, broadly speaking, were displaced persons, casualties of the processes of state formation and economic change associated with the rise of capitalism. Turned loose from the social order, they compensated for their losses through theft and extortion, supported by violence (Wallerstein 1974: 141–143). In the peripheral regions especially, state institutions were weak and unable to police the countryside. Neither were they able to control the causes of displacement or provide adequate welfare for persons who were displaced. So banditry spread and the large property owners, unable to find protection in the state, made their own terms with local bands. The private army of ruffians and brigands attached to a local magnate was very common in peripheral areas.

In Sicily, particularly western Sicily, the strength of banditry reflected above all the displacement of herding interests, as the specialization in wheat advanced after 1500. For, to the extent that wheat expanded at the expense of pasturage, it caused a reduction in the animal population; yet urban markets for animal products, both in Palermo and abroad, continued to be active. If anything, population growth, urbanization, and a rising standard of living caused these markets to expand. As a result, animal rustling was an extraordinarily lucrative activity, which lined the pockets and bolstered the courage of those who were adept at it. Spanish legislation required that livestock sales be conducted publically, with the seller showing proof of ownership. But the police powers of the state were poorly organized. The viceroy appointed a public security officer to each community, and strong viceroys tried to place Spaniards in these positions but were frequently unable to do so because of local protest. Most of the officers were from the localities and found no difficulty in collaborating with local brigands (Mack Smith, 1968a: 296). Unable to extend its police powers, the state allowed any owner of 10 or more cattle to carry arms "on foot or horseback, except in the city streets [D'Alessandro 1959: 164]" (see also Mack Smith 1968a: 149 ff., 187 ff.). Travelers could not have relished the thought that the government had no monopoly of arms unless, of course, they were themselves armed or accompanied by an armed escort. Pitrè records, for the eighteenth century, that even under escort no one set out on a trip into the interior without first making his last will and testament, having himself confessed, and taking communion (Pitrè 1944: Vol. I, 165). As a further precaution, travelers would pay protection money to bandits along the route of their trip.

In the late eighteenth century the Neapolitan Bourbons

launched a program of road construction in Sicily which was in part intended to deal with the problem of rural insecurity. But their resources were meager relative to the task. Erosion and landslides, the by-products of latifundism, added to the challenge of the Sicilian landscape, with its anarchic mountain terrain. Geographers and engineers who came to build roads in Sicily considered road construction there more difficult than in the Alps (Trasselli 1962: xv). Between 1777 and 1824, 250 miles of roadway was built but much of it was poorly constructed and fell into disuse (De Welz 1964: 146–207). The problems of internal communication and security in the countryside thus carried over into the nineteenth and twentieth centuries, while in the core areas of Europe effective state governments had long before laid such problems to rest.

BROKER CAPITALISM AND
POLITICAL STRUCTURE

Poor roads, armed bandits, and a virtually uninhabited countryside combined to reinforce the apparent isolation of the rural towns and further retard their integration. But the isolation of the towns from one another and the state by no means indicated the isolation of Sicily from the world, any more than the "feudal" titles of lords indicated participation in a precapitalist or self-sufficient economy. The agrotown was little connected to other nearby settlements not because Sicily was autarchic but because it was held firmly in the magnetic field of foreign merchants and cities, by the export of primary products and the import of manufactures. Morse's analysis of Latin America applies equally well here: This condition of foreign domination "militated against the emergence of a stable network of towns and villages, producing a variety of economic surpluses and linked in commercial exchange [1962: 479]."

If producers were not linked to indigenous market towns by regular commercial exchanges (because there were no market towns and no varied surpluses to trade), commodities nevertheless moved throughout the island toward the coasts, destined for foreign trade. The result was widespread opportunity for entrepreneurship. Who were the entrepreneurs? In the Sicilian interior they were not foreign merchants who were rooted in Palermo or abroad, nor were they the great landowners, most of whom preferred to live far away from their land. They were distinctively *rural* entrepreneurs who spent days or weeks on end at the *massaria*—the ranchlike establishment which coordinated the agricultural and pastoral activities of the latifundium. They were, in any event, familiar with the rural landscape and the people who controlled it, from the bandits in the mountains to the landlords in the cities. They personally provided the integration which the state bureaucracy and indigenous infrastructure lacked. For Sicily, especially western Sicily, they were the most important broker capitalists. They are discussed in Chapter 4.

In conclusion, we would suggest that (*1*) a diarchic form of government in which barons shared power with the crown; (2) a feeble bureaucracy understaffed and undercapitalized from the center; (3) a poorly articulated infrastructure of relations among towns; and (*4*) the proliferation of banditry in the countryside all gave support to the pursuit of profit by short-lived, task-specific coalitions employing extralegal means. Neither feudalism nor isolation can explain these phenomena, for western Sicily was neither feudal (in the usual sense) nor isolated. It was not a traditional society. Rather, its particular role in the capitalist world economy created the political structure so congenial to broker capitalism.

chapter 4

Peasants, Herdsmen, and Rural Entrepreneurs

The specialized production of wheat and animal products for export from Sicily to the metropolitan centers of Spain and Italy led to the formation of social groups which would have to face a new set of pressures in the nineteenth and twentieth centuries: the pressures of an English-dominated, industrial, global system of exploitation. To understand the Sicilian response to these pressures, it will help to be familiar with the way of life, the activities, and the problems of three broadly defined groups—peasants, herdsmen, and rural entrepreneurs. Our information about these groups derives largely from fieldwork, from written accounts of rural life in Sicily dating back to the 1700s, and from local archival material covering roughly the period 1870 to World War II. From these sources two themes emerge: First, in the face of external pressures, herdsmen had more leverage than peasants; and second, rural entrepreneurs (more oriented toward pastoralism than agriculture) had the most leverage of all. For this group, the specialized colonial role of Sicily as a producer of primary resources opened up more opportunities than it frustrated.

THE *MEZZADRIA* SYSTEM—DIFFERENT FROM
SLAVERY, SERFDOM, AND FREE LABOR

Several forms of land contract coexist in rural Sicily; they are complex enough to bewilder the untutored observer. By distinguishing contracts associated with diversified village agriculture from contracts associated with latifundism, we can resolve some of the confusion. Through the Arab–Norman period, in addition to privately owned allodia, there were two common arrangements by which peasants could gain access to the land. One guaranteed access to public land or land held collectively by residents of a community, with the right to pasture animals and collect whatever the land bore: wood, stones, wild berries, and vegetables. Covered by the legal concept of servitudes, *usi civici,* or use rights, this type of access implied a communal domain. These were ascriptive rights available to all citizens of the community (Pupillo-Baresi 1903).

The second arrangement guaranteed the peasant access to arable land on a long-term basis (several decades or even generations). Known as *emphyteusis,* it involved a fixed rent in money or kind but no obligation of military or personal service. The peasant was free to rent or sell his holding and to hire labor for its cultivation. Investments and improvements were his responsibility and any increase in productivity was exclusively his to enjoy. In addition to the annual rent, the landlord's rights extended to a percentage of the selling price should the holding be alienated, and the right to repossess the holding should it be abandoned or unimproved, or should the tenant default on his rent (Bloch 1962: 179; Boyd 1952: 70; Corleo 1871: 11).

The contract of emphyteusis, like the copyhold contract in England, gave security and freedom of movement to the peasant. Use rights similarly supported peasant autonomy. They enabled local householders to keep a few milk and draft animals and to collect supplementary food and construction materials. Both types of holding existed all over Sicily. In western Sicily, however, the Catalan expansion of the fourteenth and fifteenth centuries dealt a heavy blow to both, such that emphyteusis contracts were thereafter concentrated on the northeastern coast and thinly distributed throughout the rest of the island (Garufi 1946–1947: Vol. 1, 35–51). Use rights continued to exist in the west, but in a weakened form. As new communities were founded in the late sixteenth and seventeenth centuries, contracts in emphyteusis and use rights on common land were offered to attract settlers. The eighteenth-century resurgence of latifundism, however, caused many landlords to abrogate those arrangements which were favorable to peasants (Mack Smith 1968b: 278–279).

There were three major types of contract under the latifundist agrarian regime: sharecropping (*mezzadria*); a rental arrangement known as the *terratico*; and hourly or daily wage labor contracts. Until the late nineteenth century, when thousands of peasants became day laborers, *mezzadria* was the most common form. Sharecropping spread through Italy and parts of France as these areas declined relative to North Atlantic Europe in the seventeenth century. Wallerstein contrasts it with the "second serfdom" in eastern Europe during roughly the same period. There, peasant labor was more rigidly coerced, as peasants were forbidden to leave the land to which they were assigned and seek employment elsewhere, under threat of violence. They were virtually slaves. While sharecroppers did not have the leverage of yeoman farmers, who owned their own land, they were not so constrained as were slaves or serfs. They contributed a share of the capital investment in a holding, participated in the risks and profits, and to some extent worked on their own initiative. The existence of sharecropping rather than serfdom probably reflected a ratio of population to cultivable land that was higher than that in areas like Poland, where specialization in wheat led to enserfment (Wallerstein 1974: 103–105).

Serfdom in Sicily played quite a different role, having been introduced under Norman rule when the island was relatively autonomous vis-à-vis foreign markets. The state then was strong in relation to the feudal lords, some of whose fiefs were unpopulated. Thousands of peasants belonged to the royal domain, holding property in emphyteusis or as outright owners. Populated fiefs housed the peasants in villages, or *casali,* and when the villages and peasant properties fell victim to the Catalan advance, so did serfdom, to be replaced by sharecropping and day labor on the latifundia. Only some aspects of the lord–peasant relationship characteristic of feudalism remained: the *angherie* (annoyances) which burdened Sicilian peasants well into the twentieth century, such as the obligation to deliver "gifts" of produce to the lord and the greeting "I kiss your hand, excellency."

In summary, the relegation of Sicily to the periphery of an expanding world-system deprived peasants of their rights to communal domain and secure tenures in emphyteusis, although it completely eliminated neither of these forms, just as it did not completely eliminate the allodium, or small private holding. It eliminated serfdom of the earlier, Norman, period but not the *banalités* and tokens of deference required by the lords of their tenants. It replaced or supplemented these earlier forms of land contract with a plurality of new forms, the most common of which was the *mezzadria* sharecropping contract. We have yet to assess the extent to which the resulting conditions were exploitative, for in fact they were. In many respects Sicilian peasants were closer to their East European counterparts than were the peasant *mezzadri* who sharecropped the land in northern and central Italy.

LATIFUNDISM AND PEASANT INSECURITY

The economic decline of northern Italy in the seventeenth century resulted in the decline of industry and the ruralization of the economy, but it did not turn this region into a specialized producer of primary products for export to world markets, as in Sicily. In southern Italy and Sicily the *mezzadria* contract worked differently from that of northern and central Italy, for only in the south did it serve to organize production for export to foreign markets. Sydel Silverman's comparison of *mezzadria* in north and south Italy is a useful guide (1968). In central Italy, where sharecropping became the dominant agrarian contract, peasants were granted stable long-term tenure on their plots of land. They and their families lived on dispersed homesteads or farms which were in turn passed on to their heirs. They owned almost all the other means of production and received approximately half of the yield as their share. In Sicily, by contrast, sharecropping peasants lived in agrotowns and negotiated to cultivate several small scattered holdings for a year at a time. Because the land lay fallow or in pasturage after each harvest, the peasant had always to sharecrop different plots in successive years. Nor did his family participate as on a farm. The young unmarried sons helped with the agricultural labor but once married they were on their own. Nothing like the extended family characteristic of central Italy existed among the peasants of the south. The women of the family, meanwhile, had no gardens, or barnyards, no real productive resources which they controlled except, perhaps, their capacity to produce children. Though they processed food and raised chickens which foraged in the streets and courtyards of the town, though they spun and wove flax and wool and may have made brooms from palm leaves collected by their husbands, peasant women in the latifundist region of Sicily did little agricultural labor.

South Italian and Sicilian sharecroppers owned very few of the means of production. Well-capitalized rural entrepreneurs, called *gabellotti,* typically rented whole estates from the barons and divided the portions to be cultivated into small plots for sublet to peasant sharecroppers. The *gabellotti* owned the plows and draft animals, while peasants owned little more than their hoes and were constantly in debt to these overlords. Citing Takahashi's observation that share-croppers who work for usurious landowners are "semi-serfs," Waller-stein suggests that coercion by debt is hardly less harsh than the coercion of the Polish second serfdom (1974: 104).

THE PROBLEM OF FRAGMENTATION

The conditions of Mediterranean agriculture compounded the insecurity of Sicilian peasants by promoting the fragmentation of land and the fragmentation of social units such as the family and the com-munity. Mediterranean grain farming required a light scratch plowing. The transalpine heavy plow would have destroyed the crust on the surface which is essential to the soil's capacity to retain moisture in an arid climate (Wolf 1966b: 32–33). With light plowing a wheat field could take on virtually any size or shape; it could be cultivated according to a rotation cycle quite out of step with that of contiguous fields, and it could be plowed by one animal without the use of a team. Even on the great latifundia which coordinated planting and harvesting over wide areas, fragmentation of land and labor was the rule. *Gabellotti* and landlords did not impose uniform rotation cycles. The quality of land, its altitude, and its distance from the town, together with market forecasts, dictated one of several alternate cycles, as well as the terms of the rental or sharecropping contracts. Most estates were divided into three to five portions. In some cases, a portion comprised noncontiguous lands. Often, different portions underwent different cycles of rotation which varied in length from 3 to 6 years. According to Ziino, regular rotation was almost never car-ried out and contracts varied from one lot to another (1911: 78–102).

Once a *gabellotto,* in negotiations with the landlord, had decided on rotation patterns, he divided the portions of the estate to be cultivated into plots of 1–6 hectares for distribution among share-croppers. The majority of sharecropping contracts stipulated an even division of the harvest: half to the *gabellotto,* half to the peasant. But the contracts were almost always embellished by various additional burdens on the peasant: interest on borrowed seed, plows, and work animals; contributions to the estate guard's salary and to the priest who said Sunday mass at the *massaria*; fees for the cost of transporting grain to the threshing floor; and so on (Sonnino 1925: 35–36; Ziino 1911: 85). The peasant who cropped good land within easy distance of the town paid more dearly for his contract than the peasant whose plot was poor and inaccessible. Some contracts, particularly in periods of pressure, gave the peasant only a third, a fourth, or a fifth of the annual yield. To negotiate contracts, the landlord or *gabellotto* chose a peasant of "good faith" who presided over a kind of auction as peasants competed for the good lots. The terms varied from peasant to peasant and from lot to lot. Contracts were made to fit individual situations (Ziino 1911: 75–78). Since few plots were ever cultivated for more than a year at a time, peasants were faced with the anxieties of an open-ended negotiation after every harvest. Surely because the contracts were so idiosyncratic and complex, the *gabellotti* often twisted their terms on the threshing floor the following July. Peasants had to be forever on their guard; yet, they were often cheated. In Villamaura peasants recall how the typical *gabellotto*—now a figure of the past—used to measure the grain in units which differed from those in the contract, advantaged of course by the absence of uniform standard weights and measures in Sicily.

Because of the insecurity inherent in the *mezzadria* contract of latifundist Sicily, peasants naturally wanted to supplement it with other kinds of landholding: straight rental (more common in eastern than in western Sicily), land in emphyteusis, and, wherever possible, outright ownership. Poor peasants owned little or no land and probably rented very little. They supplemented their income with day labor. Middle and wealthier peasants (the latter called *borgesi*) owned one to a few scattered plots and held the majority of long-term emphyteusis contracts. But how much security rested in these holdings? The exigencies of latifundism and the Mediterranean climate impinged on them, too. Either they were on poor, stony land near the town or they were on good basin land far away from the peasant's house. Both conditions discouraged capital investment and improvement (Chisholm 1962: 60–65). People were also crowded on the land, and agriculture was crowded by pastoralism. Land disputes between kinsmen and neighbors were common.

Men who farmed contiguous holdings (whether as owners or as sharecroppers) were potential competitors. In Sicily, anyone whose land did not border on an established road or path had the right to an access path through his neighbor's land. Similarly, he was entitled to construct a drainage ditch from his field across other fields to the nearest runoff point. The man who depended on another for access to his holding worried that his neighbor might sow grain in the path, while the neighbor worried that the path would be widened by passing men and animals. Should one peasant inundate the other's field when trying to drain his own, or deprive the other of water, a quarrel might ensue. Quarrels were undoubtedly most bitter during periods when advancing landlordism, pasturage, or population growth caused contraction of the available land.

Sicilian peasants (but not the nobility) practiced partible inheritance of land, for males and females in theory, at least for males in practice. The result was to accelerate the fragmentation of land and with it of families. Given that agricultural technology placed no limit on the minimum size or the shape of holdings, the overriding consideration in property divisions was (and is) the mutual satisfaction of all the heirs. In partitions involving more than one holding, each plot of land in each location was divided, usually among all the legitimate claimants.

One inheritance and division which we followed in Villamaura offers a good example of the process. A deceased smallholder left five plots to be divided among nine heirs. One plot, an olive grove nearly 0.5 hectares in size, was 3 kilometers from town. Two other plots, each 0.75 hectares, were about 5 kilometers from town. Both were good wheat land, but only one was on the public road. The remaining two plots, each a little over 1 hectare, were 8 and 10 kilometers from the town, one on a mule path, and the other not, and both with mediocre, stony soils, suitable mainly for grazing. A surveyor was hired to create nine purportedly equal quotas, which he did by leaving the olive grove intact and dividing the other four holdings into four or five portions each. The quotas were put in a hat and, in the presence of a notary public, the claimants drew. Eight of them received various combinations of good and bad land in at least two and sometimes three locations; the ninth drew the olive grove and the obligation to compensate the others in cash. Among the eight, some had to grant rights of access to others. Although all nine heirs had agreed that the quotas were of equal value, one of the eight was doubtful after the drawing. Having received in his quota a stony plot with no access to a public road, he accused the winner of the olive grove of collusion with the surveyor. It would have been better, he argued, to divide that half hectare of olive trees nine different ways. Such conflicts are not unfamiliar, and the outcomes might occasionally seem odd. In the land register for Villamaura, one woman appears as owner of 231/832 of a plot consisting of 0.05 hectares. Her cousin owns the other 601 parts. Occasionally, multiple ownership of single trees occurs.[1]

Property divisions multiplied the boundaries which a man had to defend against the encroachment of others; furthermore, they complicated rights of access. As they increased the likelihood of conflict, the security which presumably attaches to ownership declined. Landowning peasants, with very few exceptions, thus had to supplement their holdings with sharecropping contracts and sometimes with day labor for others. There were, it is true, several gradations of Sicilian peasant, ranging from poor to wealthy, but they did not fall into clearly separate categories. In the latifundist sector the majority were simply plurally occupied sharecroppers and tenants, most with a little land on the side but some with none at all, and each additionally burdened with various feudal dues and obligations to a lord. As Goubert has suggested for the Beauvaisis region of seventeenth-century France, plural occupation meant semi-proletarian status (1967: 156–158). Whether semi-proletarian or semi-serf matters little. The basic feature was an overriding insecurity of land tenure which, although quite different from the "second serfdom," nevertheless had the same effect—to coerce peasant labor.

In the eighteenth century, north Europeans—Englishmen, Frenchmen, Germans—traveled extensively as northern Europe expanded its sphere of influence. In Palermo, foreign guests sat down to meals at the tables of the aristocracy on which upward of 24 courses were served, not counting appetizers, desserts, and sherberts. In the interior of the island they discovered the conditions of the peasantry to be more appalling than anywhere else in Europe. Peasants ate no meat and few vegetables, except for fava beans in season and the wild vegetables they gathered on communal or fallow land. They made thin soups of these "grasses"; they did not eat pasta; and the bread

---

[1] In instances of extreme complexity such as this, the holding in question usually remains intact for purposes of cultivation, its proceeds going to each heir according to the quota owned. Peasants in Sicily can also mitigate fragmentation by arranging appropriate marriages with first or second cousins. This strategy, however, seems less effective in Sicily than Davis (1973) reported for Pisticci, a south Italian agrotown. An inquiry we made into cases of cousin marriage going back to 1850 revealed that in the great majority of cases cousins who married either owned bits of land in different rural zones or owned no land at all (see pp. 76–78 of this chapter). We encountered no instances of land transactions specifically intended to consolidate holdings, although there may have been some. In the minds of both peasants and land brokers in Villamaura, fragmentation seemed to loom as an irreversible tendency of rural life.

they ate was of poor quality. Bread and soup were augmented, according to season, by onions or by poor quality cheese and by the fruit of the prickly pear cactus. Unlike the aristocracy, peasants consumed very little wine or milk and no coffee or chocolate. Their beverage was water and their special treats were *baccalà* and tuna. Observers were universally shocked by their poor health (Pitrè 1944: Vol. I, 331–339; Pontieri 1933).

THE POSITION OF HERDSMEN COMPARED TO THAT OF PEASANTS

The arid climate of Sicily made it difficult to contain the movement of animals, and transhumant migration of herds required pastoral specialists who constituted a subgroup of the rural labor force. If we can judge by the genealogical data obtained from Villamaura, this pastoral subgroup overlapped with the peasantry. Herdsmen as a rule had peasant kinsmen, some of them in ascendant and descendant generations, many of them collaterals, and herdsmen also cultivated the land as day laborers or sharecroppers. Their primary activity, however, had to do with animal husbandry. They worked individually or in association with other herdsmen.

Herdsmen had varying degrees of relationship to the great latifundia. Some formed an integral part of the *massaria* complex, which organized the pastoral as well as the agricultural components of a large estate. Others—the minority in western Sicily—remained outside the *massaria,* although dependent upon it for some of their grazing land. All of them, however, felt the impact of the latifundist agrarian regime. As it massed large herds of animals and lengthened the routes of transhumance so as to link coast with interior in vast pastoral enterprises, independent shepherds and goatherds lost their access to land. They, too, were excluded from common land by the lords' *difesi,* or enclosures. Moreover, as wheat cultivation spread, it intensified competition for pastures, driving the most vulnerable herdsmen onto the least productive grazing land.

Herdsmen, whether associated with the *massaria* or independent of it, also competed for access to cultivated land—land which could be grazed after a harvest or in the second or third year of a rotation cycle. Unlike transalpine agriculture, in which communities strictly regulated the opening up of harvested fields for grazing (on a fixed date all farmers with fields in this condition were obliged to open them up), the Mediterranean system meant that herdsmen had to make their own arrangements. Over the centuries, an open, unfenced countryside in which herdsmen and cultivators used the same or contiguous spaces gave rise to a complex set of social arrangements. Where herdsmen grazed animals on fallow land or on the stubble of harvested fields, they did so through contracts which they negotiated with individual landholders. Because their entry into the zones of cultivation was not timed or regulated by the community, it often happened that small herds had to pass through cultivated fields to graze on neighboring fields which happened to be in the fallow stage of the rotation cycle. The resulting delicately balanced (and tenuous) arrangements degenerated into conflicts of interest during periods of pressure. Then, negotiated access gave way to trespass as herdsmen grazed their animals abusively on land that was not theirs and retaliated with violence against those who disputed their actions.[2]

In the long run, stock raising gave way to agriculture in western Sicily, but not until the twentieth century. Up to that time pastoralism prevailed, not so much by preventing agricultural expansion as by ensuring that it would take a form compatible with continued joint exploitation of the land. In the status hierarchy of western Sicily, shepherds and cowherds ranked lower than peasants. After all, they spent most of their time with animals in the "barbarian" countryside, away from the "civilization" of the towns. In many ways, however, they had greater freedom of movement and more power than the peasant cultivators. It was their mobility in particular that gave them leverage in their conflicts with peasants. Of the two categories, herdsmen were most likely to carry arms. The rural entrepreneurs, whom we discuss next, were mostly of pastoral rather than peasant background.

RURAL PLACES AND RURAL ENTREPRENEURS

Of all the broker capitalists in western Sicily, by far the most important were those who controlled the production and circulation of the primary exports of the region. Their operations were head-

---

[2] Conflicts of interest between herdsmen and cultivators also existed in the European countryside, especially in certain regions and during certain periods (see, for example, Goubert 1967: 156). However, they never approached the intensity or pervasiveness of conflict in the Mediterranean (see Chiva 1963; Peristiany 1965; Pitt-Rivers 1961, 1963, 1965).

quartered not in town but in four types of rural place: monasteries with their surrounding arable land, rural inns (called *fondaci*), the water driven flour mills, and the *massarie*. Each of these places had a resident staff, depending on the season. Those who lived in the countryside usually had a house in town where their families lived, as there were virtually no women and children in the countryside.

Physically the *massaria* is a rude complex of buildings which form a square around a courtyard, perhaps containing a well. The principal building housed the apartment and offices of the estate owner or his chief administrator. Other buildings contained stalls for draft and transport animals; storerooms for seed, equipment, and cereals; quarters for the permanent residents, including a kitchen and bakery; and straw pallets for agricultural laborers and sharecroppers who would sleep over during the harvest season. Some housed peasant labor in straw shacks or simple mud dwellings (*cassette di muro*), and some also featured a small chapel. The permanent hands usually planted vegetables near an underground spring so they could irrigate the garden during the summer months. But there were few trees to soften the surrounding landscape. On the contrary, for want of wood

The interior courtyard of a massaria. *"In all, the* massaria *bore little resemblance to the villa, chateau, or manor house familiar in other regions of Italy and Europe."*

bread was baked, water boiled, and cheese manufactured over fires of straw and brushwood. In all, the *massaria* bore little resemblance to the villa, chateau, or manor house familiar in other regions of Italy and Europe. Uncomfortable and unhygienic, it was clearly not intended for family life. Its windows and doors opened mainly into the courtyard and it was, if anything, as much a "fortress" as it was a farm (Scrofani 1962: 241–242; Ziino 1911: 50–55).

Rural monasteries and inns were equally rustic. A monastary was often only a glorified *massaria* staffed by monks; whereas the typical inn (in some cases part of a *massaria*) consisted of two rooms—a tavern for eating, drinking, and playing cards, and a large stall in which men, animals, and carts shared lodgings. Not just the inns, but also the monasteries, mills, and *massarie* were places where travelers would get together—they vibrated with the comings and goings of rural entrepreneurs. Noteworthy among these were the men primarily responsible for transporting and marketing the island's major commodities: merchants who bought and sold grain, fleeces, cheese, and animals; mediators and brokers in the sale of the same goods; muleteers who transported and dealt in grain; and after 1800, when roads were being built, carters who replaced the muleteers; butchers from the towns who were also animal dealers; bandits who stole animals for profit and vendetta; and finally the innkeepers, monks, and millers.

Most of the rural entrepreneurs, however, were directly connected to the *massaria*. The *massaria* permanently housed estate guards (on large estates, a head guard, a custodian of the magazines, and several subordinate guards) and other men responsible for supervising peasant labor. Depending on its size, the *massaria* employed various other specialists: operators of stores, mills, and bakeries, grooms and stall boys for the transport animals; a lead muleteer and subordinates; a smith who made and repaired farming tools; and others who cared for draft animals and supervised the plowing (Blok 1974: 60–64; Sonnino 1925: 42). In addition to salaries paid in money and kind, plots of land and the free use of plows were granted the guards, overseers, and specialists. If they owned a few head of sheep or goats, which they often did, they might also be granted pasture rights. Owners or administrators of the latifundia preferred to hire on such terms for it gave their salaried employees a stake in the total operation and, they thought, reduced the need for supervision. Like the tax farmers and judges discussed in Chapter 3, the employees of a *massaria* were expected to work hard for profit; at least the profit motive would ensure that they stayed on the *massaria* through the harvest season (see Platzer and Schifani 1963).

According to Sonnino, who studied the administration of latifundia in 1876, perhaps half the livestock of a given *massaria* belonged to small-scale entrepreneurs who were also employees of the estate: cattle, sheep, and goat herders, some of whom were experts at various phases of animal husbandry and cheese production. Often four or five shepherds formed a "joint stock" association which itself had an administrative structure and was attached in the course of the year to more than one *massaria*. The head of such an association, the *curatolo,* specialized in preparing and marketing the cheese and other milk products. This man was among the most powerful of those who lived in the countryside, his influence being matched only by that of a chief guard or overseer (1925: 43–44).

Although he rarely lived in the countryside, the *gabellotto,* or chief administrator, was the prime mover in the *massaria* complex. In return for rent paid to the landowner, he controlled vast landholdings, sometimes consisting of several latifundia. First used in the sixteenth century to encourage better-off peasants to cultivate pastures, the contract of *gabella* (literally prebend) was widely in use by the mid-eighteenth century (Aymard 1973; Garufi 1946–1947: Vol. 2, 36–37; Romano 1964: 210). Like tax farmers and other prebendal officials in any peripheral society, the Sicilian *gabellotti* were ambitious and ruthless men who accumulated wealth by a great variety of means: at the expense of peasant sharecroppers and day laborers who were dependent on them for access to land and employment and who were forced to borrow plows and draft animals, seed and cash at usurious rates of interest; and also at the expense of the landowning noblemen whom they cheated and, indeed, on whose land they may have held the mortgage. Because *gabellotti* paid fixed rents, rising prices worked to their advantage. Many moved into the gentry stratum during periods of inflation. The landlords tried to protect themselves with short-term leases of 3, 6, or occasionally 9 years (an average rotation cycle was 3 years), but short-term leases only encouraged the *gabellotto* to milk a property for maximum short-run gain, rather than invest in improvements for the future. *Gabellotti* also took tax collecting concessions and other municipal services *in gabella* and trafficked actively in grain and animals. Many either owned or leased facilities for storing and elaborating agricultural products— flour mills, bakeries, wine and olive presses, warehouses, etc. Most important, the typical *gabellotto* owned large herds of animals and devoted parts of the latifundia he rented to grazing. His animals, in return, fertilized the landlord's fields on which they grazed. Upon his death in the seventeenth century, the *gabellotto* for the archbishop of Monreale left some 800 head of cattle, 800 pigs, 3000 sheep, and hundreds of asses, mules, horses, and bulls.[3] He was extremely rich, but not atypical (Garufi 1946–1947: Vol. 2, 58–59).

Animal rustling further strengthened the relationship between pastoral enterprise and rural capitalism. One of the most important of all indigenous commercial activities, it was organized and financed by rural entrepreneurs. Not a solitary occupation, rustling was profitable and secure in proportion to the speed with which livestock, once stolen, lost their identity in the slaughterhouse or on some distant *massaria*. This meant that a group of men had to work well together, and quickly, first to gather information about herds and flocks which might be vulnerable and about owners of animals who might be powerless to retaliate because they were weak or absent; then actually to steal the animals; then to find shelter and grazing for them en route to cooperating butchers or dealers (Alongi 1886: 111–133; Blok 1974: 138–139, 148–153). Influential rural entrepreneurs—especially *gabellotti,* head shepherds (*curatoli*), and estate guards (*campieri*)—organized these profitable operations. Even when they did not themselves steal the animals, they gathered and transmitted information, arranged the illicit commerce, and secured refuge for the shepherds and others who did the actual work.

Rural entrepreneurs also dominated the animal markets, or fairs, held in the late summer and early autumn in one interior town after another. According to our informants, before they ever owned trucks or cars, livestock owners and dealers attended fairs within roughly a 50-mile radius of their respective home towns. Mediators, brokers, wholesalers, and butchers also went to these fairs. In transit these men used routes of transhumance that were little known to the population at large and sought lodging and pasture for their animals at *massarie* along the way. Their close ties to this institution protected them against banditry and theft, which ordinary people greatly feared. Peasants who wished to make some transaction at a fair outside their own town usually traveled in the company of rural entrepreneurs who could arrange the necessary protection and sustenance for them.

It is interesting to compare the fairs of western and interior Sicily

[3] Pigs were unusual in western Sicily. A forest (one of few) in the territory of the archbishop of Monreale must account for their presence in this case.

with those of the northeastern coast, where the distances between settlements were small and there were no latifundia. Here peasants used to own two-wheeled carts in which they transported goods to market and their families to festivals and fairs. The carts could be converted into sleeping shelters and no one worried too much about accommodations or security. In western Sicily, by contrast, only carters owned carts; at best, peasants owned a mule or donkey and many were without any means of transportation other than their feet. They could commute to their fields (at no small cost in time and energy), but they could not transport their wives and families to fairs. In any event, the animal fairs were strictly for men, as were virtually all the activities of rural entrepreneurs. In 1929, says Chapman, women of the west Sicilian town that she studied never set foot in butcher shops (1971: 33, 38). With few exceptions this practice remains true of Villamaura today.

The ability of rural entrepreneurs and their associates to command the routes of transhumance, the rural places, and the people of the interior gave them a considerable advantage over other social groups. People who were based in town depended on them for help in transactions that occurred beyond its borders. In Villamaura artisans told us that their forerunners acquired supplies through the carters who regularly visited Palermo. They themselves rarely went to the city. One of our friends, a tailor, did go regularly to buy cloth and other supplies, as his father and grandfather had done before him. What seemed remarkable to us, however, was the relative poverty of this man's network compared with those of the rural entrepreneurs. He went always and only to Palermo. Along the way he knew only one person, the host of the inn where he stayed en route. For his supplies he visited the same firm that had provisioned his father and grandfather, and he always stayed in the same pension in Palermo, owned by an ex-Villamaurese. Rural entrepreneurs had more friends and contacts in the city, and many more along the way.

Even the landowners were significantly less mobile in interior Sicily than rural entrepreneurs. Because of their class position, the landlords' networks were extensive, yet many of them were quite ignorant of the countryside. Like a true dependence elite, they lived in Palermo or abroad and some of them never set eyes on their rural estates (Pitrè 1944: Vol. I, 204–216; Pontieri 1933: 64–65). They left their affairs in the hands of their *gabellotti* and were, needless to say, vulnerable to the *gabellotti's* machinations.

Rural entrepreneurs appropriately had a spirit and know-how

which set them apart from the rest of the population. Unlike most townspeople, for example, they could identify landmarks in the treeless and uninhabited expanse of a latifundium: Red Rock, Mint Cave, Oil Ridge, Hill of the Dead, Donkey's Grotto, and so on. Someone had been shot here; someone else had found shelter there. What look like undifferentiated hills and valleys to the untrained eye are rich in history to those who are knowledgeable.

The muleteers and their functional descendants, the carters, took to the road (or path) in great style. Prior to the late nineteenth century, when the interior was still without roads, wheat destined for the coastal cities and for export was carried out by mule pack. The status of a landowner or *gabellotto* was measured by the number and appearance of his mule trains, so the animals were decorated with brightly colored woolen pompoms and jangling bells. The carts that eventually replaced the mule trains were even more vividly decorated. Craftsmen painted the sides and back of the cart with brilliant scenes depicting tales of feudal love and combat. Every other aspect of the cart, from the intricate iron lattice which formed the axles to the carved and painted handgrips was spectacular (Fagone 1966).

The carts have in turn been replaced by motorized vans of every size and description (some of which are painted in the style of traditional carts). But we came to know some of the ex-carters of Villamaura, many of whom still gather in a small storefront on the main street to play cards, gossip, and reminisce. They described how the carters used to travel in caravan, singing and telling stories to each other. En route they ate together and slept in the stables of the rural inns, each next to his own cart and mule to guard them against theft.

Perhaps the best-known aspect of a rural entrepreneur's esprit was the theme of violence—his association with violence and with those who regularly used it. Not only bandits but *gabellotti,* estate guards, and owners of large herds habitually carried arms, often demonstratively. The writer Emanuele Navarro della Miraglia described a typical animal dealer "leaning on the barrel of a rifle with one leg crossed over the other to expose the butt of a revolver in the waistband of his trousers [Navarro della Miraglia 1963: 49]." Violence was part of animal theft and part of the protection of animals from rustlers. It was part of banditry. In general it belonged to the world of the *massaria* complex and the men who were associated with the *massaria.* So long as the state was unable to monopolize violence in western Sicily, this institution and those men enjoyed a relatively autonomous way of life in which they responded to opportunities as they occurred.

RURAL ENTERPRISE AND KINSHIP

Another characteristic distinguished the rural entrepreneurs from the rest of the population and, like the factors already discussed, enhanced their capacity to accumulate capital and power. It was their ability to form fraternal associations made up of adult, married brothers who jointly exploited land and animal resources.

It is unusual in western Sicily for brothers to work together. If anything, ties between brothers are cool and sometimes hostile. Throughout the Mediterranean this condition reflects the strain that partible inheritance places upon the relationship between father and sons and between close male heirs. The establishment of new and independent households when children marry undermines the viability of old households. Ethnographies from many different regions attest to animosity between father and sons and to an emotional distance between brothers, particularly after they marry. Conversely, the most enduring and solidary bond is that which unites a mother with her children. The brother–sister tie is also close, as are relations between a mother's brother and her children and between cross, as opposed to parallel, cousins (Barth 1961: 32 ff.; Campbell 1964: 103–104; Chapman 1971: 76–77; Peters 1963: 184; 1970: 389–391).[4] Referring to the status of in-laws, west Sicilians say, "The bride's side is sweet like honey, the groom's side is sour like vinegar." Parents expect to lose their sons when they marry, whereas daughters will eventually bring them sons—this in spite of a definite preference for male offspring and a tendency for newlyweds to settle near the family of the groom. A proverb heard often in western Sicily affirms that "a father can care for ten sons but a hundred sons are inadequate to care for one father." Contemporary Italian law usually permits a father to dispose of at least one–third of his property as he sees fit, and aged fathers are often thought to use this provision to exact loyalty and support from at least one son (Chapman 1971: 78–80; Cronin 1970: 103–119).

Despite these divisive tendencies of Sicilian kinship, cousin marriage is common (or at least relatively so) in Villamaura, and we found that the incidence of patrilateral parallel cousin marriage was much

[4] Since women inherit property in Sicily, one may perhaps wonder why the brother–sister tie is close. Notwithstanding partible inheritance, property divisions traditionally had a patrilineal bias. Women more often received houses or money; men more often received land (Chapman 1971: 70). In addition, women took their portions as dowry and hence were usually out of the running by the time the father made his last will or died.

higher in *massaria* families than in the rest of the population. Although most cousin marriages were between children of a brother and sister—an outcome one would predict from the structured intimacy of the brother–sister tie—among the families of rural entrepreneurs there were a number of cases of marriage between children of brothers. Moreover, the brothers in question continued to work together, even after they had married, and under the direction of their father as long as he was alive. This situation is remarkable for it contradicts the general case that there is little fraternal association and patriarchal authority in Sicilian kinship.

Common in many Middle Eastern and North African societies, marriage between the children of brothers, i.e., patrilateral parallel cousin marriage, operates less to reflect economic and political solidarity among brothers than to help maintain such solidarity in the face of strong competing centrifugal forces (Barth 1961: 33–36; Cunnison 1966: 96). Armed with this interpretation of marriage between children of brothers, we designed a small study to test the hypothesis that such marriages, although unusual in the general population, would be relatively common among livestock owning rural entrepreneurs, and to find out why.

The study was conducted in Villamaura during the summer of 1971. It was based on two research populations: a random sample of all households in the town and a census of *massariotto* families— families which had long administered the ex-latifundia in the communal territory and whose heads were once called *gabellotti*. In these families were the majority of Villamaura's most notable rural entrepreneurs. Because the latifundium is much changed today, the *massariotto* is rarely a *gabellotto* (rentier), but in the past this was his most likely role. We interviewed a mature adult in each sample household, either the head of the family or his wife, and from each respondent we recorded the genealogy of his or her paternal grandfather.[5] Limitations of time prevented us from acquiring a given genealogy from more than one person. Where there were gaps in the information, however, or where we doubted its validity, we sought

---

[5] The sample was drawn from a file of approximately 2500 households, kept by the town secretary. The file was arranged alphabetically by street, and there was no reason to expect any systematic periodicity in the list which might have biased the sample. There were 40 households selected and 4 families refused to participate. We interviewed members of 11 out of the 12 *massariotto* families that we were able to identify. We should have taken a sample of marriages, rather than households, perhaps using parish records, but this would not have been feasible given the time and personnel at our disposal.

confirmation from persons other than the respondent.[6] As we recorded the genealogies, we asked our respondents to discuss the reasons for each cousin marriage that had occurred. For each generation in the genealogy we asked about the relationships between brothers, before and after their marriages (did they work together, for example), and how succession to property (land and houses) was handled. We also collected occupational, economic, and emigration histories for each adult male named (including those who married in) and for the father of each woman who married into the family.

A few respondents (all of them rural entrepreneurs) could construct a complete genealogy ascending to their great grandfather; most, however, could not and a few (none of whom were rural entrepreneurs) had difficulty naming all of their grandfather's descendants. With the exception of one family of potters (one of three such families in town) and one family of small holders (who had at one time owned a small herd of animals), none of the families in the household sample reported that brothers worked together once they were married. Several men when asked if they worked together with their brothers answered, "Oh no, we're all married." Among the *massariotto* families, however, brothers worked together on a continuing basis in 9 of the 11 families studied.

There is a good reason for this fraternal solidarity among *massariotto* families: Upwardly mobile "shepherd-ranchers" raised livestock in partnership with others to get an efficient ratio of manpower to herd and flock size; to allow for separating the animals by age and sex; and to achieve the better quality and greater variety of cheeses that a large herd yielded (Colonna 1852: 228; Morici 1940: 18). Also, the bigger the livestock enterprise, the faster it accumulated capital with which to buy land. According to the old-time *massariotti* of Villamaura, it is preferable to build a partnership with close agnatic kinsmen because they are more trustworthy than non-kin. With kinsmen it is possible to form what they call a "perfect partnership" (*società perfetta*), in which all expenses and all profits are divided among the partners according to the proportion of animals each contributes to the common herd. Once the herd is pooled, no attempt need be made to measure and record the productivity or consumption of each partner's animals. Under other, less than

[6] The *massariotto* families are well known "establishments" in the town. There were only a dozen of them and they tended to intermarry. Thus, their genealogies overlapped and we were able to get "better" and more detailed data from the census than from the sample. This is a methodological problem. Its existence also supports our hypothesis.

"perfect," forms of stock-raising partnership, division of the profit depends on the actual measured productivity of each partner's animals. Such arrangements are often unstable because they generate uncertainty and suspicion. How can partner A, for example, be sure that partner B is not giving preference to B's animals when it is his turn to supervise the grazing? Under these conditions, the division of the product and the profit were tense occasions.

But why could not any group of animal herders form a società perfetta, and why did brothers have some advantage in this respect? The answer was suggested to us by Morici's description of pastoral associations in Sicily (1940: 17–24). A perfect partnership can work only if the animals that are initially pooled are roughly equal in quality and productivity. Then a partner can be sure that his share of the profit will be roughly equivalent to what he would have received if his animals had been milked separately and their milk had been elaborated and then marketed separately. Non-kin who pool their herds cannot be sure that their animals are equally productive, but brothers can, because brothers inherit their stock from one common herd, that of their father (Morici 1940: 21, n.1). Indeed, our massariotto informants told us that most often the fathers actively promoted such an arrangement among their sons, in an attempt to keep them together in control of a unified patrimony of animals and land. Unlike the general population, the children of upwardly mobile rural entrepreneurs grew up with the idea that fraternal solidarity is important. One shepherd in the random sample lamented that although his father had owned enough animals to launch a small-scale partnership, he had lacked the "courage" to organize his sons. They had all married, gone their separate ways, and had not improved their economic positions.

Consistent with the patriarchal role of the father is an established division of labor in the massariotto families: One son, almost always the oldest, administered the enterprise; another attended to its affairs in town; another supervised the shepherds and peasants on the massaria. The oldest sons of the two largest and most influential families inherited substantially more than their brothers and appear to have moved into their fathers' shoes as organizers and patriarchs. The daughters of massariotti were dowered in houses and money, but rarely in land and animals. So in this subgroup there was a tendency toward primogeniture, preference for males in succession and patriarchy, in spite of the general norm that stressed partible inheritance and fragmentation of the family of origin.

As we anticipated, the genealogies in the census of massariotto families showed a much greater tendency to consolidate kin groups through marriage than was true of the population at large. The 33 genealogies in the general sample yielded 7 cases in which a brother and a sister married a sister and a brother; 5 cases of marriage between the children of sisters; and 10 cases between the children of a brother and a sister. There were no marriages between children of sisters in our census of 11 *massariotto* families. However, this census yielded 10 cases in which siblings married siblings and 9 cases of marriage between children of a brother and a sister—both significantly higher percentages of the total number of marriages. Most striking of all was the differential distribution of patrilateral parallel cousin marriage—that is, marriage between children of brothers. There were 5 in the sample of 40 households, and 12 in the census of *massariotto* families. In other words, the most common form of cousin marriage in the population at large was marriage between children of brothers and sisters or between children of sisters. Among *massariotti,* cousin marriage in general, and patrilateral parallel cousin marriage in particular, was more pronounced.

Our other major source of data about cousin marriage in the past was the diocesan archive of the province, where we examined papal dispensations for cousin marriages which occurred in the period 1850–1905 in Villamaura. Dispensations were required for marriages between persons related to each other within the third degree. Occupation and social standing were not clearly indicated on the records, but it was possible to make a rough distinction between wealthy *massariotti* and other families based on their names, the titles that were used by the priest who filled out the application, and his frequent reference to the applicants' wealth or poverty. Of the 64 first cousin marriages recorded during this period, 20 were between children of brothers. We were able to trace about half of these patrilateral parallel cousin marriages to clearly identifiable *massariotto* families, in spite of the fact that such families represented a very small proportion of the total population. The picture for patrilineally biased second cousin marriages was similar.[7]

Although limited in scope and depth, our genealogical and

---

[7] Of 32 marriages between second cousins whose grandfathers were brothers, 15 were contracted within *massariotto* families. There were 19 second cousin marriages in which the father of one mate and the mother of the other were children of brothers. Ten of these were in *massariotto* families. We would guess that in the case of a *massariotto* family, the father of one of the marriage partners had been brought into the *massaria* (along with his land and animals) as the functional equivalent of a natural son. The marriage of his child to his wife's cousin's child might have served to reinforce his commitment to the establishment while it contributed to the continued unity of the patrimony.

archival data allow us to draw a few conclusions about the meaning of cousin marriage in Sicily. In poor families, cousin marriage reflected already existing patterns of intimacy between two families. That few of the families in the general population produced patrilateral parallel cousin marriages is symptomatic of the tenuous nature of relations between brothers, as compared with the bonds that united brothers to sisters and sisters to each other. Most cousin marriages in this population occurred between children of a brother and sister or between children of sisters. In many of these marriages, little or no property was involved, so their scope could not have been the reunification of property that had been fragmented, though this sometimes was the case. In the archival record we found only three instances in which the parties to marriages between non-*massariotti* possessed landholdings in the same rural district. In the applications for dispensation that were filed by the parish priest, he most often wrote that the bride was too poor to attract another spouse and, besides, the groom had been at liberty to visit her house through their youth and had probably compromised her honor. In the applications filed for the wealthy entrepreneurial families, the rationale changed: It was argued that wealthy people had to marry their cousins because the rest of the population was too poor to provide eligible marriage partners.

Obviously, there is more than this explanation to cousin marriage among the prosperous, where its purpose seems clearly related to the consolidation of family enterprises. As one of our informants explained in reference to parallel cousin marriages, brothers stayed together on the *massaria* even after they married, but they experienced increasing strain as their children reached maturity and prepared to marry. Some intermarriage between these children prevented the strain from coming to the surface, thus preserving the enterprise intact until the brothers retired. At this point the enterprise either disintegrated or was taken over by only one or two members of the second generation, usually those who had married a paternal uncle's heir. By the third generation, descendants were dispersed in a variety of occupations, including high status occupations in government, the clergy, and the professions. In sum, fraternal association and parallel cousin marriage were organizational strategies for advancement of the strongest group of rural entrepreneurs, those who owned large herds of cattle and sheep.

Finally, although fraternal solidarity was not favored by all rural entrepreneurs, two of Villamaura's carter–grain merchant families did manage to create lineagelike organizations. Today, male descendants of these families pursue various occupations. Some are in the professions, some in commerce. But they still cooperate through the exchange of economic and political assistance and as partners in various business ventures. In neither family has there been patrilateral parallel cousin marriage, but both families are heavily intermarried with notable *massariotto* families. It is likely that fraternal solidarity, a necessary strategy for ambitious "ranchers," was available as a model to other entrepreneurs closely associated with them and likewise intent on building up a patrimony.

Not all rural entrepreneurs were as wealthy and powerful as those who belonged to the large family enterprises just described. Many were of modest means and some merged with the impoverished category of ordinary shepherds and goatherds. Rural entrepreneurs, moreover, pursued a variety of different occupations: butcher, carter, tax farmer and *gabellotto*, mediator, estate guard, bandit, head of a pastoral association, and so on. Some of them engaged in more than one activity, while others were more highly specialized. For these reasons we cannot argue that rural entrepreneurs constituted a single class. Nor were they a status group. Internally they had their own status hierarchy which was isomorphic to the hierarchy of the population at large. *Massariotti* and *gabellotti* were at the top. Propertyless mediators were near the bottom. For the most advanced and successful rural entrepreneurs, an important distinguishing characteristic was the ability to organize patriarchal fraternal associations and to build great family enterprises on this basis.

In the network of relationships that bound rural entrepreneurs to each other, the areas of greatest density, the nodal points in space, were located in the rural places of the countryside, particularly the *massarie*, and not in the towns. It was their common familiarity with the life of the countryside, their ability to cope with its violence, and their shared involvement in the *massaria* which engendered in them that special solidarity which leads us to define them as a group. This solidarity, their networks, and their critical roles in the *massarie* distinguished them from everyone else in the society. Ultimately they, in contrast to both landlords and poor peasants, were able to hold their own in the face of nineteenth-century, postindustrial imperialism.

chapter 5

Cultural Codes

Peasants, herdsmen, and rural entrepreneurs do not fit the conventional image of social strata in a traditional society. Peasants were not firmly rooted in the land by dint of inertia or custom, nor did they love the land. On the other hand, much entrepreneurial activity was located in the countryside rather than in towns and cities. Nevertheless, these nontraditional groups did have traditions, cultural codes that are for the most part still followed today. This chapter examines three of these codes in western Sicily—honor (*onore*), friendship (*amicizia*), and cleverness (*furberia*)—and attempts to assess their relationship to Sicily's position in a changing world.

The approach here differs from that of many other treatments of culture. It does not view cultural codes in peasant societies as quaint manifestations of a stable and remote rural–agrarian past, different from and opposed to the "urban" culture of modernity. Rather, we assume that like the social groups and political structure described in the preceding chapters cultural codes are also products of forces set in motion by core area expansion in the past. Broadly speaking, the continuity of cultural codes is to be understood in terms of the continuity of Sicily's role in a world division of labor, even though that role has undergone many changes in the industrial age. In the face of these changes, politically successful rural entrepreneurs have furthered the conditions for perpetuating the codes.

Our approach to the analysis of culture is guided by the idea that cultural codes are fashioned collectively by people who are responding to their changing natural and political environments. Code setting, however, may be the special province of some, and the interpretation and implementation of codes will vary across the major fault lines that define a population (class, region, ethnicity, sex, age). Our analysis of culture in western Sicily takes particular codes of more or less general salience to the entire population and describes them on the basis of ethnographic research. Then we look for analogous codes in other places; we find them, for the most part, in the Mediterranean and in Latin America. Comparing the histories of these places with that of Sicily has enabled us to put forward some tentative hypotheses about relationships between their common colonial experience and the codes in question.

FURBERIA

The American and English troops that occupied Sicily during World War II used insecticides, principally DDT, to eliminate malaria. Following the war, the Italian government continued to spray DDT throughout the island. For awhile, mosquitoes and house flies virtually disappeared, but in spite of regular annual treatments the insects have begun to reappear, increasing in number each year. Many people are well aware that successive applications of DDT can produce a strain of mosquito resistant to DDT, but the most common explanation for the return of the mosquitoes offered in Villamaura was quite different (and equally tenable): The firm that had been awarded the contract to spray insecticide was said to be cheating on the contract by decreasing the amount of DDT in proportion to water in the solution.

The problem of the defective oranges is even more to the point. Every year, toward the end of the growing season, truckloads of oranges arrive from the orchards around Palermo for sale in the interior towns at low prices. The oranges contain sections that are dry and mealy, and this fruit must be the worst of the crop, unsuitable for export. From several different people in different towns we learned that the Palermitani had extracted some of the juice from the oranges with a hypodermic syringe. This juice was used to manufacture soft drinks, and the rest of the orange, still intact, was then sold to the "unsuspecting" peasants of the interior. With some of our friends we argued against the hypodermic hypothesis and even arranged a test with syringe and orange, but we could not shake their faith in the corruptness of the Palermitani ("They must use a special syringe").

These views on the DDT and the oranges reflect a widespread reciprocal distrust, a mutually shared expectation that it is likely, indeed proper, that each person will pursue his own interests to the detriment of others if necessary. This is what it means to be a devil with a pocket full of money, rather than a fool with five cents. People can be *furbo* or *fesso*. The *furbo* is shrewd and cunning; he uses his astuteness to serve his own interests, to manipulate others, if possible without alienating them in the process. Of course, the *furbo* requires a *fesso*—one who is naive or gullible, easily taken for a ride (*preso in giro*; see Davis 1969: 75–76; P. Schneider 1969: 146–147). This dichotomy embraces many other expressions. For example, the words *buono* and *sincero* most often mean "good" and "sincere," respectively. In certain contexts, however, they have a derogatory meaning which borders on *fesso*. The expression *tre volte buono* ("three times good") means "fool" and is an insult. Similarly, in myth and proverb a respected man is one who looks after his own affairs (*chi fa i fatti suoi*) and takes advantage of the opportunities that present themselves, without being too concerned about the needs or feelings of others. A generous person may be respected, provided that he does not let his generosity endanger his own position and that of his immediate family. A completely selfless person would be a fool, as would anyone who neglected an opportunity to aggrandize his own position solely out of concern for legality or the common good.

It is not surprising that many people feel ambivalent about *furberia*. Most people most of the time are neither *furbo* nor *fesso*, but when the chips are down most would rather be *furbo* than taken for *fesso*, that is, taken for a fool; this is as true of women as it is of men. People mistrust and fear the *furberia* of others, yet they admire clever strategies so long as they themselves are not the immediate victims, and Sicilians often take vicarious pleasure in the aesthetics of the plot and in its success. In Villamaura we noticed that people generally rewarded *furberia* in their children (irrespective of social class), and parents often overtly and self-consciously favored a rebellious or mischievous child over siblings who were less "turbid" (regardless of sex or birth order).[1] Anecdotes Sicilians tell about themselves also celebrate the shrewd manipulator who can maneuver others who are more rich or powerful than he. A classic story tells of the Sicilian astronaut who demands that a space agency administrator pay him 9 million lire to fly to the moon, compared with only 3 million requested by a German astronaut. When asked to explain the amount, the Sicilian astronaut tells the administrator, "Three million are for me, three million for you, and three million to send the German to the moon."

Furberia, or shrewdness, has its counterpart in Latin American societies, particularly among middlemen, broker capitalists who maximize profits by using their wits (Wolf and Hansen 1967). South Italians share in it, too, using the words *furbo* and *fesso* as do Sicilians (Davis 1969: 75–76). An interesting distinction related to shrewdness and to lack of respect for the law exists within Sicily itself, where concepts like *furberia* are used to distinguish the eastern from the western and interior regions. West Sicilians call the northeastern province of Messina and the southeastern province of Syracuse the *babbo,* naive or "square," provinces of the island. Westerners are said to be shrewd and self-interested, while the easterners are law-abiding, public-spirited, and *babbo.* (The central eastern province of Catania—more influenced by foreign domination than either of the others—is something of an exception: Catanians are praised for their skills as counterfeiters.)

Legend celebrates the difference between western and northeastern Sicily which throughout the Spanish period were strong political and economic rivals. In 1783, an earthquake crippled the northeastern city of Messina. The viceroy, a Neapolitan Bourbon, asked the Palermitani to shorten the festival of their patron saint, Santa Rosalia, in order to contribute relief funds to Messina. The outraged people of Palermo refused and to show their disrespect for the easterners sent a nocturnal delegation to Messina to break off the thumb and middle fingers of one hand on the statue of Neptune which adorns the center of the city, thus symbolically cuckolding the good people of Messina. The Messinesi retaliated by breaking the noses of the praetorian guards who surround a fountain in the municipal piazza of Palermo, symbolically making pimps of the people of Palermo. (In the Middle Ages, procurers were punished with a

---

[1] When it is someone you love and respect, his behavior is *torbido;* the same behavior in an outsider makes him *prepotente,* a bully.

broken or severed nose.) It is appropriate that the Messinesi were cuckolded, since cuckolds are *fesso,* while procurers are known for their ability to manipulate others. In the nineteenth century, a west Sicilian landowner complained that "the citizens of Messina . . . are better patriots than we Palermitani. . . . The statue of Neptune . . . is seen today without defect, with the palm intact and hand resculpted. . . . Our statues, through our natural disrespect for the public welfare, still have broken noses [quoted in Pitrè, who also records the legend, 1939: 351–354]." Today the noses of the praetorians have been replaced, but the cracks are evident and that "natural disrespect" still seems more pronounced in the west than in the northeast.

The geographical distribution of this cultural code which celebrates astuteness, even—indeed especially—when it contradicts the public welfare or legal norms suggests that it was elaborated in response to the same conditions that produced broker capitalism: the conditions which were created by a peripheral colonial role in the world-system of the Spanish Empire. We recall that the colonies of Spain were governed by a weak and ineffectual central authority whose commands were increasingly contradicted by the evolving market forces of North Atlantic capitalism. On the periphery of the Spanish Empire capitalists could not enhance their own power by supporting the power of the state. On the contrary, private and state interests were at loggerheads, so that one could serve the first only by antagonizing the second, and there was a constant repetition of governmental force circumvented by private fraud.

Clearly, an activity like the contraband grain trade worked to the advantage of landlords and foreign merchants—the former as producers, the latter as financial backers and exporters. Yet it was not confined to these groups for it also supported countless rural entrepreneurs engaged in transport, mediation, administration, and other ancillary functions, both legal and illegal. For the rural entrepreneurs, self-serving cleverness, or *furberia,* often shaded into *prepotenza* (only approximately translated by the English "prepotency"). A *prepotente* backs up his shrewd strategies with the use of superior power, tinged with a threat of violence. He intimidates or bullies others into the role of *fesso* by structuring situations which allow them few alternative options. This illuminates the common use of the passive voice when one complains, "I was taken for *fesso.*" The close ties of rural entrepreneurs to the *massaria* complex, with its pastoral bias and remoteness from the police arm of the state, explains their ability to support *furberia* with *prepotenza* when the need arose.

More often than not victims of *furberia* and *prepotenza,* the peasants of western Sicily nonetheless respected this code. Perhaps it was largely a matter of survival, since the fluidity and insecurity of the peasants' tenure on the land meant that they continually faced difficult bargaining situations with sharp-dealing entrepreneurs. The sharecropping contracts negotiated each August, the sale of an animal in the fall, and the sale or purchase of wheat and seed during the year all were occasions that raised the peasant's level of anxiety and put him on guard. What humiliation for him if he emerged roundly cheated, taken for *fesso* by a grain merchant or *gabellotto*. (And, on the other hand, what humiliation for the grain merchant or landlord who was cheated by a peasant in the same tense situation.) By the same token, a peasant would have good reason to be proud if others recognized him as a man who held his own.

So most peasants tried to hold their own in this game, even though the odds were against them. Indeed, the loose and manipulable structure of dominance characteristic of colonies like Sicily left enough room so that a nominally powerless peasant could occasionally outmaneuver his oppressors. Perhaps that is why most peasants, no less than the rural entrepreneurs, subscribed to the code of shrewdness and elaborated no contradictory class ideology appropriate to their overall life circumstances. Or were they fooled here, too, hoodwinked by an ideology of cleverness which served the interests of entrepreneurs and landowners?

ONORE

Generally speaking, honor refers to a person's worth as judged by others. One's virtue, dignity, morality, and status constitute one's honor. To be rich in these qualities presupposes personal autonomy—the freedom and capacity to act. As in medieval Europe, honor in Sicily implies a quick response to offense, intolerance of any encroachment upon one's person or patrimony or the person and patrimony of others to whom one is loyal. In Mediterranean societies, honor is an attribute not only of individuals but of kinship groups, whether extended families and lineages, as in North Africa, or the nuclear families of Greece, Italy, Sicily, and Spain. Taken to its extreme, the Sicilian code of honor implies a society organized into so many autonomous and competing equivalent nuclear family units. "The family is the Sicilian's State," says a character in Leonardo Sciascia's novel, *Mafia Vendetta* (1964: 95). This being the case, honor is a "national anthem," an ideology of citizenship and loyalty to the family. It defends the family, as it were, in three respects: (1) in respect to property; (2) in respect to prestige or status; and (3) in respect to the loyalty of women. Let us examine each in turn.

In Sicily, the nuclear family is the basic property exploiting unit of the society. (Land and animals are technically owned by individuals, a man and his wife, but they are administered by the husband in his capacity as family head.) In the past, and to some extent even now, heads of families, like heads of state entrusted with territorial defense, protected their patrimonies by making a general claim for respect, while convincing others that any attempt to trespass on the property of the family would provoke swift retaliation. Disputes over land and water, abusive grazing, boundaries, and rights of privacy all were inflamed as much by the problem of honor as by the particular utilities at stake. This explains why a technical solution that maximized the legal rights to equity of both conflicting parties was no solution at all if it were not also an honorable solution for everyone concerned. In all future transactions, a family's credibility rested upon its honor.

In addition to being the basic property exploiting unit, the Sicilian family is also the object of moral evaluation. As Chapman pointed out, "misfortune or success which affects one member of the household brings sorrow or joy to all [1971: 73]." Sometimes reputation extends beyond the nuclear family to other close kin (especially when the reputation has been sullied). Nicknames, for example, may spread from husband to wife, and occasionally from wife to husband, or through a mother to her children. Usually, however, they spread through males and identify a minimal patriline, two or three generations deep (see Chapman 1971: 71–72). People often refer to the whole patrilineal group by its nickname (but rarely in the presence of its members).

Moral evaluation by the community and its gossips encourages rivalry for status in which families and individuals representing families are the actors. People reckon their net worth by noting who comes to the wedding with an appropriate gift; who visits them in case of an illness or death in the family; who offers coffee or an aperitif at the bar; who shows respect by insisting that you walk to his right during the evening *passeggiatta*; and so forth. Most people take these questions of etiquette seriously and are concerned lest the slightest offense signify that one's claim to status is not recognized by significant others. A denial of respect, when respect has been claimed, is functionally the same as abusive grazing: It calls for retaliation to avoid some greater offense.

When a denial of respect occurs, however, whether through encroachment on property or through a lack of deference, the offended party has a problem of interpretation. He is reluctant to mount a counteroffense for fear that the original slight was not intended and that his reaction will cost him a potential ally. On the other hand, if it was intended, then to let it pass is a sign of weakness. As Vinogradov and Waterbury explained in their discussion of segmented systems in Morocco "intelligent defense is assured through a maximization of options and the avoidance of situations of mutually exclusive choice [1971: 35]." Sometimes there are formulas for determining intent, as among Sardinian pastoralists where theft motivated by necessity is distinguished from theft with intent to harm. There, when someone steals an animal whose milk is used by the shepherd's family, this is prima facie evidence of intent to harm. If an animal is stolen from the common herd, then the theft is deemed motivated by necessity, therefore impersonal and less serious (Musio 1969: 85–88).

Where such formulas do not exist, a decision must be made. A slight or a trespass may have been deliberate and provocative; it may have been intended as a retaliatory measure or warning; it may simply have been an accident. Before they make a decision, the victims must weigh the available evidence, perhaps seek advice from kinsmen, and, most important, assess their own power in the situation. In general, public offenses are more likely to demand retaliation than are offenses that go unnoticed. Julian Amery's description of conflict among Albanians makes this point well.

> Under anarchy, as in international relations, the importance of a crime lies less in its intrinsic character than in the challenge which it represents to the victim's prestige. All crimes, therefore, be they murder, rape, theft, or merely insult, are of equal weight. Prestige, however, can only suffer from a public slight; and it was said among the Albanians that though a rough word in company would often lead to a feud of years, a blow unseen by third parties might well be forgotten [Amery 1948: 8].

In their replies to offense, or presumed offense, Sicilians seek to ward off future aggression by convincing others of their capacity to protect their own interests. But they also try to avoid an unnecessary escalation of reprisals, a protracted vendetta which might jeopardize their families and cut off sources of support and information. "The probable need for allies in the future makes it impolitic to eliminate adversaries in the present [Vinogradov and Waterbury 1971: 35]." A compromise between these goals is to break off relations, refusing to acknowledge or speak to an enemy, but exhorting only members of one's immediate family to do the same. The Sicilian dialect provides a word for this stalemate: *sciariarisi*—to be on "nonspeaking terms."

Such vendettas rarely spread beyond the close kinsmen of the major protagonists. Nonpartisan observers recognize the situation and avoid it without attempting to assess blame. *Iddi sugnu sciariatti*— "They are not speaking"—is a matter-of-fact expression one often hears in a west Sicilian town. Sometimes mutual friends who are placed at a disadvantage (both expressive and instrumental) by the fact that two families are not speaking will attempt to arrange a peace between them. Often the mediation is successful, but sometimes the positions harden, and severed ties may last a lifetime and into the next generation.

In contemporary Villamaura, people are constantly evaluating one another; their relative positions at any moment are represented by an implicit balance sheet that expresses social debits and credits. To be able to compete in the first place, a man must be a "good father to his family" (*buon padre di famiglia*). Within his means he must see his daughters well married and his sons securely employed. He must command the respect of his family and ensure that they meet the minimal obligations of their familial roles. Above all, he must promote and defend the chastity of the women in his family. At least until recently, male members of the west Sicilian family considered themselves responsible for their women's virtue, and women's comportment was an important yardstick by which the family honor was measured, as well as an important symbol which proclaimed its honor. Good fathers preserved the virginity of their daughters until they were married. Brothers were also enlisted toward this end, for brothers traditionally did not marry until all of their marriageable sisters were dowered and then wed. In many cases they could receive no share of the inheritance until this happened, and they had to sacrifice their own earnings to the accumulation of dowry (Cronin 1970: 113–115; see also Friedl 1967).

People used to believe that women's sexuality when not confined to wedlock and procreation was a danger to the community at large (some still think so). Female sexuality had to be carefully controlled for women were thought incapable of controlling their own strong impulses toward sexual gratification. From the time of their confirmation—which itself is a symbolic lesson in modesty—young girls were given special treatment to impress upon them the importance of restraint. At puberty they went into semi-seclusion, under surveillance by their parents and brothers. A girl would spend as many hours each day as the family could afford embroidering linens for the marriage bed, in the company of other women and girls. By their quantity and the intricacy of their design, sets of sheets, bedspreads, and pillowcases would represent a bride's family wealth and the magnitude of her dowry. A "12-sheet" wife came from a better family than a "10-sheet" wife and probably brought a better house or land to the marriage. The importance of dowry and the difficulty of preparing it led some Sicilians to observe that daughters were not children but "burdens." An extreme statement is the proverb reported by Chapman, "Blessed is the door out of which goes a dead daughter[1971: 30]."

From puberty to marriage (the number of years varied with social class and with the historical period in question), a young girl's activities were closely watched. Once there was a fiancé, he visited with her or took walks with her in the presence of her brothers. Should he or anyone else manage to claim her virginity, her father and brothers were technically supposed to kill her and her lover (in that order), for virgin daughters symbolized the honor of the family and the loss of virginity plunged all its members into shame, especially if the loss were publicly known. As Chapman put it, "if one of the women is guilty of misconduct, all the men are equipped with horns and the other women tend to share her bad reputation [1971: 73]."

The loss of a daughter's virginity spelled failure of the family in two ways. First, by assuming the complicity of the woman, the community suspected her of treason, of aiding and abetting the expansionist policy of a competing family, and of subverting the interests of the group to which she owed allegiance. Thus, the solidarity of the family—its capacity to control and protect its members—was brought into question. Second, the outsider who successfully attacked the sanctity of the family by violating one of its women was, in effect, publicly and most dramatically proclaiming his disregard for the honor and dignity of its men. For these men faced with dishonor there were few remedies. The usurper could renounce his attack on the dignity of the family and remove the stain on its daughter's virtue by marrying her posthaste. Failing that, the only way for cuckolds to lose their horns was to kill the people who placed them there. "Only blood would wash blood"; hence, the legendary crime of honor.

Women who did not marry fell into several categories. Some became nuns. Others, including some who could not afford the costs of the novitiate, took informal vows of celibacy and became "house nuns" (bizzocche). These women wore black, attended church everyday, and carefully avoided men. Some imagined themselves wed to Christ or to a saint (often Saint Paul). People in the community usually considered them foolish but tolerated their strategy (Chapman 1971: 42–43, 88–89). The risk was that an unmarried woman might go astray, becoming a prostitute or a maidservant to the aristocracy. In a society where the sexuality of young women was so rigorously disciplined, young men usually had their first sexual experience with such women. Even today, well over 50% of the men in Sicily and the Italian south have their first sexual encounter with women whom they consider unmarriageable (Parca 1965).

In the past a Sicilian bride was expected to submit to a virginity test on her wedding night, the well-known test of the bloodied nuptial sheet (Chapman 1971: 105; Pitrè 1939: 99–100). First and most eager to inspect the sheet, as it hung from the young couple's window the morning after their marriage, were the close kinsmen of the husband, for the stained sheet now symbolized not only her purity but also his honor and that of their future children. A new family had been created, with the wife at its center. Once a mother, a woman no longer posed the danger of unbridled and seductive sexuality as she once had. She could still commit adultery, however, in which case, too, it would be appropriate for the husband to respond with a crime of honor, killing her and her lover.

The comportment and status of women is relevant to the problem of family honor even when the woman becomes a widow (obviously a *young* widow is more dangerous than a young virgin). Women married younger than men, often by as much as 10 years or more, so that most wives outlived their husbands. The rules of mourning, enforced by her in-laws and children, ensured that she would not be a ready candidate for remarriage (which in any case the church prohibited). Widows were expected to seclude themselves totally for 1–2 years after their husbands' deaths, to close the windows and doors of their houses, and to remain indoors except in the early morning before dawn. Children and other close relatives kept them supplied with food. During this period and for the remainder of their lives widows shrouded themselves in black: A black scarf covered their heads at all times indoors, and they wore an additional black shawl when they went out. Similar if less extreme customs governed the behavior of the wives of prisoners and migrants (Chapman 1971: 108). Mourning customs for the deaths of relatives other than the husband, and mourning customs imposed upon men, were considerably less rigorous. If a woman failed to show proper respect for her husband by mourning his death publicly and passionately, it would reflect badly on his honor—ex post facto—and on the honor of his survivors.

It appears, in view of these many restrictions, that women had lit-

"Widows shrouded themselves in black." [Photo by Nicola Scafidi.]

"Houses were small, and much domestic activity took place outdoors, in courtyards, streets, and doorways."

tle individual freedom. One might even argue that they passed at marriage from imprisonment in one nuclear family to imprisonment in another. Yet Sicily was a sex-segregated as well as a familist society. If men shopped and congregated in public and political arenas, women were not entirely isolated at home. Houses were small, and much domestic activity took place outdoors, in courtyards, streets, and doorways. Sewing, spinning, embroidery, and laundry were done in the company of other women. Much food preparation also took place this way. Women freely borrowed and lent, had access to one another's houses, minded one another's children, and, most important, provided one another with information and with emotional and moral support. Nor was their gossip limited to "women's affairs" and empty of economic and political content. It was the vehicle by which reputations, including the reputations of men, were made and broken. Mutual aid and solidarity (especially among sisters and cousins), plus access to information, combined to make many women formidable figures behind the scenes. One suspects that they had more to do with arranging their children's marriages than men. In addition women participated in crucial decisions affecting the household economy and were as knowledgeable as men about real estate transactions and inheritance laws. In Villamaura we observed that women often accompanied their husbands to the office of the notary public, before whom all kinds of economic transactions were settled.

Finally, although rigorous in theory, the code of honor was flexible in fact. Most cuckolds were not murderers and therefore not disposed to follow the rule that "blood washes blood," especially if their predicament were not widely known in the community. Restrictions on widows and the use of virginity tests had as much a ritual as a practical significance, and it is often the outward form of a ritual more than its substance that matters. People were well aware that the blood on the sheet could have come from the bride's thumb. Nor were young women necessarily sexually naive or repressed since the code of virginity rested upon shame and not guilt. Constraints were public and publicly enforced, with the result that young girls embroidering matrimonial sheets might have defined their sexuality as a source of pride.[2] If anything, their fantasy life may have been enriched by the men's theory that women have strong erotic impulses that they cannot themselves control: "A match held close to the fire will eventually light [quoted in Chapman 1971: 40]." Widows, too, were sometimes thought insincere. "The widow weeps for the dead and thinks of the living [quoted in Chapman 1971: 110]." One man in Villamaura who doubted his wife's fealty twice feigned death in order to see for himself whether or not she would mourn him properly.

Origins of the Honor Code

The concepts honor and shame are widely diffused throughout the Mediterranean and have existed there for centuries. Throughout the area, however, the seclusion of women is associated with quite different social arrangements in different societies: on the European side with nuclear families, monogamy, dowry, and rules prohibiting cousin marriage, the remarriage of widows, and divorce; on the North African side with extended families and lineages, polygyny, bride price, a preference for patrilateral parallel cousin marriage, the levirate, and the possibility of divorce. In truth we can put forth only some very tentative ideas about the origins of a complex normative system that exists in so many different social contexts.

---

[2] The bedroom is important in a new household. Couples purchase bedroom furniture before furnishing other rooms and take great pride in its display.

The temporal and geographical distribution of honor in Mediterranean societies suggests that its origins go back to classical antiquity. From the Bronze Age, the Mediterranean basin was a cradle of empires because the sea provided easy transportation for accumulation of wealth through trade. Unfortunately, the land surrounding the sea was mountainous and arid, not well suited to feed the populations of great imperial systems, the more so as these systems promoted deforestation and pastoral uses of land. In the Mediterranean area, all world-systems—past as well as present—put a great strain on the land. We have seen how in Sicily pressure on land intensified competition between herdsmen and cultivators and how, together with partible inheritance, it fragmented peasant holdings. Under these conditions, the code of honor has helped the Sicilian family maintain the integrity of its flocks and fields against the encroachments of others. It was all the more necessary because, despite imperial pressure, the legal apparatus of the state functioned poorly at the local level. Perhaps the same was true of societies throughout the area, pressured by empires from the beginning of historical time (J. Schneider 1971).

Other possible origins of the honor code concern features of the ancient empires which distinguished them from later, capitalist, world-systems. Two such distinguishing characteristics—one political and the other economic—will be discussed here. The political distinction relates to Wallerstein's observation that ancient empires attempted to extend administrative control to the limits of their economic domain; whereas the core societies of world capitalism rely principally on market mechanisms (Wallerstein 1974). Within their respective domains, the ancient imperial bureaucracies did their best to break down or retard the formation of private accumulations of property. Unchecked, such accumulations could become the basis for a challenge to the central power, as in feudalism. Imperial policy typically promoted the practice of partible inheritance of property, including inheritance rights for women in the form of dowry.

Supplementing and reinforcing the strategies of empires to centralize control over domain were two great Mediterranean religions, Catholic Christianity and Islam. Both sought to undermine the solidarity of corporate kinship groups and the property accumulations which supported that solidarity, as they "subordinated the community of blood to the community of faith [quoted in Mintz and Wolf 1967: 179]." The Church went further in this than Islam, but both religions had the same aim: centralized power and the integration of society on a higher level. Where Islam demarcates sacred zones in which blood may not be shed, Christianity tells its followers to turn the other cheek in response to offense. The Church, moreover, barely recognizes patrilineal descent. It forbids marriage within several degrees of relationship, thus effectively neutralizing the capacity of kin groups to retain control over property and to organize politically. It forbids widows to remarry kinsmen for the same reason. It gives religious sanction to relations of coparenthood which, although they rest on a metaphor of kinship, are voluntary and contractual. It further rules out as marriage partners all ritual kinsmen, a rule that weakens fictive kin groups, too (Mintz and Wolf 1967: 179–180). Unlike Islam, Catholicism celebrates the family of procreation, in which women as mothers (not daughters) are repositories of honor. In a sense, Catholicism preempts the symbolism of virginity by attaching it to the Holy Family, where it is fused with motherhood and bilateral descent (Lea 1907).

It seems to us that in their confrontation with lineal descent groups, both the Church and Islam sought to buttress the position of women against that of men. They granted women rights and status denied them by their families and in the process created allies who could bore away at the solidarity of the domestic group from within. As in the case of blood vengeance, Catholic Christianity went further in this than Islam. Where Islam, for example, permits women to inherit half as much property as men, Catholicism insists upon full inheritance rights. Where Islam protects women from arbitrary divorce, Catholicism outlaws divorce altogether. Women in contemporary Sicily are more religious than men. Unlike men they attend church regularly and are more likely than men to vote for the party of the priests. In a way, the Church was and is their patron in a figurative "battle between the sexes."

If this interpretation is correct, then we must assume that familism and the code of honor not only bolstered domestic groups in their rivalry against each other but also defended the family against the hegemony of Church and state. In other words, men with interests in family sovereignty did not fully accept the Church's view that a woman could be sacred but clung instead to the duality in which they, the men, were descended from God and the women from the devil (see Campbell 1964: 31–32). As the Church reached out to women, men doubled their efforts to control them. And up to a point they succeeded. Men rarely granted full inheritance rights to women. In addition, they refused to yield the privilege of blood vengeance or to yield to any suprafamilial monopoly over the use of violence. That kinship groups are the principal units of conflict in traditional Mediterranean societies points to something quite different from mere continuity with a "tribal" past. It tells us that although challenged by the great religions these groups found a relatively successful way to fight back. We are suggesting that the honor code initially defended the family against the political pressure of ancient empires and religions aimed at limiting the power and autonomy of kinship groups in society. To the extent that the state apparatus remained weak and centralization did not occur, honor prevailed and the "family is the state."

Perhaps the code also responded to economic conditions that distinguished the ancient empires from the capitalist world-system. In contrast to the core industrial societies of the modern world, which export cheap commodities for mass consumption, metropolitan centers of the ancient world exported luxury goods almost exclusively. The ancient empires further differed from a capitalist world-system in the way they mobilized labor. Capitalism has advanced technologies by which it displaces labor from the countryside, forcing workers to migrate into industrial areas. Its technologies have also produced a staggering explosion of population. The core societies of the ancient Mediterranean were chronically short of labor, particularly in relationship to the labor-intensive luxury manufactures they produced. They mobilized labor directly and indirectly through conquest, through the importation of slaves.

Not nearly enough is known about the ancient and medieval slave trades, but two fairly well established features seem extremely important to us. First, in contrast to the late Atlantic slave trade, which concentrated on males of working age, the ancient and medieval trades sought women as much as, and perhaps even more than, men (Fisher and Fisher 1972: 116, 119 ff.). Captured women served as concubines or worked in craft production in the core societies where they were eventually purchased. The second important feature of the early slave trade was that the very peripheral societies that exported slaves, imported luxuries manufactured in the core.

This suggests a second hypothesis about the origins of honor: that families secluded women, defended their chastity, and retaliated with violence to attacks on female "virtue" in response to the threat posed by the agents of local and foreign slave markets. The strong undercurrent of asceticism implicit in the honor code even suggests that the family unit further cut itself off from those markets by resisting their exchange utilities—foreign luxuries. Women were secluded not only from men but from the temptations of the courtly way of life as well. Perhaps the seductiveness of women and the seductiveness of luxuries were symbolically linked to a single foreign evil that threatened the resources of the family group and of the indigenous society. Women were evil because, tempted by luxury commodities, they were potential accomplices in the larceny of their own productivity in children and labor. Could this be why men claimed that women came from the devil and could not be trusted to control their own sexuality? Interestingly, the Sicilian dialect word for widow is *la cattiva,* which also means prisoner or captive slave. Both meanings derive from the Latin *captus,* suggesting a symbolic equivalency of status (Traina 1868: 178). One was either a prisoner of the family or a prisoner of foreigners.

If we could pursue this line of reasoning further, with additional evidence, it might help explain the appearance of similar codes of honor in other, disparate places at other times, such as medieval Europe and among the Plains Indians of North America in the nineteenth and twentieth centuries. Both areas were ravaged by luxury-bearing traders in search of captive labor. Perhaps the conditions in both areas were similar enough to those of Sicily under early imperial domination to account for analogous preoccupations with virginity.[3]

The Renaissance cities of northern Italy, for which Sicily served as a periphery, also manufactured luxuries for export. Although Sicily did not regularly exchange slaves for luxuries during the Spanish period, it did export wheat, the production of which required Sicilian labor. In addition, the Sicilian aristocracy practiced a kind of informal polygyny, staffing their great homes with concubines and female servants. Carmelo Trasselli has uncovered evidence that in sixteenth-century Sicily women were often captured, kidnapped, held for ransom, subjected to acts of violence, and taken as concubines (1973). Barons and local notables seem frequently, although not exclusively, to have been the perpetrators of these acts, which occurred in rural towns as well as in Palermo. They did not enjoy a right of *jus primae noctis* with women of their tenants and sharecroppers, but—and this is worse— they encroached upon these women as they encroached on peasant land. In Trasselli's view, barons took women from their dependents neither as a right nor by customary law but as an act of violence and prepotency. He also has presented data to show that illegitimacy was common in the sixteenth century, particularly as the consequence of

[3] Slavery and slave trading were common in Europe from the fall of the Roman Empire and the rise of its eastern successor until the ninth and tenth centuries, in some places even longer. The capture or sale of slaves for export to Near Eastern markets indicated that the European economy was subordinate to the luxury-exporting empires of Byzantium and Islam, although historians are only beginning to examine the implications of this imbalance in trade (see Misbach 1972).

unions between single women and married men or priests. Many men kept concubines, and venereal disease was spreading. Manuals of confession warned of extraconjugal affairs, adultery, incest, rape, affairs with celibate clergy, homosexuality, bestiality, "and worse." The manuals also pointed to the use of contraception and abortion, both apparently ancient practices in Sicily (along with infanticide) despite religious prohibitions against them (Borruso 1966).[4] It is difficult to judge whether one purpose of woman-capture by the landed class was to increase the number of their dependents—a conclusion suggested by the fact that they apparently legitimated many of their bastard offspring. At any event, Trasselli's research permits us to consider the continuity of the code of honor as a means of protecting women against encroachment.

The idea that women were more vulnerable than men to dominance by external forces might also explain certain aspects of custom and costume that impress the outsider in Sicily. Women who embroider are familiar with patterns that circulated in the royal courts of Europe (Fagone 1966). Their enforced isolation from the luxury manufactures of foreign metropolitan centers is suggested by their ability to copy and elaborate upon—but not buy—expensive foreign goods. With regard to their own wardrobes, the strictures of mourning ran counter to much courtly fashion. North Italian courtiers, for example, indulged in brilliant polychrome themes for cloth and clothing, emphasizing floral patterns, rich brocades, and parti-colored garments. Sicilian aristocrats emulated these metropolitan court styles with gusto. Pitrè recorded for the eighteenth century how aristocratic women used perfumes and brightly colored silks (now French) in a way that foreign observers thought was extravagant, even going so far as to import their hairdressers from France (1939: 305–320). They also enjoyed a freedom of behavior unknown to upper-class women elsewhere in Europe (Vaussard 1963: 92). But other Sicilian women wore somber styles except on their wedding days and on holidays. They dressed in clothes spun from flax or wool and dyed in dark hues, or else in the more severe black garments of mourning. Even colored ribbons were shunned (Vaussard 1963: 49). Although sometimes in the history of European fashion black has been a courtly color, it nevertheless stands most consistently and explicitly for withdrawal

---

[4] Until the twentieth century, the Church distinguished between abortion conducted before or after the fetus was blessed with a soul. A male fetus received a soul in the fortieth day, a female fetus in the eightieth to ninetieth day. Early abortions were not considered criminal and required only a year of penitence (Borruso 1966: 82–83).

from the rainbow of luxury. Its association with night and death confirms the message of restraint and self-denial.

In the community studied by Chapman in 1929, the typical Sicilian bride preferred to wear a brightly colored silk dress on her wedding day rather than the white dress, stockings, and slippers prescribed by the Church. A black shawl, however, covered her head. Moreover, "for a week [after the wedding] the bridal couple keep to their home, and on the following Sunday they make a formal appearance together at church. For this the bride wears a special dress which her husband has provided. Frequently this is black, and will serve as her best mourning dress when she has the occasion to go into black . . . [1971: 105]."

Honor and Inequality

Although the code of honor might have arisen in response to threats to the family posed by predatory local and foreign elites, it is doubtful that the seclusion of women and the defensive posture associated with honor were effective against any but near-status equals who also engaged in predatory tactics. Certainly, data from contemporary Sicily suggest that it is in competition between near status equals that honor plays a significant role. Peasants were powerless to redress the inequalities of latifundism; they could not effectively challenge baronial usurpations of land. A man could, however, challenge his peers when they attempted to move against the integrity of his property, for example, through abusive grazing. The same was true of honor as it applied to women.

One way to escape the dishonorable consequences of rape or seduction was for the father of the violated daughter hastily to arrange her marriage to the culprit. Such an alternative was especially likely if the man were of higher status than she. Likewise, if a young man still wanted to marry a woman who had been refused him by her parents, he could sometimes force the issue by kidnapping her. The girl's father would then be constrained to permit the marriage in order to reestablish his and his family's honor. Similar qualifications applied to adultery. As Davis has written about Pisticci, a south Italian town like Villamaura, set among ex-latifundia, "a man can seduce the wife or daughter of his social inferior with relative impunity." Moreover, "since the 'reasonable adulterer' is known to take care to select his partners among his honour inferiors, we could say that a man who cuckolds another *ipso facto* claims to be his honour-superior; and it is only when this is not the case, or when the cuckold rejects the claim, that homicide is appropriate behavior. . . . Indeed, in the absence of evidence to the contrary, a poor man is assumed to be a cuckold [Davis 1969: 70–73]." Cuckoldry, then, comes in different conditions. There is the *cornuto contento,* who in effect sells his wife or daughter to a status superior, and the *cornuto bastionato,* who is powerless to respond. Both imply the continuance of woman-capture.

In relations between the powerful and the powerless, the powerless live in a more or less chronic state of mortification for which there is no feasible remedy. But when the transgressor is of roughly equal status and power, then one can hardly fail to retaliate even against the most superficial denial of reciprocity. Thus, honor functions literally to even the score among people who are close enough to each other to feel envy. In one case, a blacksmith envied his neighbor, a peasant's son who had managed to acquire stable employment as a civil servant. The blacksmith's resentment intensified when the neighbor arranged a good marriage for his daughter. He began to feel (rightly or wrongly?) that the neighbor and members of his family were snubbing him, finding very subtle ways to show disrespect and violating the simpler etiquettes of everyday life. The blacksmith, though invited, did not attend the wedding of the neighbor's daughter, offering a lame excuse. Of course the neighbor replied in kind, by failing to visit the blacksmith when he was ill. Their relationship deteriorated in a downward spiral of reciprocal affronts until finally they and their respective families were no longer on speaking terms (they were *sciariatti*). This was not a happy state of affairs, but each man felt that he had recovered his honor and had preserved his moral equality with the other.

Preoccupation with honor, and envy, are thus closely related. Envy is institutionalized in belief in the evil eye (*malocchio*), which was common in the past. Even today one encounters the occasional sorcerer (*mago*) who can neutralize spells cast by witches and otherwise innocent but jealous neighbors and relatives. When guests come to such joyous occasions as weddings or baptisms their host or hostess will give them a little nosegay of candy-coated almonds. Barth suggested that this practice, which is common throughout the Mediterranean, may be intended to neutralize the potential harm which might have been created by the guest's envy (1961: 145).

In many ways, rural entrepreneurs were specialists in honor. They were, after all, upwardly mobile, striving for wealth, power, and position, and therefore supersensitive to the etiquettes of proper behavior and the tokens of respect embodied in those etiquettes.

Since, however, they were powerful persons with more than the usual access to violent means, their reaction to the problem of honor was more aggressive, less defensive and passive. Their lives exhibited a spirit and levity that contrasted with the somber tone of honor and shame in the towns. The contrast was dramatically symbolized in the vivid primary colors that were used to decorate the carts and animals that served the great *massarie*: dyed wool pompoms and paraphernalia for horses and mules, and vivid descriptive paintings for the carts. The opposition black versus bright colors was consonant with a more fundamental division of priorities. The black, somber, austere mode meant withdrawal and isolation from the marketplace; whereas the gaily colored mode meant commercial activity. The former was female and sedentary; the latter, male and mobile. Men mediated between women and the outside world, and among men the most important mediators were the rural entrepreneurs.

AMICIZIA

Recall that the most important activities of rural entrepreneurs involved moving agricultural products into distant, sometimes clandestine markets. Crucial to this process was their ability to organize commerce between towns, that is, from place to place throughout the interior. Until the late nineteenth century, however, the interior lacked roads. It was barely penetrated by the police powers of the state, and the settlement pattern, fixed during the Catalan hegemony of the fourteenth and fifteenth centuries, had eliminated market towns, break-of-bulk points, and intermediate centers of commercial attraction. To cope with these conditions, rural entrepreneurs needed some form of organization that would transcend the local nucleus of family and ritual kin—godparents and coparents. They needed a form of organization that transcended even the patrilineal extended family enterprises of the *massariotti,* described in Chapter 4. In order to go beyond their local domains, rural entrepreneurs cultivated vast networks of personal contacts which extended to many and distant locations.

Friendship was the critical relation which defined networks of exchange in western Sicily, and the operative social structure was (and is) the coalition of friends. The coalition is one kind of noncorporate group: a group of persons who are mutually interdependent and have a shared normative orientation but do not have a common interest in property (broadly defined) which is vested in the group per se. Such a group has no charter and no bank account or treasury, and individual members are not legally bound by the collectivity. Other forms of noncorporate group are the clique and the patron–client chain.

Coalitions are temporary, ad hoc, and task specific, i.e., they are formed to accomplish specific ends, after which they disband. New members may be added as new resources or skills are needed and, depending on his relationship to the others, a member can withdraw, taking his assets with him. Since the coalition is fluid and task specific, it does not ask too much of its participants. Rarely does one commit all of one's energy, time, or capital to a given coalition. Status differences among members of a coalition may be relevant to the way it is organized and then functions, but such differences are not, as in a patron–client chain, a universal and defining characteristic. If anything, there is in the coalition a tendency toward "democratization," as the idiom of friendship serves to neutralize differences in power. Thus, two members of unequal status, effectively related as patron and client, refer to each other as friends.

Coalitions are initiated by one or a few persons. If the person who initiates the coalition cannot find the allies he needs in his own network of friends, he will work through that network to reach friends of friends. Sometimes, a coalition's most important or effective participant will be someone who was several networks removed from the initiator and totally unaware of his existence. As a result of their joint effort, however, both the initiator and the other participants will enlarge their respective networks. Indeed, the shifting composition of many networks in Sicily is related to the involvement of their members in successive coalitions.

Obviously the coalition had some limitations as an organizing device for business ventures. Since it had no legal status, and members could unilaterally withdraw their assets before a task was completed, it was liable to disintegrate. It was less stable than the joint stock associations through which merchant capitalists in medieval and Renaissance Italy financed sea trade even though these also were characterized by a lack of continuity and trust—each partnership covered one voyage (Lane 1944; Lopez and Raymond 1955). It was certainly less stable than the large corporate structures of industrial northern Europe. In the mid-nineteenth century, one Sicilian complained that association requires good faith and easy credit, neither of which was possible in Sicily because there was no real government (Majoranna 1855). Yet for the same reasons that the coalition was unstable, it met the demands of broker capitalism under conditions of colonial dependency. For it enabled rural entrepreneurs to adapt to shifting market conditions that they could not control, with a minimum of organizational overhead. Furthermore, what business associates lacked in terms of reliable legal protection, they made up for by celebrating friendship.

In western Sicily, the friendship tie seems to be self-serving in the sense that people do not make the distinction between "business friends" and "social friends." Thus, there is no contradiction in having a friend and using him or her as a resource. Cultivation of a network of friendship (*una rete di amicizia*) is a widely celebrated strategy for getting ahead, while purely expressive bonds are the luxury of young people, before they enter the marketplace as adults.

Nevertheless, as Wolf has pointed out, instrumental friendship has an emotional component (1966a: 12–13). Friends like each other, find each other *simpatico*; the resulting good feelings add another dimension to their association. Reciprocity need not be immediate or balanced because cooperation and trust are sufficient to override most day-by-day transactions. In business ventures where exchanges cannot be regulated by contracts enforceable in courts of law, adherence to the norms of friendship provides a source of stability and predictability, especially as many of these exchanges are made between strangers who have no basis for reciprocal trust except that they are recommended to each other by a mutual friend.

So friendship is important to rural entrepreneurs, and the ideology of friendship is often celebrated when they gather to exchange information, create coalitions, and simply enjoy one another's company. Such gatherings, usually exclusively male, often occur at banquets, some of which are inspired by a newly established or newly repaired alliance. Important in the past, as well as today, they typically took place in the countryside. Rural entrepreneurs from different towns met at the banquet table on the *massaria* or at one of the water driven mills. They slaughtered, roasted, and ate sheep or goats, along with vast quantities of freshly made pasta as well as cheese and wine. Unless the families were present, the men who hosted the affair did the cooking (Alongi 1886: 151; Cavalieri 1925: xxv; Chilanti 1959: 117–163; Romano 1966: 10–35). Today the automobile and new standards of consumption have combined to make a variety of other locations—restaurants, bars, private homes, summer villas—more attractive than the *massaria* as meeting places. In spite of this shift, however, the nature and purpose of the gatherings appear much the same. Men come together to eat, drink, and make merry—this is its own reward. But these occasions also facilitate the broadening of a participant's range of friends and contacts and allow for the creation or modification of temporary goal-specific coalitions. Equally important, we think, the banquets provide a context for elevating friendship to an ideology, thus lending additional stability to alliances formed in its name.

P. Schneider had the opportunity to participate in a number of such occasions, the most notable of which was a series of five banquets (held in restaurants and summer villas on the outskirts of four towns) to celebrate the resolution of a quarrel between two influential persons, a merchant from Villamaura and a wholesaler from a nearby community, Solera. The truce had been negotiated by mutual friends from the towns of Palazzoverde and Montebello. The first banquet was held in a rustic house on the outskirts of Palazzoverde by one of the peacemakers and several of his close friends. In the weeks that followed, this banquet was succeeded by four others in as many different places. Two were held in summer villas, two in resort area restaurants. None was held in town. In all but the last, the hosts prepared the food themselves, each group trying to outdo the hosts of the previous week's banquet. And the meals were lavish: antipasto, soup, pasta, two or three fish and meat courses, salad, fruit, and cake, all accompanied by great quantities of wine. (Indeed, at one of the villas the wine flowed from barrels on the second floor through a hose and spigot which hung over the table on the ground floor.) Consistent with tradition, no women attended these affairs.

By the last banquet about 100 people were involved. There appear to have been three major categories of participant: (1) close friends of the principals (the two people who had quarreled and the two who had negotiated the truce); (2) friends of people in group 1; and (3) friends once removed—i.e., friends of friends of people in group 1. Among the participants were many notables from the towns involved—mayors and councilmen, priests, veterinarians, and doctors.

The banquets brought together small, well-knit cliques from different communities, as well as individuals who had never before met. Each person there was recommended to the others by his very presence, and each seemed intent on expanding his contacts. Upon arrival at the celebration, most paired off to discuss private matters, "making the *passeggiata*," strolling slowly back and forth across the room, a tactic that ensures privacy. (There is tacit recognition that a group which is not moving in a public place is open, but a walking group is closed to outsiders.) At this point one had a clear picture of the extent to which dyadic relations are salient in the social structure. Of course no one kept the same partner for the entire evening and much of the time the dyadic pattern gave way to a collective one, but no one should doubt that the modern feast, as were those in the past, is an important occasion for network building and a proving ground for anyone who would like to be a "fisher of men."

In the course of the banquets people made deals and formed coalitions to accomplish a great variety of goals that had nothing to do with the issue that brought them together. Two carpenters from Palazzoverde made arrangements to get contracts in Villamaura and Montebello; a butcher arranged for an official to put pressure on provincial authorities to raise price ceilings on retail meat; the mayor of one town renewed his friendship with a dignitary from another town; and so forth. The banquets, in other words, served the useful purpose of rounding up like-minded entrepreneurs from several towns. Since all were invited by friends, each could see the others as potential allies—if not entirely trustworthy, then at least constrained by ethical obligations to mutual friends.

Once the solidarity broke down in a way that further illustrates the salience of friendship to the occasion, and the salience of the occasion to friendship. The son of the Solera wholesaler invited three young men of his own acquaintance to the third banquet. Although these young men also knew Don Totò, the peacemaker, they did not known anyone else present. Their host was responsible to the others for their comportment; in addition, he felt obliged to see to it that his guests were treated with proper respect. During the course of the evening the young men became increasingly exuberant and, it seemed, quite insensitive to the etiquette of deference which the situation required. They began to mock Don Totò while he was making a toast to friendship, whereupon one of his close friends stood up and exploded, "You people are not part of this company and should show proper respect to Don Totò!" (Having consumed more than his share of wine, Don Totò was in no condition to defend himself, which is why he drew their mockery in the first place.) The young men were offended and left the house; immediately, the man who had invited them turned on Don Totò's protector and furiously accused him of insulting his friends and offending him in the process. It appeared as if several weeks of peacemaking and three banquets were going up in smoke, until a respected guest, a notable from Villamaura, took the floor and made a soothing speech about the importance of friendship. The situation was calmed, and the three young men were persuaded to return. It is interesting that they attended the following banquet, but Don Totò's protector did not. Nevertheless, their behavior on subsequent occasions was much more subdued.

Reflected in this incident is the quality of life associated with the code of honor. But the incident was transcended, and in this we see the real meaning of the banquets. They seemed designed to create orderliness and predictability in the uncertain world of rural entrepreneurship. At the banquet tables, men were arranged by town. At the first gathering the merchant from Villamaura and the wholesaler from Solera sat at opposite ends of a long table, while the peacemakers and their close friends sat in the middle. Many toasts were drunk and speeches delivered (sometimes sung in rhyme)—impassioned odes to the importance of friendship. "It is harder to find friends than money," said Don Totò, "but they last longer and are worth much more." Another theme was respect for age, which is consistent with the patriarchal bias of families that had their roots in the *massaria*. The oldest man present was given the honor of cutting the cake, while Don Totò proclaimed that the old are "our teachers and masters." His conclusion that "we owe them an enormous debt" elicited applause and embraces all around.

Serious speechmaking was supplemented by another form of solidarity based on entertainment and horseplay. At the first banquet several persons performed a parody on the Catholic mass in which one, robed in a lace tablecloth as a priest, cleverly wove vulgar commentaries into an otherwise official sounding liturgy. This "profane mass" was repeated at subsequent gatherings, each time with more attention to costumes and props until, on the third repetition, it included a fireworks display. The themes of the mass were oral and genital, but they did not stress the sexual exploits of the men present so much as their vulnerability to the evil ways of women. Great emphasis was placed on eating and drinking and on the fraternal bonds created when men break bread together. Some of the participants then parodied women, dancing erotically alone and together, applauded and encouraged by the others. We have no way of knowing whether these themes were typical of banquets in the past. We can nevertheless imagine that gatherings of men in country places often chose priests and women as targets of their humor—the prescribed religious behavior and prescribed sex roles. What better way to reinforce solidarity among men who belong to the town, church, and family but who have also an important and exclusive life beyond?

In sum, rural entrepreneurs managed the wide-ranging circulation of commodities without the benefit of such structural supports as a hierarchy of central markets and effective presence of the state. They faced a problem of trust: They were dependent upon one another, but they came from different communities and different kindreds, and they were operating in a barren and insecure countryside exposed to banditry. Their structural solution to these problems was the ad hoc coalition, generated out of a matrix of friendship relations and supported by a cultural code of friendship. That is why this code was so enthusiastically celebrated on the many occasions when entrepreneurs feasted together (P. Schneider 1972).

In this chapter we have sought the origins of cultural codes important to western Sicily in the relationship of that region to its geopolitical environment over several centuries. In the case of honor, pressures emanating from world-systems as far back as the ancient empires of the Near East and Italy would seem to account for possible origins. The ancient empires threatened the existence of the family by creating land shortages, fragmenting kin groups, and making claims on women. These pressures continued to a large extent under Spanish dominance. We think that the honor code was part of an overall strategy of resistance at the local and family levels.

The code of *furberia* (astuteness, shrewdness) was linked to the specific conditions of dominance under Spain. A loose, manipulable structure of colonial rule, coupled with evolving capitalist markets, was its hypothesized source. The code of friendship, we suspect, originated in the same context, although for somewhat different reasons. This code and the ways in which it was celebrated are reminiscent of other types of business association. Marc Bloch demonstrated how "peace associations" and "drinking fraternities" in medieval France and Germany solved problems of protection and trust for itinerant merchants and businessmen similarly unable to count for support on the state (Bloch 1962: 345–355). Latin America and west Africa provide other examples of elaborate cultural supports for capitalist activity (see Cohen 1969; Leeds 1964; Pi Sunyer 1967; Wolf and Hansen 1967). Nor was Sicily alone in combining business with pleasure. In all of these examples, business partners ate and drank together, possibly because men who do this will have second thoughts about cheating one another. The word *company*, first used for the trade associations of ancient and medieval Italy, comes from the Latin *campanis*—to break bread together.

An ideology like *amicizia* was most likely to flourish and be critical to business activities where it was the only, or major, basis for trust. In the colonies of the Spanish Empire, with ineffective state power, no market towns, and no hierarchy of settlements through which the circulation of commodities could be articulated and controlled, friendship played this role. It did for the ad hoc coalition of friends what the state did for business associations elsewhere: It lent credibility to contracts and a modicum of predictability to affairs. The friendship code, in short, may be understood as a response by rural entrepreneurs to the opportunities that opened up for them when Sicily became a source of primary products under Spain.

The point of exploring the possible origins of shrewdness, honor, and friendship is not merely to satisfy our curiosity. It is to show how these codes might have been products of the relationship between Sicily and its external environment, rather than inherent attributes of the "Sicilian character." The chapters that follow, in the second part, examine what happened to west Sicilian society during and after its confrontation with postindustrial imperialism of the nineteenth and early twentieth centuries. As is well known, the island emerged from this confrontation an exporter of raw labor instead of raw wheat. It failed to develop its own diversified agriculture or industry. Cultural codes like shrewdness and honor have often been held responsible for this fate, partly because no one ever questioned their origins. Given the possibility that they resulted from the same forces that gave rise to the social, political, and economic institutions of the preindustrial society, and are thus an integral part of what Sicily as a colony became, we can now go on to explore how these institutions, plus a variety of new forces, influenced the path of recent postindustrial change.

Sicily in
a Postindustrial
World-System

chapter 6

From the Export of Wheat to the Export of Labor

Western Sicily's early colonial experience had an enduring impact upon environment, land use and tenure, and social and political organization. We have argued that it also helped shape cultural codes, some of which are still intact today. Between that early experience and the present, the regional society confronted and adapted to a new set of pressures that derived from the expansion of increasingly industrial North Atlantic Europe—especially England—and from the efforts of northern Italy to industrialize along "North Atlantic" lines—that is, to become competitive with the North Atlantic. The time period for these new pressures overlaps with the time period of Spanish dominance, for already in the seventeenth century the North Atlantic countries rebelled against Mediterranean influence and assumed an apparently irreversible lead in European development. The new pressures, however, reached a peak in the nineteenth and twentieth centuries, under English and then American supremacy. In Part II of our book, we will examine the impact of these new pressures on west Sicilian society: on the peasantry, on herdsmen, and on rural entrepreneurs. Our intent is to illuminate areas of continuity—in particular, the failure of land reform and the persistence of broker capitalism—and to account for the rise of mafia as a distinctive feature of the transition of western Sicily from a preindustrial to a postindustrial peripheral region.

NEW TYPES OF PRESSURE

Three decisive changes in Sicily's world environment occurred in the nineteenth century to transform the island—again, primarily its western region—from a source of wheat to a source of unskilled labor, thus establishing a relationship with the outside world more unbalanced and disadvantageous than that of the past. One change was a decline in the export market for Sicilian wheat; another was the import of cheap (as opposed to luxury) manufactures; and the third was a combination of factors producing rapid population growth. Together these changes proved hard to resist. Containing them would have meant the development of alternative agricultural and industrial enterprises that would absorb Sicilian labor at home. This chapter, after considering the three new pressures, will trace and analyze the failure of efforts after 1800 to develop any significant export other than labor.

As the industrial revolution in the nineteenth century wrought changes in transportation and agriculture, Sicily's specialized export, hard wheat, became less and less competitive in foreign markets. It yielded first to Russian competition, then to New World grains produced in America, Argentina, and Canada by capital intensive, mechanized means. Grown and harvested without fertilizers or machinery, transported out of the interior by mule train, Sicilian wheat could no longer satisfy the bread makers of distant cities. In 1819 the Bourbon government ended export licensing in wheat as Italy and even Sicily began to import wheat (Mack Smith 1968b: 388; Scrofani 1962: 107–109). From 1840, the steamship made it feasible to transport soft wheat quickly, thus negating the advantage of hard wheat's resistance to spoilage. In the twentieth century, chemical additives to soft wheat further undermined markets for the hard variety by making it possible to manufacture pasta without it. Pasta used to be exclusively a hard wheat product (the very best pasta still is).

Simultaneous with the decline of an external market for Sicilian wheat was the invasion of the island by cheap manufactures—also products of the industrial breakthrough in northwest Europe. In world-systems of the past, Sicily had imported manufactures, but they were primarily luxury goods that did not displace many indigenous crafts. In the nineteenth century, Sicilian craftsmen faced a much wider range of mass-produced goods, aimed at poor as well as rich consumers. In spite of import duties, shoes, nails, buttons, glass, rope, wool, and other cheap textiles entered regularly (Pitrè 1944: Vol. I; 27). Local crafts disappeared, and we read reports of economic decline in such varied activities as candle- and tile-making, ceramics, hide-tanning, fish conservation, boat building, and coral polishing (Ciaccio 1900: 78–96; Scaturro 1926: Vol. II, 468). In the early eighteenth century, the coastal town of Sciacca in western Sicily had a small but thriving textile factory; by the end of the nineteenth century weaving and embroidering were done entirely at home. The only industry to receive mention in a nineteenth-century description of the coastal city of Mazzara was the preparation of plaster for house construction (Nicastro 1913: 1–28). Clearly the livelihood of many artisans was at stake.

At the same time that the decline of wheat led to job losses in agriculture and as the avalanche of manufactured imports took away work from craftsmen, the Sicilian population began to grow at a cruelly accelerated rate. Historical demographers and social scientists are just beginning to understand the population explosions which occurred in some, but not all, parts of the world in this period. Whatever the dynamics of so complex a change, it led to a new situation: the existence of labor surpluses rather than shortages and the "voluntary" movement, the migration, of labor from one area to another (in contrast to the mobilization of labor through capture and enslavement as before). In Sicily, population increased by 50% in the eighteenth century, from 1 million to 1.5 million. Population density almost tripled in the western region, where it increased from 25 to 74 persons per square kilometer. In the southeast, around Syracuse, growth was slower, from 31 to 59 people per square kilometer. The northeastern region, around Messina, registered the smallest gain: from 38 to 55 people per square kilometer (Pontieri 1961: 46). After 1800, the rate of growth everywhere in Sicily picked up: A population of 1.5 million jumped to 3.5 million by 1900; in 1950 it was 4.5 million, notwithstanding massive emigration. Clearly, this rate of expansion worsened the problems of displacement mentioned earlier.

THE BOURBON *BONIFICA*: A FORMULA FOR CONFRONTING THE NEW WORLD-SYSTEM

In the first half of the nineteenth century, deteriorating conditions in agriculture and the competitive pressure placed on local craftsmen by imported consumer goods forced the ruling Neapolitan Bourbons to seek a solution. Some government advisors advocated free trade. Basing their arguments on the assessments of Europeans who had visited Sicily and the southern part of the mainland in the 1700s, they suggested that competitive trade would lead to improved productivity in agriculture and manufacturing. They noted that England was promoting a free trade policy, and the dramatic increase in her national product seemed to prove their point. Critics argued, however, that a policy which would serve England's interests would not necessarily work to the advantage of the Bourbon Kingdom. If trade barriers were to be removed, England could more easily claim the primary resources of other regions as well as flood these regions with her manufactures. Indeed, European traders—English, French, and Spanish—had long claimed exemption from customs duties in Sicily (Mack Smith 1968b: 380).

But the protectionist alternative was equally unattractive. Given the absence of an infrastructure for development in the form of a well-integrated state and market, and given the fact that Sicily and southern Italy were poor, it would have been difficult in the extreme to maintain a protective wall around nascent industries until such time as they could compete with foreign imports. The Bourbon administration took a compromise route, which the Italian nation would later briefly follow after unification in 1860. This route was to improve agriculture in the hope of accumulating capital from agricultural exports, the capital in turn to finance improvements in transport and communications, state services, and the like—essential preconditions for future development.

How was agriculture to be improved? Even if wheat growers were protected by a tariff from external competition, it was unlikely that their methods of cultivation could ever be improved to the point of making wheat a significant export again. The Bourbons recognized that to be competitive, the new agriculture would have to emphasize intensively cultivated, "luxury" crops—wine grapes, vegetables, fruits—not easily grown in colder climates or in the absence of constant human attention and labor (Scrofani 1962: 225). Toward this end they instituted a program called a *Bonifica*, which, had it been successful, would have resulted in a shift from latifundism to a diversified type of agrarian regime—a shift, in brief, from interior-dominated, extensive agriculture and long-range cycles of transhumance to coast-dominated, tree crop agriculture, with capitalized animal husbandry in the interior.

Planners of the *Bonifica* stressed the need to reforest mountains in order to stem erosion and restore a ruined hydrographic system. Water control would have to be removed from private vested interests since irrigation and drainage in the coast and lowlands depended upon water conservation in the interior and mountains (Scrofani 1962: 217–229).[1] Peasants of the latifundist west would be resettled in villages or hamlets on the land, supported by construction of buildings and roads, and drainage of malarial basins. According to legislation passed between 1836 and 1853, landholders who joined the program, alone or in cooperative association, would receive tax exemptions for a period of 20 years. The participants, for their part, would not be the titled owners of large estates but a new class of ambitious, investment-oriented, yeoman-type "improving" farmers, recruited from below. What Sicily lacked in wheat, it could acquire by using the new export crops as exchange.

The kind of reform envisioned by the Bourbon planners required far more organization, energy, and capital than the government of the two Sicilies could possibly muster. After all, its immodest goal was to reverse over five centuries of latifundism, as if the *casali,* or villages, of the Arab period, together with their varied crops, were still intact. The government's most substantial contribution was a series of laws, begun in the late eighteenth century and continued under English rule, that abolished so-called feudalism. As a result of these laws, land became more strictly a commodity than it had been, and promiscuous, overlapping claims to land were curtailed. The aristocracy could no longer legally entail land or practice primogeniture. Control by single families over vast extensions came to an end, as the component estates were alienated from the holding. For the first time, the law enabled creditors to claim these estates in settlement of debt, and this, too, accelerated transfers of property. Most important, legislation focused on promiscuous grazing rights. Decrees of 1807–1810 required partition of feudal and demesnial land, whether open or

---

[1] Carlo Afan De Rivera, one of the Bourbon planners of hydraulic rehabilitation in Sicily, noted that the mountainous topography had long contributed to private as opposed to public control of water. Cooperative efforts to control this resource, such as had evolved in the Po valley of northern Italy, were unknown in the southern and island regions (Scrofani 1962: 220–221).

cultivated, on which such rights were exercised. Subsequent legislation (1838–1841) provided for partition of some communal domains (Scrofani 1962: 217).

Consistent with the *Bonifica,* partition was intended to facilitate more intensive uses of land, above all by excluding animals and by creating a class of small to medium landholders loyal to the central power. Peasants with capital, helped by low interest loans, were to acquire the partitioned land outright, or in emphyteusis. Thus they would be compensated for their loss of use rights. As with the eighteenth-century effort to control the export of wheat, however, the results of the *Bonifica* were almost opposite to those intended. Few peasants benefited and many suffered from it. The real beneficiaries were rural entrepreneurs, especially the *gabellotti.* Either directly or as creditors of peasants, they acquired the bulk of partitioned land in the nineteenth century and emerged as the backbone of a new landowning class, the gentry, or *civile* class. From the beginning of the century until 1860, the number of large landholders increased tenfold (Mack Smith 1959: 38). A class of small and medium holders, small-scale capitalist farmers, did not form.

Peasant losses will sound entirely familiar. Losing the right to use communal domain, peasants could no longer pasture a work animal or the family goat, nor could they cut brush or gather stones and wild vegetables. As had happened to peasants elsewhere, the abolition of "feudalism" left Sicilians more vulnerable than ever to the markets of the world (see Wolf 1969). Most serious of all, they lost access to arable land through indebtedness and usurpation. Several times under the Bourbons, peasants rose up to occupy appropriated communal land, set fire to tax records, and attack agents of the state.

1860–1880: THE PATTERN REPEATED AGAIN

Although the Bourbon government's plan for Sicily was overambitious given the resources it was willing to commit, it may have been the only feasible way to avoid an eventual surplus of manpower. Significantly, every subsequent effort at agrarian reform at least paid lip service to precisely the same goals. In addition to breaking up latifundia, it was necessary to *transform* agriculture: reforest mountains, launch irrigation projects, build villages, hamlets, and roads, and plant diversified labor-intensive crops—in short, to change the ecology of western Sicily. Sicily, in addition to confronting the obstacles that past latifundism posed for this course of action, after 1860 became vulnerable to the often conflicting interests of north Italian industrial development.

Unified in 1860 under the hegemony of a north Italian kingdom, the kingdom of Piedmont, Italy as a whole was an underdeveloped society vis-à-vis the industrial North Atlantic. The manufacturing and commercial cities of the Po valley, which in the sixteenth century had dominated much of Europe, were now far behind other European centers of industry. Nineteenth-century Italy, relative to France and England, was a poor and still primarily agricultural country—part of Europe's semi-periphery, in Wallerstein's terms (1974). Its first government, after unification, advocated free trade and an open economy, thus maintaining the support of France and England. The leaders of this government, known as Moderates, also depended heavily upon foreign capital to integrate their country. Some of this capital was English; most of it came from France. French capital built the railroads which knit the new Italy together. French financiers owned 20% of Italy's national debt and 80% of its foreign debt. French capital also contributed to a number of private enterprises in Italy (Cameron 1961: 284–302; Romeo 1959: 30). A major Italian export was raw silk to France.

The Moderates' scheme for economic growth, consistent with their advocacy of free trade and similar to the Bourbon *Bonifica*, was to accumulate capital for industry out of agricultural exports, largely by improving agricultural production. As a group, they represented the interests of progressive north Italian landlords, and their efforts were largely concentrated in the north. Although Sicily exported intensively cultivated cash crops in this period, the state did little more to improve Sicilian agriculture than partition Church lands (Romeo 1959: 35–36). And with the same results as under the Bourbons: In 1867, the Italian government legislated the partition and sale of Church lands in Sicily. Ecclesiastical domain had already been divided in southern Italy but it still occupied 10% of the island's surface. Parcels of around 50 hectares each were sold at auction, almost exclusively to *gabellotti* and *civili* (Cavalieri 1925: xxxviii–xxxix; Corleo 1871; D'Alessandro 1959: 87–92). In Villamaura, eight *civile* families acquired nearly 80% of a vast latifundium owned by the Knights of Malta. Four of them held over 50%.

Consistent with the sale of Church lands, other policies of the new Italian government exacerbated conditions for the Sicilian peasantry. In a stroke it eliminated tariff barriers throughout the peninsula and islands, subjecting several hundred small-scale industries to competing foreign manufactures. It unified the national debt to the disadvantage of Sicily and the south; it demobilized Bourbon soldiers and introduced conscription; and it reimposed the onerous grist tax on grinding flour (the tax had been collected by the Bourbons but was eliminated briefly in the early 1860s). From the late 1860s until 1877, demobilized Bourbon troops and displaced peasants staged a "brigand war" to regain lost land (and eliminate the grist tax). Bandits organized large federated groups and planned operations that were increasingly bold. They kidnapped landowners and held them for ransom, forcing them to act upon carefully penned letters of extortion. Holdups and robberies multiplied not only in the countryside but in the towns as well (D'Alessandro 1959: 92–93). The mails became vulnerable, crop theft spread, and everywhere defiance of bandits led to arson and property damage if not to murder. For the province of Palermo alone, D'Alessandro reported 81 homicides, 164 robberies, 65 thefts in the countryside, 18 fires, and 26 assaults on the mail in a 6-month period of 1871 (1959: 94). As in southern Italy, but with considerably more difficulty, the Piedmont-centered state intervened militarily to suppress the brigand war.

1880–1900: A CLOSED ECONOMY PHASE OF ITALIAN DEVELOPMENT

The moderate scheme for advancing the Italian economy was, like the Bourbon *Bonifica,* a necessary but also limited first phase of development. By concentrating on agriculture, it maintained the imbalance between "rich nations and poor nations." Its reliance on English and French capital further reinforced Italy's dependence vis-à-vis the North Atlantic, and dependency made Italy vulnerable to the great depression which began in the North Atlantic in the early 1870s—that is, shortly after the southern United States withdrew from the North Atlantic sphere of influence. This depression undermined the stability of the Moderate government in Italy. In the south and in Sicily its effects were compounded by the appearance of mechanically produced American wheat in European markets following the Civil War, in turn a contributing factor to the brigand war. In the parliamentary elections of 1874–1876, *gabellotti* and the *civili* voted the Piedmontese Moderates out of power and replaced them with a center–left government in which Republicans and Radicals had a larger voice. South Italian and Sicilian votes were decisive in this shift

(Graziano 1973: 13). Francesco Crispi, a Sicilian lawyer and nationalist, became minister of the interior, the most powerful national position below that of prime minister.

Between 1876 and 1887, the Piedmontese prime minister, Depretis, managed a series of governments through a process that became known as *trasformismo*—a process of co-optation in which conflicting interests were transformed, through grants of patronage, into more or less willing government supporters. No clear-cut scheme for development characterized this period, during which the government provided little direction, and certain conditions deteriorated of their own accord. In particular, the price of wheat fell after 1880 from 30 to 22 lire per quintal. (By 1894, it was 13.5 lire a quintal.) In 1887 the Sicilian Crispi left the Ministry of the Interior to become prime minister, and a policy of economic closure was forged. Italy would become an industrial nation equal to France if not England. Crispi, responsive to north Italian heavy industrial interests, was well suited to pursue this goal. His experience as interior minister, hence patron of prefects throughout Italy, and his roots in Sicily, enabled him to mobilize parliamentary majorities to support the development of iron and steel industries. He became, in effect, the tool of an alliance between northern industrial and southern agrarian interests. The alliance had nothing to do with agricultural exports. Instead, its quid pro quo was a protective tariff on wheat which, as we will see, reversed earlier efforts to return western Sicily to a diversified, coast-dominated, agrarian regime.

In marked contrast to the Moderates, Crispi was a militant protectionist and militantly anti-French. His program became a rallying point for all the politicians and businessmen who had resented the intervention of foreign capital during the preceding decades. Under Crispi, French capital was withdrawn from Italy although German capital replaced it to some extent. In Sicily and the south, German and north Italian capital spurred a change in the milling process as steam driven mills replaced water driven mills in the countryside (Ciaccio 1900: 94). (Subsequently, gas and electric power replaced steam, although a few water mills continued to operate until the 1950s.)

In addition to wheat, the commodities most heavily protected against foreign imports were cotton textiles, iron, and steel. Shipbuilding was also protected (Neufeld 1961: 153). But the actual effect of this protectionist policy is difficult to assess. Consumers bore the cost of protection and one may well question the extent to which methods of production were actually improved. Certainly wheat was produced as before, on large estates in rotation with pastoralism. According to the economic historian Alexander Gerschenkron, protection in general bred inefficiency and corruption. Subsidized by the government, banks overextended credit through low interest loans to industry, and bank scandals were the inevitable result. Moreover, the economy developed more rapidly in the early 1900s, after a series of scandals brought down the Crispians and their tariff policy (Gerschenkron 1955). Yet, given the hegemony of France in late nineteenth-century Italy, the free trade (open economy) alternative was also problematic. Perhaps the industrial growth recorded for the first decade or so of the twentieth century was a consequence of the preceding, protectionist era. One needs to know more about the relationship between the two phases.[2]

At any event, the Crispian era was an unequivocal disaster for the latifundist regions of the south and Sicily. Protectionism necessitated abrogation of a commercial treaty with France, and this resulted in a trade war in 1887. The French not only withdrew capital from Italy but also closed their markets to Italian imports. This was a severe blow to the wine and citrus fruit industries so recently built up in the south. Many growers and investors went bankrupt. French capitalists meanwhile restocked French vineyards, earlier destroyed by a phylloxera infestation, with a plant developed in California, and invested heavily in Algerian vineyards as well. The phylloxera then came to Italy to deal a final and virtually unresisted blow to wine production there. Between 1833 and 1880–1885, the extension of land in vineyards had doubled in Sicily, largely as a consequence of the Bourbon *Bonifica* and French demand. Between 1885 and 1903, however, almost all the gain was lost as hectares in vineyards declined from over 320,000 to 176,000. In the same period, the extension in grain increased from 663,000 to almost 800,000 hectares—a gain of about 20% (Scrofani 1962: 235). Fruit and vegetable growers, while less severely hit, were unable to mobilize the capital necessary to remain competitive with other producers. Citrus groves did not disappear in Sicily, and in fact expanded again after 1900; yet the island, and especially its western region, failed to become the major producer it might have become.

The most tragic consequence of Crispian policies for the south

---

[2] Wallerstein has raised a similar question about Tokugawa Japan. Whereas many historians would agree with C. R. Boxer that this regime's isolationism retarded Japanese involvement in the European industrial revolution, Wallerstein has suggested an opposite interpretation: "Could one not argue that only because Japan went into its shell so effectively at that time was it able to emerge in the 19th century in a form strong enough to resist playing a peripheral role in the world-system, and hence to industrialize rapidly [1974: 343, n.202]."

and Sicily was the rapid deterioration of peasant conditions, for the protective tariff on wheat and the new milling techniques stimulated more encroachment on land. Use rights were abrogated, commons appropriated, and vineyards destroyed. The number of people who owned land was lower in 1901 than it had been in 1860 (Mack Smith 1959: 149). In the same period the population of Sicily climbed from about 2.4 to over 3.5 million. As the wheat tariff inflated the price of bread, the peasant diet worsened, and the death rate became extremely high (Mack Smith 1959: 240; Neufeld 1961: 153, 213; Rochefort 1961: 65–66). Records of the communal council of Villamaura in the early 1890s indicate that many citizens could not pay their taxes, that the annual religious festival was deeply in debt, and that the town had to loan money to peasants in order that they might marry off their daughters. Bread riots were always a threat. The notary's archive for the same years contains numerous cases in which a member of the *civile* class made loans to 10 or more peasants at a time at usurious rates of interest. Others loaned seed to groups of around 50. The peasants used their small holdings as collateral, all too often losing them in the end. The typical peasant probably still cultivated two or more fields under a variety of arrangements: sharecropping, rental, emphyteusis, or outright ownership and worked as a day laborer on the side. He was, however, increasingly driven into a growing class of *braccianti*—day laborers without any means of production save their arms (*braccia*). All types of peasant were idle much of the time, while landowners, disregarding the abolition of "feudal" institutions, continued to demand and collect a variety of *banalités*.

The Sicilian peasantry was restive in the nineteenth century, and several times during the unfolding Risorgimento disturbances had broken out: 1820, 1837, 1848, 1860, 1866, and 1875. Local groups under local leaders burned buildings that housed tax and land registers, occupied partitioned land, and supported brigands who kidnapped wealthy landowners for ransom. In the early 1890s, the ferment acquired more persistent organization as squads, called *fasci,* formed and federated. In the process of federation, a few leaders of broader background emerged. Socialist and anarchist intellectuals argued for court proceedings against local mayors who were responsible for illegal appropriations of communal lands. Attempting to weld the *fasci* into a trade union movement, these leaders called farm labor strikes. In 1893, a regional Socialist congress met in Sicily, but not long afterward Crispi, on the advice of Sicilian deputies to Parliament, imposed martial law and dissolved the *fasci* by force. A second uprising in 1897–1898 was similarly repressed.

That a socialist movement should have failed to coalesce among Sicilian peasants is consistent with Wolf's observation that peasants must have leverage if they are to sustain a revolt (1969). They must have enough freedom from their oppressors to grow their own food and food for their guerrillas and leaders (see also Alavi 1965). Such leverage was impossible for Sicilian peasants, who had lost their villages and village lands by the fifteenth century. By that early date land had already taken on a commercial aspect, albeit camouflaged by feudal forms. Except for the practice of use rights and the existence of communal domain, collective rights in property were negligible and the barons created illegal enclosures (*difesi*) on common, as well as feudal, land. The removal of cultivators from arable land to be settled in agrotowns not only ensured their dependence on the latifundium; it exposed them directly and daily to "urban" powerholders. While it is true that these towns were not much influenced by state institutions, they were by no means closed and well-defended like the Russian *mir*. To the contrary, they were permeated by market forces to which local entrepreneurs were intimately tied.

In addition to the economic and military constraints that obstructed peasant revolt, the government that sent in troops was not foreign, nor was it illegitimate to most Sicilians. Its prime minister was himself a Sicilian and the electoral majorities that he put together drew heavily upon his home constituencies. Indeed, it was under Crispi that rural entrepreneurs and new landowners in the south and Sicily organized a far-flung system to deliver national patronage and that, in Sicily, rural entrepreneurial interests were consolidated in mafia. As Anton Blok has argued, the failure of peasants to change their society through socialism was intimately related to the success of mafia (1969c). Mafiosi in particular, and broker capitalists in general, not only assisted in the repression of the *fasci*; they held out the alternative of jobs, favors, and protection to at least some client peasants. They could do this because of their government connections—connections which in turn demonstrated the importance, the status, and the power of brokers in a society shaped by the experience of dominance under Spain. Again we encounter the dual aspect of that experience. On the one hand it was oppressive, but on the other it offered rewards that filtered down into strata below the landed aristocracy.

The ultimate response of Sicilians and south Italians to the repression of the Crispi era, and to the deteriorated conditions which it forced upon them, is well known. Between 1876 and 1925, over 1.5

million people left Sicily, principally for North America. The peak period of this massive exodus was clearly 1900–1914. In other words, emigration followed the failure of the *fasci* and the spread of bankruptcies through the vineyard zones, although artisans also numbered among the migrants (Neufeld 1961: 521; Renda 1963: 48; Rochefort 1961: 71). In retrospect, it seems an ominous portent of Italy's uneven future that the Americas, rather than northern Italy, harvested so much surplus Sicilian labor.

LAND REFORM IN THE TWENTIETH CENTURY

At the beginning of the nineteenth century, Sicily's role in the world economy was unsettled by changes in the export market for wheat. Yet, for the better part of a century, the island's new role remained unclear. Only after the mid-1890s did it become apparent that the major export of this peripheral area would be manpower. One alternative, diversified agriculture producing luxury crops for export, was alive until the Crispian era. Its demise in that period, moreover, did not immediately lead to emigration, as landlords, eager to increase efficiency in the production of wheat, had every reason to retain a large pool of underemployed laborers at home (provided they could control them). Under Crispi, the Italian government attempted to restrict emigration by making it bureaucratically difficult. After the repression of the *fasci,* peasants, enticed by the American labor market, began to agitate for the "freedom to migrate."

With the fall of Crispi, and the turn of the century rise of Giolitti, all this changed. Replacing the protectionist policies of the Crispian era with another phase of economic liberalism, the Giolittian government not only sanctioned emigration, it defined the export of people as a reasonable substitute for the export of manufactures, as well as a spur to the luxury crop trade, since Italians overseas would demand many of their favorite foods from home. During the period 1900–1914, shipping companies and "agents of emigration" (whether official or informal) operated with a relatively free hand. The Italian government levied taxes on their "traffic," which financed government efforts to encourage emigrants to send wages home to Italy, and eventually to return to live. It is estimated that roughly one-third of the Sicilian migrants to North America did return (Dore 1964; Foerster 1969: 474–501; Nitti 1958: 303–459; Renda 1963).

"The peasant loses his donkey [or mule] . . ."

". . . as the rich man loses his wife [Lorenzoni 1910: 139]."

Moving away from economic closure, the government of Giolitti reduced the wheat tariff and once more encouraged the expansion of intensive agriculture. Yet the latifundist regions of southern Italy and Sicily required a large-scale capital intervention before they could produce luxury crops competitively, and the funds for reforestation and irrigation projects were not forthcoming. In addition, emigration drained labor away from vineyards and orchards, making these enterprises unprofitable for small producers. The Giolittian government did not launch an all-out attack on the latifundium. But during the Giolittian period the size and coherence of the latifundium began gradually to change as a consequence of emigration remittances. Slowly in the twentieth century remittances from America came to play a major role in the creation of a new kind of agriculture, one which involved modest advances in tree crops but whose thrust was to intensify the cultivation of wheat.

Between 1891 and 1895, emigrants' remittances accounted for 0.5% of depositor credits in Italy's postal savings system. In 1910 they made up 20.9%—an indication of the increasing importance of this new source of income (Neufeld 1961: 290). With remittance money, peasants began to acquire their own means of production although not, at first, land. The most important of these means was an animal for transport—rarely a horse (rural entrepreneurs rode horses), usually a mule or an ass. In 1881, the Sicilian donkey population was 83,000; in 1908 it was almost 200,000 (Lorenzoni 1910: 128). Proverbs described the donkey as the peasant's best friend and companion: "The peasant loses his donkey as the rich man loses his wife [Lorenzoni 1910: 139]." The mule population climbed, too, although less dramatically: It was 112,000 in 1876 and 153,000 in 1908.

The mule and ass were adjuncts to the new cultivation. They allowed peasants almost daily access to the holdings that they share-cropped or rented on large estates, as well as to the meager holdings they owned. By working 10–12 hours a day with a hoe, peasants improved the soils of these holdings. Gradually, too, they began to purchase chemical fertilizers which enabled them to eliminate the fallow year in the rotation cycle. It became possible to plant wheat for 2 consecutive years—a different variety each year—on land that had earlier produced a crop only once every 3 or 4 years. Chemical fertilizers, moreover, allowed for cultivation of one or two forage crops without irrigation and these crops—the fava bean or sulla—began to replace the year in the rotation cycle that had once been left to pasturage. Whereas once the latifundium had been run from the *massaria* as an integrated estate, it was now fragmented in production, if not fragmented in ownership. Supplementing—indeed, displacing—the *gabellotto's* entrepreneurial role were hundreds of small-scale peasant entrepreneurs (Lorenzoni 1910: 133–145; Scrofani 1962: 253–256).

This shift in the basic nature of the latifundium, to what is sometimes called "peasant latifundism," was advanced by a cooperative movement that slowly gathered strength. The "transformist" policies of the Giolittian years (1901–1914) created an atmosphere in which peasant leagues could form. On the national level, Giolitti sought inspiration from the labor and welfare policies of more advanced societies and tentatively opened communication with Italian Socialists. After World War I, and under fascism, leagues and cooperatives organized by Catholics and war veterans (although not by Socialists) became instruments of the first transfers of land to peasant ownership. Other cooperatives simply replaced *gabellotti* as administrators of large estates, which they ran with a membership of peasant entrepreneurs rather than semi-proletarians. Cooperatives also purchased and sold fertilizers. A few leaders of the movement were Socialists. They advocated reclamation and transformation of land, as had the Bourbon planners, but with the additional feature of collective control. They were, however, but a small minority and no cooperative was able to collectivize land (for southern Italy see Tarrow 1967). Because the tariff war with France had ended, vineyards and tree crops did return in the coastal zone of western Sicily. The overall nature of change, however, was different: It was change within, not change of the latifundist regime.

Even so, change met serious, if not official, resistance. Landowners and *gabellotti*—both increasingly parasitic on production—bitterly opposed the peasant movement and, through their henchmen—their mafiosi and retainers—they managed to retain a large number of latifundia intact. The conflict reached a peak after World War I when, all over Italy, mass occupations of factories and land occurred. In Sicily, peasant leagues of every stripe took over large estates. Cooperatives signed contracts with landlords which excluded *gabellotti*. In Villamaura, as elsewhere, the homicide rate was high for the years 1920–1926, partly because of the struggle for land. In the end many large estates were unaffected, especially the predominantly pastoral estates of high altitudes. In Villamaura, for example, four such estates, all largely exceeding 700 meters in altitude, have resisted division until the present day. A fifth, also located in the mountains, was divided in a violent confrontation between *gabellotti* and peasants at the close of World War I.

Occupations of land and factories at the close of World War I were symptoms of economic underdevelopment in Italy. They showed that demobilized soldiers had nowhere to go, especially as North America was beginning to restrict immigration, and that the military efforts of the war years had not resulted in an expansion of Italy's domain. But, in spite of Socialist and Communist party leadership, the occupations did not culminate in an overthrow of the Italian government. Perhaps this was because, as Gramsci insisted, revolution required an alliance of northern industrial and southern agrarian masses (1949). Except in the north, land occupations were detached from the mainstream of left wing radicalism in Italy. In the south they aimed at an expansion of peasant small holdings. The consequences for northern Italy are well known. In its moment of failure, the northern labor movement lay open and vulnerable to the angry repression of all who had been threatened by it—factory owners, landowners, and ordinary citizens who felt themselves victims, or potential victims, of an organized labor force. By mobilizing these repressive elements, a new elite consolidated the base for fascism.

Italian Fascists advocated economic closure. Much like Crispi, only with more support, they assumed a hostile stance toward the outside world, especially France and England. The government favored iron and steel as well as other industrial and landed interests hostile to organized labor. It cut off emigration to foreign countries and even from region to region within Italy, while at the same time actively encouraging a high rate of population growth to further colonial expansion in Africa. Fascism also declared that Italy would be self-sufficient in wheat. When Italy was open to the outside world, as under the Moderates and Giolitti, it imported wheat and exported luxury crops—wine, fruits, olives, and vegetables (and, after 1900, also labor). When it became committed to development from within, these crops were sacrificed to wheat.

At first the Fascist wheat policy strengthened peasant latifundism, and there was some further erosion of large estates. Between Lorenzoni's inquest in 1907 and 1927, Sicilian territory in latifundia (defined as extensively cultivated estates of 200 hectares or more) fell from 29.7% to 22.2% of the total area (Molè 1929). In 1833, there were 682,658 landholdings in Sicily and in 1938 there were 1,224,531. According to Scrofani, the number of small holdings (as distinct from proprietors) grew at an average rate of 2110 per year between 1853 and 1908, but at an average rate of 14,194 per year from 1908 to 1938 (1962: 251). In the 1930s and 1940s, however, fascism increasingly protected large landholders. Moreover, because the growth of small holdings occurred in the absence of agricultural transformation, many of the most serious problems of Sicilian agriculture remained.

THE POSTWAR LAND REFORM:
A TYPE OF WELFARE

Following the second world war, peasant rebellion broke out again in Sicily. Bandits threatened landlords with theft and extortion and peasants formed cooperatives which sought to occupy land on the latifundia. In 1946, when the Communist party was represented in the national government, with a Communist minister of agriculture, a law was passed that legalized the occupations. Subsequently, however, Italy embraced the Marshall Plan, the Communists were excluded from the government, and a series of more conservative reforms was passed. New laws limited landholdings to 200 hectares, outlawed the *sub-gabella,* and subjected to expropriation any landholder who failed to cultivate and improve his property and hire a certain number of peasants in the process. Large holdings left to pasturage were against the law. A land reform agency, ERAS, was set up to distribute expropriated holdings to small holders organized in cooperatives. The sharecropper's portion of a crop was increased from 50% to 60% and *banalités* were prohibited.

In 1947, more than 600,000 hectares, or 25% of Sicily, was in holdings of more than 200 hectares each (an increase from 1927), while 1% of the proprietors owned half the arable land (INEA 1947). Fifteen years later, 1% of the proprietors owned 35% of the land (Parisi 1966: 4–5). In this period, ERAS assigned some 76,000 hectares to land-hungry peasants, while 147,000 hectares were purchased with financial help from the government. An unknown quantity of land was purchased with emigration remittances, bringing the total to over 300,000 hectares (Rochefort 1961: 162). In Villamaura in 1860, there were approximately 3200 landholdings on approximately 10,000 hectares of land in the town's territory. In 1960, the number of holdings had increased to 8000.

Although the land reform of the postwar period attacked large estates with a vigor new to Sicily, it, too, failed to provide the support system which would transform latifundism into diversified agriculture. As a result, many estate owners successfully resisted the reform, and changes that did occur had more the quality of erosion from below than a planned assault on an outmoded regime from above. In 1940, for example, there were 87,000 hectares of irrigated land in Sicily amounting to 3.6% of the agro-forest surface (compared with 32.9% in Lombardy and 27.7% in Piedmont). As a consequence of the reform, an additional 10,000 hectares were irrigated and 20,000 more scheduled for irrigation (Rochefort 1961: 133). But, as Rochefort pointed out, it should have been possible to irrigate twice that much land. In addition, irrigation canals were often completed but for lack of financing and organization were not linked up to existing supplies of water.

In Villamaura, the agrarian reform agency expropriated a large tract of valley arable to construct an artificial lake. Its water, however, was not available locally for irrigation because funds were never allocated to build canals and a pumping station. Cultivators on a plain to the south of the lake had no need of a pump and even were blessed with the necessary aquaducts, but their land was not irrigated either because of a dispute between the agrarian reform agency (now ESA) and the regional electrification agency (ESE) over priority of access to the water. (ESE has constructed a power generating station below the dam and wishes to retain control over the water even though it no longer uses the station to generate electricity.) The dispute was still going on in 1971.

Reforestation was also very limited. The most immediate benefit created by most reforestation projects was the 30–80 days' employment they gave to otherwise unemployed day laborers—meager pickings, but enough to qualify these workers for unemployment insurance during the rest of the year (Rochefort 1961: 127). Although there was a great need for reforestation to reverse the environmental deterioration caused by the latifundia, these projects often suffered from undercapitalization and from the failure of some subcontractors to complete the plantings for which they were paid. To this day new forests are poorly maintained, not pruned or cleared of dead wood, so that they become highly susceptible to fire. Every summer several thousand hectares burn, sometimes ignited by displaced shepherds whose loss of grazing land to reforestation was never compensated to their satisfaction.

During the 1950s millions of lire were spent on road construction in Sicily (Rochefort 1961: 118) but few funds were allocated to rural roads, many of which are still routes of transhumance, ill-suited to the movement of crops and agricultural machinery and often virtually impassible during the rainy season. The reform agency similarly spent millions on the construction of hamlets which are located in the countryside and designed to return the peasants to the land. Each is equipped with small houses, a church, a school, and a police station. Some of these hamlets were constructed during the Fascist period but most have been built since the war. The most striking feature of the hamlets to one who visits them today is that they are empty, except for a few weeks during the harvest. Many lack adequate supplies of water and electricity, and the land that surrounds them is no more intensively cultivated than before (Blok 1966; Rochefort 1961: 116).

Nor did the land reform program of the postwar period strengthen the peasant cooperative movement. Quite the contrary, the land reform agency may have undermined the cooperative associations it was supposed to organize and assist. In the past, cooperatives had been relatively independent peasant organizations. Now, they became appendages of the land reform agency which supplied leaders, lawyers, accountants, and so forth. Peasants joined in order to qualify for land allotments, credit, and other services, but their participation was strictly nominal. In effect, a cooperative consisted of several bureaucrats of the land reform agency and a roster of members. Being included in the roster was often a matter of political patronage; loyalty to the government party was the quid pro quo (Bernabei 1972; Schneider and Schneider 1976; Scrofani 1962: 253–256; Tarrow 1967: 222–224, 351, 365).

The postwar land reform also failed to alter significantly the distribution of wealth in western Sicily, as landlords, some of whose land had been expropriated, were eager to sell or mortgage the rest. The proceeds were quickly invested in urban real estate. Sons and daughters of this class are among the few Sicilians to receive elite educations and arrange marriages in Palermo and northern Italy. Our sample of households (see Chapter 4) included two families of *civile* standing. Children of both held such occupations as dentist, doctor, businessman, lawyer, and official, in Palermo, Turin, and Milan.

Perhaps the most telling sign that agricultural transformation has not occurred in Sicily lies in the relationship between wheat and other crops (for detailed information see Parisi 1966). According to Mack Smith, between 1947 and 1963

> the area under wheat declined a little (about 10%), although cereals continued to take up well over half the agricultural land. . . . Grape and wine production by the early 1960s was worth as much as that of cereals. The production of tomatoes tripled by 1960 over the prewar figure, that of potatoes doubled, that of artichokes went up five times. . . . Citrus growing improved a good deal, though not nearly so fast as in other Mediterranean states [Mack Smith 1968b: 533–534].

These developments, however, were not accompanied by a proportionate increase in agricultural revenues, nor has the yield per hectare on intensively cultivated land kept pace with that of northern Italy, Israel, Morocco, and elsewhere. Today, growers, especially of citrus fruits, find themselves outdistanced by their competitors and at the mercy of north Italian and other foreign merchants (Milone 1959; Parisi 1966: 17–19; Schneider and Schneider 1974). We will see that in western Sicily, mafiosi have burdened marketing structures and the production process with parasitic middlemen, thereby creating a serious obstacle to competitive pricing. In some years fruit is left on the trees because of these problems. Meanwhile, wheat subsidies militate against wholesale conversion to intensive agriculture and preserve the essential features of peasant latifundism.

Like the Bourbon planners over a century ago, agronomists and development experts today argue that were Sicily to abandon the mountainous interior to capitalized ranching and become competitive in the production of luxury crops, it could both accumulate more capital from foreign trade and employ more labor at home. Just why the national government and Common Market have opted to perpetuate hard wheat is a complex problem the solution of which is political as well as economic. Price supports and subsidies put a brake on rural unemployment and displacement, hence on peasant unrest, without the expense of transforming the land. In the absence of transformation, northern Italy and the Common Market countries have enjoyed Sicily's pool of cheap unskilled labor.

The postwar land reform was in effect a type of welfare designed to soften displacement by subsidizing peasants who stayed in the wheat producing interior, buying off peasant rebellion by redistributing parcels of land (Franklin 1969: 174; Tarrow 1967: 272–291). In the 1950s, emigration, restricted under fascism, began again. Official estimates, almost certainly low, place the number of out-migrants between 400,000 and 450,000 for the decade 1951–1961 (Magagnini 1966: 3; Renda 1963: 139). Our 1965 sample of Villamaura families revealed that over one-third of the local households were missing at least one member to migration, and that over 12% of the local population had left. (Around 1900 the population was 11,000; today it is about 7500.) In some towns over 50% of the population emigrated (Renda 1963: 99–106, 114). Perhaps half of the migrants ended up in the industrial zones of northern Italy or in urban centers within Sicily itself, but the rest went elsewhere, a few to Canada, Australia, and South America, the majority to Switzerland, France, and West

Germany. Sicily, in short, maintained its dependency in today's world-system as an exporter of its own manpower. As before, a national government policy defines emigration as a "necessary evil" and a solution to the balance of payments problem.

INDUSTRIAL DEVELOPMENT

Given that the land reform in Sicily left the island poorly pre-pared to accumulate capital out of agricultural exports, it should not surprise us that industrial development in the postwar period has been weak. This is not to say that there are no industries. Since the war, government policies have attempted to encourage industrial growth by offering tax exemptions and credit facilities, by reducing railroad tariffs, and by channeling national funds through develop-ment agencies such as IRFIS (Istituto Regionale per il Financiamento del'Industria in Sicilia), SOFIS (Società Finanziaria Siciliana), and the Cassa per il Mezzogiorno. According to Denis Mack Smith, the number of public corporations in Sicily rose from 218 to 1576 in the first 15 years following the war (1968b: 535). In 1953, Gulf discovered oil off the southeastern coast. Since then several refineries have been constructed in eastern Sicily, together with such secondary establish-ments as thermoelectric plants and factories for manufacturing plastics and other petrochemicals. Modest expansion has also occurred in textiles, synthetics, furniture, paper, and construction materials. By the 1960s, two deposits of natural gas had been opened and were being exploited, and potash was being refined for fertilizer (Mack Smith 1968b: 535-537; Rochefort 1961: 228-230). During the period 1953-1963 "the tonnage handled in Sicilian ports increased six-fold. . . . Cement production went up ten-fold. Sulphuric acid production rose from almost nothing to nearly half a million tons, and potash from nothing to one million tons. Electricity production went up nearly 100% in 1960-63 [Mack Smith 1968b: 537]."

Yet this "minor industrial revolution," as Mack Smith has described it, has had relatively little impact on the economic potential of Sicily itself, particularly that of western Sicily. The major portion of new investment is north Italian and multinational and devoted to primary extractive industries—principally, oil and potash—which do not contribute to the local economy in proportion to the resources they extract. The new refineries, derricks, and factories are highly automated. They require few employees and many of their workers are skilled technicians imported from northern Italy or the United States. With the exception of minimal taxes paid to local governments profits are not reinvested in Sicilian enterprise, and the existence of new primary industries has not given rise to the proliferation of secondary and tertiary activities which are necessary to alter significantly the island's economic base. In effect, the new investment is a colonial enterprise, exploiting Sicily's raw materials to the benefit of outside metropolitan powers, often the same outside powers which import Sicilian labor.

THE CAUSES OF UNDERDEVELOPMENT

Looking back over the nearly 200 years in which Sicily has confronted the pressures of a postindustrial world, perhaps we can draw some conclusions about the island's condition. Two factors have emerged in our discussion to account in part for Sicily's underdevelopment. First we noted that past latifundism, because of its impact on the environment, complicated the transformation of agriculture and made it costly. Centuries ago, Sicily's Arab rulers erased the scars of Roman latifundism from the western interior, but after the Spanish period the damage was more profound. In addition, we stressed the incompatibility of north Italian and Sicilian economic priorities. Twice in the history of the young Italian nation (under Crispi and under Mussolini) a northern industrial coalition sacrificed luxury crop agriculture to national self-sufficiency in wheat. The transformation of agriculture in Sicily was a casualty of both periods and could not enjoy continuous growth. Subsequently, emigration, by competing for manpower, made things worse. Such obstacles, when they did not ruin producers, must surely have discouraged them from making long-term capital investments in their orchards and vineyards—another reason why Sicilian fruits and vegetables are not so competitive as they might be today.

The second factor—Sicily's subordination to north Italian economic development—suggests a third, practical factor. Why did the region not demand more autonomy from Italy? Why did it have no regional elite with an articulate policy of economic closure from Italy in the interest of the general welfare of the island? Such an elite with such a policy is common in the underdeveloped world of today, where it responds to crises of unemployment and displacement similar to those faced by Sicily. It is true that these elites rarely succeed. When the costs of their programs become too high, or when the leaders cannot deliver, their positions become untenable and external enemies find internal allies who join in the plot to overthrow them. Yet, in contrast to Sicily, many poor societies appear to have a social base for the formation and reformation of leaders who are committed to altering the role of their people in the world division of labor. In Sicily, the peasant and Socialist leaders who advocated transformation of agriculture never framed a "foreign policy." They were also few in number, poorly organized among themselves, and easily repressed.

At first glance it may appear that a development elite never formed in Sicily because the island is a region, not a nation, and therefore too small and poor in resources to constitute a viable unit of autonomous economic change. Nevertheless, when pressured by a gross imbalance in trade, units smaller than this have organized politically to try to even things out. Factors like size and resource base of course influence the potential for success of a development elite, but not necessarily the formation of one in the first place. The scale of regional development planning is smaller than that of planning at the national or transnational level, but this is not to say that regions never acquire autonomy. Because of the way the world-system is organized, many social dislocations are regionally specific and require regional solutions.

More influential in the case of Sicily was the leadership structure inherited from the experience of colonization by Spain. Just as that experience blocked the formation of state institutions in the latifundist west of the island, so it left no infrastructure for the construction of a "state within a state." Consequently, in the political alignments that unified Italy in the nineteenth century, Sicilian lawyers and intellectuals, who under other circumstances might well have formed the nucleus of a development elite, were repeatedly neutralized and superseded by rural entrepreneurs and new landowners. Attached to latifundia and to wheat, and nurtured for centuries by exchange with the outside world, these interests quite comfortably accepted an alliance with north Italian industry under Crispi. As patrons of peasants, and as brokers of national integration, they stood squarely in the way not only of a socialist movement among peasants but also of regional independence.

At the close of World War II, a number of special interests coalesced in a Separatist movement in Sicily, and largely in response to this movement the postwar Italian government granted the island a regional executive and parliament, with control over such functions as mining, utilities, and land reform. But the new regional government had no taxing power and was therefore but a feeble appendage of Rome's. Rather than be a source of leadership and initiative for regional development, it has become a source of office jobs—a short-range and partial solution to unemployment in the middle class. Nor can anyone argue that this outcome disappointed the leaders of the postwar period since the Separatist movement itself failed to make a claim for regional autonomy. Its goals were more modest, to exchange one dependent relationship for another by transforming Sicily into the forty-ninth state of the United States. The Separatist emblem, stenciled on buildings all over western Sicily, depicted two soldiers of the Separatist army severing a chain that bound Sicily to mainland Italy, while others were building a new chain that would link the island to New York (Sansone and Ingrasci 1950: 56 f.). The irony of it is that while the proposed new relationship with America might have helped to reunite families split by emigration, the United States had been, to that point, the greatest importer of Sicilian labor.

chapter 7

Displaced Herdsmen

Sicily was inexorably drawn into the role of labor exporter by 1900. We must, however, correct the impression that all Sicilians were helpless victims of postindustrial pressures. Those of our readers who have seen Pietro Germi's film *Seduced and Abandoned* will recall the scene in which a police officer stationed in Sicily—but of north Italian descent—approaches a map of the nation which hangs on the wall. Placing his hand over the island, he turns to face his subaltern with a grimace, as if to say, "What a lot of trouble this place is for us; if only it could be wiped off the map." For if, throughout its difficult confrontation with a new, postindustrial world, Sicily's people supported no development elite and no well-articulated movement for regional autonomy, certain groups in the regional society nevertheless went into that period with enough power to "make trouble" for their rulers and influence the course of change. There were three major sources of trouble: herdsmen, mafiosi, and the new *civile* class of upwardly mobile rural entrepreneurs who purchased land in the nineteenth century. Mafiosi were recruited primarily from among entrepreneurs who did not become *civili,* from peasants (to a limited extent), and from herdsmen. This chapter traces the displacement of herdsmen in the nineteenth and twentieth centuries and contrasts the outcome for them with the outcome for peasants. Subsequent chapters deal with the *civile* class and mafia.

AGRARIAN REFORM AND
THE FATE OF HERDSMEN

The great latifundia of western and interior Sicily were not simply wheat producing estates; additionally they supported a pastoral industry of considerable size and scope. It is true that during the Spanish period, Sicily's wheat crop grew in relative importance. But the resulting increase in cultivated surface did not lead to irrigated meadows or the production of forage crops for animals. It reduced the quality and accessibility of grazing land and it cut radically into forest cover, but it did not alter the practice of transhumant grazing on natural pastures. Thus when Sicily became enmeshed in the crises of the nineteenth and twentieth centuries, herdsmen as well as peasants were affected. Their familiarity with the countryside, however, and their association with the *massaria* complex allowed them considerably more leverage in their response.

The first major threat to herding interests in the nineteenth century came with the Bourbon program of bonification. As vineyards and tree crops expanded, they cut into winter pastures and interrupted long-distance cycles of transhumance which linked interior to coast. Even the limited reforestation and water control projects of the *Bonifica* threatened the shepherds' access to pastures. More important, the partition of feudal, demesnial, communal, and ecclesiastical holdings curtailed promiscuous grazing rights. According to the land census of 1833, 24.9% of Sicily's territory was dedicated to naked pasture—land that could not be cultivated, even when the price for cereals was high (Milone 1959). Another 18.2% was given over to pasturage in rotation with cereals. These proportions, says Scrofani, gave the island a character "more pastoral than agrarian [1962: 126]." We have no data on the extension of pasturage from the census of 1880–1885 (the last census before the Crispian phase of protected wheat began), but we know that cereals occupied 10% less territory, and vineyards twice as much, as they had before. Olive, nut, and fruit trees, with more modest beginnings, had also spread (Scrofani 1962: 234).

It was not the intent of *Bonifica* planners that animal husbandry would simply wane. To the contrary, agricultural journals of the period were full of "physiocratic" propaganda that advised Sicilian landowners that the greatest obstacle to improved cultivation and higher yields was the continued practice of herding on natural pastures. Many articles held up for comparison European and north Italian farmers who since the eighteenth century had fed their livestock on cultivated forage in stalls (Alfonso-Spagna 1870; Balsamo 1803; Chicoli 1870). Aware of the special problems posed by an arid climate, most of the authors were, however, pessimistic. Since reform efforts at the time were directed toward expanding irrigation for tree crops, few even considered the feasibility of irrigating meadows. In the coastal zone of western Sicily, some curious symbiotic patterns developed. For example, when stronger animals for work and transport became necessary to the construction industry in Palermo, owners of oxen entered into reciprocal agreements with owners of orchards. The former ceded their animals free of charge to an orchard owner for the summer. In exchange for driving the pumps that drew water from underground sources, these animals fed on the grasses that grew along the irrigation canals (Alfonso-Spagna 1870).

And so, not only pastures, but the animal patrimony, its health undermined, declined. The more a landholding was cultivated, the more meager the grasses it yielded in years of rest. The fewer the pastures available, the more difficult it was to separate types of stock and graze each on the most suitable vegetation. Generally speaking, milk animals need green plants and work animals need fibrous plants, but in Sicily all animals as a rule got green plants only in the winter season, when they could best assimilate high energy fibrous foods, and grazed on tough dry stubble in the summer. Cattle gave so little milk between June and September that it was imperative to segregate bulls from cows between September and December, thus avoiding pregnancies that terminated in the summer months (Alfonso-Spagna 1870: 262–263). These and other problems raised the likelihood of disease, against which there was no organized quarantine. No public veterinarians existed in Sicily before the late nineteenth century and those appointed afterward had difficulty overcoming the Sicilian pastoralists' diffidence toward the law. Between 1863 and 1869, a typhus epidemic killed perhaps 300,000 cattle, creating a severe shortage of meat in Palermo; this shortage was reflected by an increase in imports (Chicoli 1870). According to Lorenzoni, the number of sheep in Sicily fell by about 70,000 between 1869 and 1881. Goats declined, too, although he gave no figures (Lorenzoni 1910: 142).

During the Crispian era, pastoralists gained something of a

breather as vineyards were destroyed and grain advanced again. Lorenzoni reported that between 1880 and 1908, the numbers of all kinds of animals increased in Sicily (see Table 1).

The distribution of the increase by province is revealing. Over half the increase in cattle between 1880 and 1908 occurred in the provinces of Syracuse and Messina, that is, in those parts of eastern Sicily where pastoralism gave way to capitalized animal husbandry. A large increase in pigs was almost exclusively eastern; whereas well over half the gain in sheep (311,745 out of 481,595) was in the west. This gain in sheep was consistent with an important western development: the dissolution of vast pastoral enterprises attached to the latifundia. For, as the *civile* class, protected by the wheat tariff, planted more and more grain, herding began gradually to assume independence from agriculture, and transhumance cycles from interior to coast broke up into shorter, less regular migrations (Lorenzoni 1910: 107, 127–145; Milone 1959: 76; Morici 1940). Goat populations increased everywhere but above all in the province of Messina, where they were raised for cheese on wooded mountain pastures.

In western Sicily goats posed a special problem for they had traditionally grazed on communal land, which *civile* landlords now appropriated for cultivation. Suddenly goatherders, called *caprai di paesi* (goatherds of the town, as opposed to the *massaria*), became targets of criticism. Partnerships of two or three *caprai* managed herds of some 30–40 goats, which they took out to graze in the daytime and kept in pens at the edge of town during the night. The goats were milked every evening and the milk was distributed to the owners of the animals or sold. In 1879, a delegation of small holders went before the mayor of Villamaura to complain bitterly that goatherds were abusively pasturing their animals on grain fields. The mayor wrote letters

Table 1
THE ANIMAL POPULATION OF SICILY: 1880–1930[a]

	Cattle	Sheep	Goats
1880–1885	125,396	477,493	171,558
1908	193,475	958,998	311,044
1918	221,357	1,077,084	476,539
1930	167,634	726,582	309,266

[a] Sources: Lorenzoni 1910: 128–132; Morici 1940: 11.

of inquiry to officials of other towns to learn how they were meeting this problem and whether or not they taxed goats or goats' milk. He also wrote to the subprefect, requesting help. His letters protested that goatherds and shepherds rented small pastures, which were hemmed in by cultivated fields, and that they were rarely owners of all the animals they watched or the sole individuals responsible for a given herd. Keeping track of their whereabouts was nearly impossible.

In the 1880s, references to the problem of "assault on property" multiplied. In 1884, amidst a wave of complaints, town authorities instructed both goatherds and shepherds that at least four animals per herd had to wear a bell and that animals could not be taken to pasture before dawn or after dusk. In 1901, national leaders considered a program that would eliminate pastures and goats throughout Italy, while local leaders resorted to renting out stretches of public roadway for grazing. In 1902–1906 the animal tax, abandoned during the epidemics in 1869 under pressure from *gabellotti,* was reinstated. The tax on goats was double the tax on sheep.

The cultivator–herder struggle worsened in the twentieth century until eventually the pastoral sector all but disappeared. The direction and outcome of this change, however, were at first unclear because emigration had contradictory consequences for pastoralism. In the absence of a wheat tariff, the prices for animal products rose relative to those of cereals. According to Morici (1940) this competitive advantage increased to the point that between 1921 and 1925 agrarian interests petitioned Rome for an adjustment. Sicilian migrants to America may have contributed to the imbalance by demanding cheese from home. In addition, these migrants reduced unemployment in Sicily, thereby enhancing the bargaining power of peasants in agricultural contracts. In response to this, and to the price situation, landowners planted less grain and allowed ever greater extensions of land to revert to pasturage. Old members of the *civile* class whom we interviewed in Villamaura recalled very clearly their decisions not to plant because of the cost of labor and their preference for pastoral exploitation of large estates. We also know from the animal census, however incomplete, that the animal population, greater in 1908 than it had been in 1880–1885, continued to grow until after World War I (see Table 1). Morici noted that after the war sheep displaced cereals in many zones (1940).

At the same time that pastoral exploitation of land advanced, however, emigration began also to undermine it, for emigration remittances encouraged the spread of peasant latifundism and this form of land use was for the most part incompatible with herding. The forage crops, fava beans and sulla, which sharecroppers and small holders planted in lieu of pastoral and fallow years in the rotation cycle, were hardly the basis for a rational animal husbandry (although when used for this purpose on high altitude latifundia, they did lead to an increase in the production of milk; Blok 1974: 70–72; Platzer and Schifani 1963). Without irrigation, these crops were meager and uneven. Of the two the fava bean was more resistant to aridity, but it was vulnerable to parasites and its cultivation required a considerable labor input (Scrofani 1962: 245). On the whole, these crops fed the mules and donkeys of the peasants and at that had to be supplemented by stubble after the harvest. In other words they did not offer the possibility of alternative pursuits to displaced herdsmen (Scrofani 1962: 245–246).

Like the goatherds of the towns, shepherds did battle with cultivators, stealing their work and transport animals, cutting or burning their crops, and allowing sheep to graze on their fields. Cultivators who reported these acts frequently withdrew their claims under pressure and were sometimes intimidated into renting land to the very shepherds who had abused them. The conflict reached a peak in the years of violence that surrounded the occupations of land after World War I. Of the 20 homicides reported for Villamaura between 1920 and 1926, 2 victims were local goatherds, 1 was a local shepherd, and 4 were shepherds from other west Sicilian towns.

Pressure on herdsmen persisted under fascism; if anything, the Fascist policy of self-sufficiency in wheat intensified the squeeze and by 1930 the animal population was once again in decline. In the animal census of 1918 there were 221,357 head of cattle in Sicily, 1,077,084 sheep, and 476,539 goats. In the census of 1930, these figures had dropped to 167,634 cattle; 726,582 sheep; and 309,266 goats. From 1926 on, the recorded proceedings of Villamaura's rural guard were concerned in overwhelming degree with the apprehension, arrest, and punishment of herdsmen. The most frequent charges were abusive grazing and illegal possession of weapons. The guard also charged herdsmen with failure to carry documents which stated ownership of animals, location of rented pastures, written permission to utilize harvested stubble, itineraries, and so on. It arrested herdsmen for the clandestine slaughter of animals, for blocking routes of transhumance, for stealing manure, for keeping dirty pens, and for failure to muzzle their dogs—charges which to some extent suggest harassment. In the same period, the captain of the guard was prosecuted, but not sentenced, for the 1921 murder of a leading goatherd. In other towns the situation was similar. According to Chapman, in Milocca "nearly every family which engaged in sheep raising had at least one member in prison [1971: 133]." The year was 1929.

At the close of World War II, the Fascist jails emptied and, supported by the American landing in Sicily, men with vested interests in the herding economy regained some influence. Yet the revival was short-lived. Together with landlords (and rural entrepreneurs grown rich from the sale of wheat on a contraband market), herdsmen became targets of renewed peasant unrest and ultimately of the agrarian reform. Uncultivated pastures, covering about 600,000 hectares in 1833, covered less than half that amount 100 years later, and in 1957 they accounted for only 250,000 hectares (Milone 1959: 55–84; Scrofani 1962: 260–261). The percentage of land in wheat in 1929 was about what it had been in 1833, but with far less time in the rotation cycle devoted to grazing (Scrofani 1962: 260–261). By 1953, Sicily, with 10.9% of the nation's total land area, raised only 4.33% of its animals; in 1964, less than 3.5% (Platzer and Schifani 1963). Today pastoralism has been relegated largely to the mountains of the northeast, where it survives as an anachronism. In the coastal zone of this region, and in the southeastern province of Ragusa near Syracuse, we find some rational cattle husbandry. In western Sicily, the importation of animals now supersedes indigenous livestock raising. Livestock enter by rail, on the hoof, and are fattened for brief intervals on expensive imported feed. The process attracts all kinds of speculators, not just herdsmen. Cheese, milk, and other dairy products are imported, too, although the last of the western shepherds continue to make ricotta and pecorino in the winter and spring (Platzer and Schifani 1963).

THE HERDSMEN'S RESPONSE TO DISPLACEMENT

Looking back over the displacement of pastoralists, we note that their response was different from the response of peasants. Where peasants joined mass demonstrations and collectively occupied estates, where they organized cooperatives in order to acquire small holdings, herdsmen pursued strategies based on acts of prepotency which were planned and executed by individuals and ad hoc coalitions. We have already encountered one of the most pervasive and difficult to control of these acts: abusive grazing. By no means absent in the Sicilian countryside before the nineteenth century, it became much more widespread after 1860. In addition to abusive grazing, the most significant "pastoral" response was banditry.

Although peasants formed bands which robbed and kidnapped during certain periods of modern Sicilian history—notably in the early 1870s and again after the two world wars—the classic bandits of the island's countryside were shepherds, and the classic act of brigandage was animal theft. Rustling was the constant manifestation, peasant uprisings the occasional symptom, of an ongoing struggle against diminishing resources. A wave of rustling followed the typhus epidemic which struck cattle in the 1860s, and animal theft was a major activity in the "brigand war" that followed (Alongi 1886: 19, 123–124; D'Alessandro 1959: 57–59, 160–164). Rustling was also pronounced in the first decade of this century, when the bandit Grisafi roamed the western interior. His men were victims of the spread of peasant latifundism and were, on the whole, more pastoral than peasant, Grisafi himself being an ex-shepherd (Blok 1974: 132–134). Meat rationing during World War I further encouraged animal theft, which continued under fascism even though hundreds of shepherds were imprisoned. In much reduced form, rustling persists today in the mountainous interior. The importance of rustling must be attributed to the fact that although pastures declined, and with them the quantity and quality of animals, the market for animal products never did. As before, in the sixteenth century, the market expanded with population growth. Herdsmen when they stole animals, no less than when they abusively grazed them, were encouraged in their *prepotenza* by this fact. Peasants, in contrast, were vulnerable to an unstable market which swung back and forth from wine and other labor-intensive crops to wheat.

In no case was animal rustling ever a large-scale enterprise: Perhaps three or four men formed a coalition to organize a given theft and then disbanded after its completion. Rustlers depended upon rural entrepreneurs and the *massaria* complex for information, refuge, and access to markets. These patterns probably characterized banditry in general, even at the height of the brigand war, when it expressed the plight of peasants. In this period, leaders of bands were often permanent residents of the countryside—shepherds or *campieri* of a *massaria* (see D'Alessandro 1959: 100). Successful leaders were of necessity well connected with the permanent residents of several such rural institutions and participated in their cultural solidarity. According to one probably exaggerated description, bandits wore clothes of blue wool or velvet, high boots, red berets, false whiskers, and carried breach-loading carbines, revolvers, daggers, and telescopes (D'Alessandro 1959: 97). The archives of prefectures, the memorabilia of many families, and newspaper accounts of the period suggest that bandits plotted kidnappings in country places and executed them with the collaboration of a landowner's rural deputies—his *gabellotto,* chief herdsman, or guards. Country places also served to hide victims, distribute booty, patch up quarrels, and host the banquet table. Contrary to Hobsbawm's argument that "social" bandits depended for food and protection upon supportive peasants, evidence points to the *massaria* elite, with its tradition of hospitality, as the critical locus of these benefits in western Sicily.[1] One *massaria* in the territory of Villamaura did the laundry of visiting bandits. Molfese's south Italian examples show bandits obtaining fresh mounts and recovering from malaria in the *massarie* there (1964).

Bandits approached their victims in different ways, depending upon whether they considered them to be of superior or inferior status. Extortion letters to landlords strained for politeness: "If you wish to become our friend, come to the watering trough carrying the money in your [own] hands. Make your estimate and we will make ours. . . . We are your faithful friends and believe me [Anonymous 1879: 28–30]." (See also Alongi 1886: 99–101.) A letter to a landholder held in captivity near Villamaura began, "Signor, excuse us, we wanted your son and in his absence we have come upon your Holy Patience (*vossia Santu Pacienza*)." A follow-up letter began, "Dearest friend. . . ." According to Mack Smith, priests may have penned these letters (1968a: 148). The most dramatic example of brigandly courtesy comes from a memoir of 1830 included in the introduction to Franchetti's survey of Sicily. It tells how a bandit leader murdered and decapitated a follower for showing disrespect to the marquis they had just robbed. The leader presented the marquis with the poor victim's head in a sack and warned that the same would befall "anyone else who dares offend you as he did [Cavalieri 1925: xvi–xvii]."

Where the bandits' targets were not marquis and counts, but ordinary people, the treatment could be subtly different. A newspaper account from the 1870s described the encounter of a small holder, Ciro, with bandits. Ciro had a little house in the countryside. Not far away a neighbor hosted bandits. The entire country district was known for its hospitality. Banquets included musicians and girls, anisette and pastries left over from weddings in a nearby town.

---

[1] For an important exchange on the relationship between banditry and peasant revolt see Blok (1972) and Hobsbawm (1972). Blok also has questioned the extent to which bandits in Sicily "represented" the peasant masses. He suggests they were more closely tied to "capital" than to "labor"—an argument supported by their close ties with pastoral enterprises and the *massaria* complex.

Bandits told stories that made their hosts cry, and groups from various towns competed to spread the best feast. One day, Ciro was approached by his neighbor, who entered Ciro's house as if it were his own. The neighbor asked to borrow 2 kilograms of pasta and a pot. "We will expect you and your wine for dinner," the neighbor told Ciro. At the appointed time, Ciro sent his wine over but did not go himself. Shortly after, he was sent for and, terrified, he went. He feared all at once the bandits, the police, and the gossip of his fellow townsmen.

During the meal, his neighbor, the bandits, and other guests ridiculed Ciro. "*Compare* Ciro," they mocked, in a parody on the intimacy of coparenthood and close friendship, "a big swallow now . . . another glass of your own good wine." Later in court Ciro testified that "the lasagna and the meat were exquisite . . . and the wine, it was my own. But I ate bile and drank vinegar, just like our Jesus Christ on the cross [Anonymous 1879: 117–120]."

Regardless of how bandits approached their victims, they backed up their claims on them with the threat of private vengeance for noncompliance, and this was the most important manifestation of banditry's pastoral, as opposed to peasant, bias. While peasants sometimes engaged in threats of this sort, they did not control the means to be convincing. Clustered in urban-dominated rural towns, and subject to the rules of local powerholders, peasants had less freedom of movement than shepherds. In contrast to shepherds, peasants found their autonomy seriously damaged by expanding latifundism in the Spanish period. Herdsmen, notwithstanding latifundism, had in the *massaria* complex a place of refuge from lord, Church, and state. They were free to keep weapons and their way of life required that they know how to use them. According to our data from Villamaura, until quite recently herdsmen were less likely than peasants to emigrate. We will see in Chapter 9 that their contribution to mafia was proportionally greater than the contribution of peasants. Mafia, however, was above all a creature of displaced rural entrepreneurs and it is to their predicament in the late nineteenth century that we now turn.

chapter 8

The Civile *Class and the Persistence of Broker Capitalism*

Sicily's encounter with North Atlantic industrial capitalism in the nineteenth and twentieth centuries resulted in serious dislocations for peasants and shepherds. What were its consequences for rural entrepreneurs? This important group was also under pressure. Industrial development in the north presented the reality of expanding state institutions, new roads and railroads, mechanized grain mills, rationalized banking and credit facilities, and centralized marketing relations, all of which were a distinct threat to the organization of broker capitalism, especially insofar as this development was financed by outsiders. In addition, land reform, to the extent that it altered patterns of land use and tenure, contradicted rural entrepreneurs' interest in a latifundist economy. We will present the evidence that this group felt these various pressures and was divided by intense competition among its members.

The focus of this chapter, however, is on the preservation, indeed the enhancement, of broker capitalism under nineteenth-and twentieth-century conditions. For, although they felt the impact of the postindustrial world, rural entrepreneurs in Sicily also formed the backbone of a new gentry class, and that class, the *civile* class, bargained successfully with north Italian interests as Italy became a nation. In a pattern perhaps best identified as bossism, its members delivered votes to different and competing segments of the north Italian industrial bourgeoisie from the early 1880s through World War I. Factionalism and corruption were hallmarks of this period and were measures of the bargaining power of the *civili*. As part of its relationship to the north, this group was able to retard and deflect the penetration of new national institutions into the regional domain and to guarantee for the future the basic structural conditions which in the past made broker capitalism possible: a weakly articulated state and hierarchy of markets. The tendency to invest capital through temporary alliances and coalitions, to depend upon a network of friends and contacts as a critical asset, and to live by one's wits, seizing opportunities even when this meant breaking the law—these aspects of brokerage remained intact and continue to be manifest to the present day.

RIVALRY AMONG *CIVILI*

By far the most successful rural entrepreneurs in nineteenth-century Sicily were those who were able to acquire large holdings in land and form a new gentry class. But, in contrast with the so-called feudal aristocracy of an earlier age, this class had some difficulty consolidating its position. It never became a stable and internally coherent ruling group. The *civili* of the nineteenth and early twentieth centuries experienced many swings of fortune in which some of them fell by the wayside, unable to expand their family patrimonies and pass them on intact. As part of their *Bonifica,* restoration Bourbons had removed the advantage of primogeniture enjoyed by the great baronial families of the past. Tactics such as parallel cousin marriage could at best retard but not reverse the fragmentation of family power, especially as the population of this group increased along with that of other groups in the second half of the nineteenth century. The cadastral record for Villamaura shows that prominent *civile* families attempted to favor one son in the disposition of inheritance: To him would go the bulk of the land, plus the holdings of celibate relatives.

By the turn of the century, however, the wheat tariff having been reduced and peasant latifundism beginning to advance, each of these families showed signs of stress. Except at high altitudes, properties were divided, reconsolidated through marriage, then divided again, often among five or more heirs: For example, one of the leading *civile* families in Villamaura purchased an estate of 500 hectares in 1835; the estate was divided into two parts toward the end of the century and again into eight parts around 1920. Even the *massaria* buildings were partitioned. Sometimes, disputes over the inheritance, purchase, or rental of land or over the refusal of a father to offer his daughter in marriage led to vendettas in which loyal dependents rallied behind the principals, who were *sciariatti*—not on speaking terms. In the archival records, words like *odio* (hatred) and *rancore* (rancor) appear with great frequency to describe relations among the *civili*.

Not only land but also the free professions suffered from overcrowding, as sons of the new gentry pursued careers in medicine and law. One or two sons as lawyers or officials in government secured the position of newly rich families in the second generation. So great was the competition for this security that all sorts of pressures were brought to bear on the schools. According to Mack Smith, "in Sicily there were cases of lecturers or even schoolmasters having to be given a police escort after the examination results were announced, and of prizes not being awarded because the master did not dare choose between students [1959: 261]." Still, many students returned to their towns without the precious degree (Mosca 1949: 191).

Status rivalry was intense. Ideally, a true *civile* owned an ex-feudal estate and sent at least one son into the free professions. Ideally, he had a title, which he acquired by marriage into the old aristocracy, or purchased from the Bourbon or Italian crown. He belonged to a local *circolo civile,* a gentlemen's social club which, in Villamaura, admitted new members only upon a favorable vote by two-thirds of the membership. Competition for space within the gentry meant, of course, that rural entrepreneurs who hoped to move up were often denied opportunities to purchase land, educate their sons, and be approved for membership in the *circolo civile*. Even the great combines of *massariotti–gabellotti* described in Chapter 4 only occasionally managed to achieve *civile* status. The club of Villamaura excluded several such families because they were "too rustic."[1]

At the very least, a proper *civile* would build a splendid *palazzo*

[1] Our census of *massariotto* families (Chapter 4) spans a status ladder: one family that clearly belongs to the *ceto civile* and has for two generations; one family that has belonged to this group for only one generation; three families that although prosperous were not admitted to the *civile* club in part because of their failure to educate any sons successfully; and six families that were never considered for membership.

(not in Palermo—only a few could afford that luxury) on a main piazza in town and build or purchase a villa in the surrounding countryside. Toward the turn of the century, the *civili* of Villamaura urged the contractor for funeral services to buy a more luxurious carriage and livery for the transport of dead gentlemen to their final resting place. Some of them (the live *civili*, that is), in their zeal to imitate the high society of Palermo disregarded both the condition of the local roads and the disapproval of their creditors as they purchased fancy carriages of their own for everyday use. Emanuele Navarro della Miraglia, a member of that class, wrote an exquisite novel in which Villamaura unfolds as a scaled down and rustic version of the eighteenth-century capital, replete with fancy weddings, baptisms, the evening *passeggiatta*, and a luxurious theater modeled after the Teatro Bellini in Palermo (Navarro della Miraglia 1963). There were 69 such theaters built in Sicily during the late nineteenth century.

We have no evidence that established *civile* families attempted to seclude women or force them to conform to norms of asceticism and modesty. On the contrary, these families looked to the Palermo aristocracy for a model, and that aristocracy in turn kept up the courtly styles of the Neapolitan Bourbons, who in their turn modeled themselves after the fashions of eighteenth-century France. The most important Villamaurese families in the late nineteenth century allowed women to dress in silk and other finery brought in from Palermo and Naples and imported from northern Italy and abroad. These families visited each other during the evenings to examine the furnishings with which each embellished its *palazzo*. They looked forward to the end of the summer season, when aristocratic and *civile* visitors came from Palermo to spend a few weeks in the country as guests of the residents of a villa. These visiting families, once Villamaurese, were notorious for their love of good times—*gente allegri* (lively people) it was said. The ball, a great aristocratic institution, was copied locally, and if the salons of the local *civili* were not yet beautified by great works of art as were the salons of Palermo, a ball was nevertheless an occasion for bustling silks, fancy coiffures, and dances modeled upon Spanish, French, and Viennese court styles (see Lampedusa, 1961: 217–245; Navarro della Miraglia 1963).

Mosca confirms our view that the status rivalry of the west Sicilian gentry revealed weakness as well as strength. Members of the *civile* class competed with each other in the consumption of an entirely derivative culture several steps removed from its Parisian source. A *civile's* position, thought Mosca, was more formal than substantial, and for that reason was quite presumptuous (1949: 188–

194). Yet the gentry were weak only in the cosmopolitan perspective of a sophisticated intellectual like Mosca. Within Italy its members secured for themselves considerable leverage, especially through an abundance of national patronage and protection. Within Sicily they were political bosses, in control of local and regional politics well into the twentieth century.

THE *CIVILE* CLASS AND THE NORTH ITALIAN INDUSTRIAL BOURGEOISIE

How did the *ceto civile* accumulate so much power on the regional level? The answer must begin with the push for industrial development in northern Italy. That push, highly organized in the 1880s and 1890s under Crispi, necessitated political mobilization since many unpopular sacrifices were involved. In this period protective tariffs led to higher prices for a wide range of commodities, including essential items like bread and textiles. The push for development further resulted in a tariff war with France and an expensive and counterproductive colonial adventure in Africa. Most seriously, it cheapened labor. The industrial interests that backed these policies in the late nineteenth century at the very least had to minimize popular protest. Their solution was the constant delivery of national patronage to win support and compliance from local notables, who in turn organized electoral majorities for parliamentary deputies loyal to Crispi. In Sicily the local notables, the *civili,* bargained from the strength of a broker capitalist past and won for themselves a virtual monopoly over police power at the local level. This power enabled them to displace peasants from land and ultimately to preserve for their outmoded forms of entrepreneurial endeavor a place in the economy of the future. The mechanism by which these outcomes were achieved is called bossism: the combined use of patronage and police power to "make elections."

In 1860, less than 2% of the Italian population could vote. After 1882, the suffrage increased from 600,000 to about 2 million, when the use of literacy tests enfranchised many artisans, small holders, and petty capitalists. Until just before World War I, when the suffrage was extended to all adult males, Italy had no mass political parties (except for a small Socialist party). Then came fascism, which outlawed all parties but its own. Between these two dates—1882 and the Fascist period—bossism overwhelmed the political scene. According to Gaetano Mosca, a Sicilian and a keen observer of the island's political life, "a conversation with a handful of bosses sufficed to gain several hundred votes, [1949: 198]." Parliamentary deputies in need of votes made themselves the clients of ministers who dispensed the state's patronage. Local bosses, as grand electors, received and distributed this patronage as they mobilized and delivered votes. "It is not the electors who elect a deputy," wrote Mosca, "but . . . the deputy who has . . . himself elected by the electors [quoted in Salomone 1945: 19]."

Often strong enough to name their own terms for supporting particular deputies and ministers, Sicilian bosses had a free hand at home. This meant tariff protection for their outmoded crop, wheat, and the right to retain, in fact to expand, the latifundium. As the Marquis di Rudinì put it, Italy was "abandoning Sicilians to exploitation by local factions [quoted in Mack Smith 1968b: 483]." Pareto, commenting on the same situation, stressed that "the government does nothing to suppress . . . abuses, because the same persons who dominate the communal [local town] councils are the chief electors of the deputies who, in their turn, employ their influence with the government to screen the misdeeds of their friends and partisans [quoted in Mack Smith 1968b: 484]." The most telling misdeeds were those of *gabellotti* and *civili* who illegally expropriated peasant, Church, and communal lands and directed local police power against those who protested. When peasants rebelled in the 1890s, it was southern Italian and Sicilian deputies to Parliament who convinced the national government to send in troops.

BOSSISM UNDER GIOLITTI

During the Crispian era, southern Italian and Sicilian bosses were well represented in national governing coalitions. They directly influenced tariff legislation (agitating for the tariff on wheat), while blocking laws that might have reformed the latifundia, and they moved the government to discourage emigration and to quell a peasant revolt. Under Giolitti, who came to power at the turn of the century and represented a somewhat different set of north Italian industrial interests, they appeared to fare less well. This government reduced the wheat tariff, promoted emigration, and established a dialogue with the Socialists. It took no steps to prevent returned emigrés from joining cooperatives or acquiring land. According to Mack

Smith, Parliament now gave "more attention to the 'Southern problem' than formerly, when debates had taken place in an empty Chamber. In 1911 the government went so far as to accept the principle that the *latifundi* were the chief cause of Sicilian poverty . . . [and] the next year a widening of the suffrage dented the oligarchic monopoly of local power [1968b: 502]."[2] All the while, however, the local bosses were furiously creating a variety of stratagems to deal with the new state interest in the south. In fact, Giolitti's regime is often cited as the most corrupt ever to govern Italy.

James Scott's analysis of corruption suggests what happened. He argues that this phenomenon occurs when private interests exert extraordinary pressure on the administration of law, rather than on the legislative process (Scott 1969). In an advanced industrial society like our own, influence over legislation takes place through financial support to electoral campaigns and through lobbying. Although both of these tactics may involve considerable manipulation of public resources to serve private ends, they are not ordinarily (or were not until recently) defined as illegal and corrupt. In this sense of the term, corruption would be most pronounced among those who are not rich or powerful enough to make law but are sufficiently wealthy and powerful to determine the application of law in their domains. Sicilian notables fit perfectly into this category from the mid-1870s on, and especially during the early decades of the twentieth century.

BOSSISM IN VILLAMAURA

From the archival records of Villamaura—minutes of town council and junta meetings, correspondence between the mayor and other officials—it would appear that municipal life throughout the bossism period was one scandal after another. In the 1890s, a newly elected mayor struck the names of some 79 voters from the electoral roll and entered 50 names of his own. He then caused the records of literacy tests, which purportedly justified these changes, to disappear. Telegrams from the prefect which urged restoration of the missing

---

[2] Mack Smith has suggested that regardless of its strong statement on the latifundium the government "continued to discourage the transformation of these ranches towards more specialist kinds of production" by its tariff policy (1968b: 502). Wheat tariffs were lower under Giolitti than they had been in the Crispian era, however, and a more significant obstacle to agricultural transformation was (as Mack Smith says elsewhere) lack of government investment in the necessary public works (1968b: 502).

documents were of no help to his challengers, who twice appealed their case in court and lost. Another aggressive mayor, after the turn of the century, persecuted a state-appointed director of public instruction who had bravely written an unfavorable report to his superiors about the local school. The mayor did not approve of three teachers who were hired by the director and he mysteriously produced doctors' certificates which stated that the teachers were not in sufficiently good health to teach. Other teachers who took the director's side in the dispute were accused of misappropriating school funds, while the director himself was suspended on the charge that he had opened a carpentry shop in the school and used the school benches for wood. As in the electoral imbroglio, state authorities intervened to question the director's suspension. The prefecture insisted that he be given back pay and the Ministry of Instruction promoted him. Yet, characteristically, the suspension stuck.

Throughout the period of boss power, prefect and subprefect intervened in local affairs. They could, for example, annul deliberations of the communal council and junta. They could point up irregularities in the budget, question new appointments, and order restoration of dismissed personnel. They could require that the town explain why it ignored certain of its debtors and spent vast sums prosecuting others. They could propose that the state take over the administration of the town. But the communal council had its own connections in high places and could in turn "annul" the deliberations of the prefecture, declaring to higher authorities that the prefect was ill-informed, out of order, "arbitrary and impetuous"; the council usually won its case. In 1881, the council of Villamaura, clearly in response to the vested (real estate) interests of some of its members, annulled the prefect's deliberation on a site for the local cemetery and wrote to the king of Italy asking for an investigation of the malarial and marshy site which this prefect had proposed. About the same time, the council wrote to the Minister of Justice to accuse a circuit judge—then prosecuting the communal secretary for graft—of having "spilt bile on the local administration."

Much of the malfeasance, scandal, and intrigue characteristic of local government in the Crispian and Giolittian eras developed out of factional struggles within the towns. As everywhere in Sicily and the south at this time, the group that won a majority on the town council elected the junta and the mayor. The mayor used his police powers and national patronage to enlarge his following and usurp communal land. Under the administration of a given mayor, all local positions were held by his clients, so the defeat of one faction by another automatically led to wholesale replacements in the municipal staff. In 1896, the incoming mayor of Villamaura, cited previously for meddling with the electoral rolls, fired 16 communal employees. His action was overruled at the provincial level, but reconfirmed by the Council of State. As administrations changed hands, contractors and personnel were replaced in the communal slaughterhouse, in the sanitation service, and on the janitorial staff of the schools. Public doctors were fired and new ones appointed; some teachers were demoted, others promoted; and so on. Tax collectors who were in debt to the commune but had not been prosecuted under the previous administration were suddenly hauled into court, and tax assessments for local citizens changed according to their political affiliation. One new administration declared the substantial back taxes of a landowner "uncollectable" and liquidated his debt. Under another, a *palazzo* that encroached on public property was declared in violation of the building code; the succeeding communal council wrote to the prefect that the *palazzo* in question "straightened and embellished the street." Another building that had "violated the rights of the commune to an unobstructed view from the windows of the town hall" suddenly became a landmark when its owner became mayor.

Although these examples of petty quarrels document the rivalry between landowning families described at the beginning of this chapter, local conflict was highly structured by external—national level—forces. The history of Villamaura's factions makes this clear. Two major groupings dominated local politics during the boss period. One was loyal to Crispi's faction, the other to Giolitti's. There were, in addition, a small group attached to the Risorgimento Moderate DiRudinì, and after 1900 an even smaller group of Socialists who initially took a position against the use of patronage for political ends. The leaders of the first three factions were all *civili* who agreed that the latifundium was sacrosanct and not to be divided or transformed. That is, the differences between them were personal, not ideological, and did not concern issues of policy. Between 1877, when the first *civile* council was elected in Villamaura, and 1882, when Crispi consolidated his position at the national level, local *civile* families were generally united in opposition to the Moderates and Bourbon aristocrats both of whom they had pushed aside. Later there was conflict within the ranks of the *civili*. It began with a quarrel between two families—one refused to grant a daughter in marriage to the other. By 1890 one of these families had mobilized a true opposition faction loyal to DiRudinì. People called these two groups *Susu* and *Jusu*—the "ups" and the "downs." Between 1892 and 1896, that is, during the years of the *fasci,* the banking scandals, and the temporary assumption of the prime ministry by Giolitti, local Crispians were so strongly challenged that they hardly functioned at all. In 1896 they lost decisively to the man who had the backing of deputies loyal to DiRudinì. This is the same man mentioned earlier who as mayor fired 16 communal employees and struck at least 79 names from the electoral rolls.

During the crisis years 1892–1896, a second opposition group (ultimately more significant) emerged. Its leader served as a compromise mayor when the *Jusu* and *Susu* were deadlocked and when Giolitti took over at the national level. This leader became mayor when the Giolittian era began in 1901. He absorbed into his following the remnants of the DiRudinì opposition and ran the town until the first world war, more or less as Giolitti ran Italy. The opposition faction now consisted of local Crispians whose ranks included a few Socialists. In 1914, shortly after an expansion of the suffrage, this faction won a majority of seats on the council. Subsequently, the Socialists split from the Crispians and a new era, less dominated by bossism, began.

Until recently, American social scientists who studied processes of "political development" were inclined to treat factionalism (and political bossism) as a preliminary stage in the integration of national institutions. Because of their emphasis on personal attachments, and their commitment to personal gains, factions such as those described in this chapter were considered an inherently more primitive, or "traditional," form of political organization than the party.[3] At the same time, students of urban and party politics were aware of the role of noncorporate structures such as cliques and clienteles in the organization of even the most advanced political systems. Indeed, we have come to realize that clientelistic factionalism is not the property of any particular society or political culture, nor is it the unique property of any particular stage in the evolution of political systems. One must ultimately question what kinds of factions will emerge under what conditions. The Villamaura council deliberations suggest that clientelistic factions—personalistic factions organized around a small leadership clique—will dominate the political process under the following conditions: (1) when two or more powerful conflicting

---

[3] The concept *faction* refers to conflict groups which emerge within a larger, encompassing unit that they tend to destroy by strife. There is some disagreement in the literature as to whether factious groups are necessarily formed only on the basis of the personal and self-interested attachment of followers to leaders (Nicholas 1965) or whether they cannot also be based on "substantive and more or less rational issues of policy and ideology [Friedrich 1968: 256–258]." We think the concept should be broad enough to cover both situations and would qualify the type of faction found in western Sicily during the bossism period as "clientelistic."

forces external to a local or regional political arena use patronage as an instrument of mobilization; and (2) when competition and insecurity at the local level make this patronage a *critical* economic and political resource to those who receive it. The number of local factions corresponds to the number of external conflicting forces, with the possible addition of groups that advocate resistance to external pressure. (Such groups would not have access to patronage, however, and would probably not function for long.) Generally speaking, the more important is patronage relative to policy in the eyes of the local population, the more likely attachment to factions depends upon short-run personal interest alone. The resulting groups are nonideological.

As described in Chapter 6, during the Crispian and Giolittian eras the major issue to divide national elites in Italy was the stance which their country should take in relation to the rest of Europe. One policy (Giolitti's) promoted free trade and the other (Crispi's) favored economic closure. Proponents of both alternatives were middle or upper-middle class and committed to defend private property from the masses. Their opposition to each other, while it mattered greatly to particular industries like armaments, steel, and textiles, was not an issue for most people, particularly in the south and Sicily. Even if he were well informed, the average person had equally compelling reasons for opposing (or supporting) either alternative; he could worry about trade wars and rising prices under protectionism, or unemployment and civil strife purportedly associated with free trade. From his point of view there was no satisfactory solution to the Italian dilemma, only solutions that favored some segments of the industrial bourgeoisie to the disadvantage of others, leaving the great majority suspended in between.

For most south Italians and Sicilians, the benefits of being connected with friends in high places were far more important than either free trade or protectionism. For in these dependent, semi-colonial regions, the choice between Crispi and Giolitti was about as meaningful as the Iroquois's choice between French, English, or American patrons (see Nicholas 1965: 47–58). Even the *civile* bosses, with their interest in a tariff on wheat, were capable of deserting Crispi in the 1890s. Crispian nationalism had run its course by then, and Giolitti's men looked rather more likely to be able to follow through on their promises of patronage. True, *civile* families competed for land, status, university degrees, government contracts, and concesssions—but these utilities had everything to do with national level favors, not with policy.

In other words, the nonideological quality of Sicilian politics during the bossism period tells us more about Italy than about Sicily. It was one of those examples of political mobilization—of which there are many—in which people had to take sides in order to survive, but the sides were defined elsewhere. Since "substantive and . . . rational issues of policy [Friedrich 1968: 256]" were irrelevant, people found themselves easily—yet unjustifiably—separated from kinsmen, neighbors, and others in their social class. Indeed, it was a frequently noted characteristic of the factions that they transcended class boundaries. The conflicts of interest and ambiguities of position inherent in such vertical chains and coalitions were undoubtedly responsible for much of the bitterness noted by those who wrote about *odio, rancore,* and "spilt bile" in the minutes of town council meetings.

HOW THE POLITICAL STRUCTURE THAT FAVORED BROKER CAPITALISM WAS PRESERVED

Bossism, and the flagrant corruption that accompanied it, enabled Sicily's rural entrepreneurs and *civili* to retard the penetration of state institutions into their island society. They twisted its roads and railroads as they ignored its prefects and police. Although its overall presence was vastly expanded, the post-unification Italian state perpetuated in Sicily the political structure of Spanish domination. In particular, the state remained weak in relation to private interests, which easily circumvented any mandate they did not like, living as before by their wits and *furberia.* Furthermore, the settlement pattern retained the equipotentiality of communities, and the lack of a division of labor and integration between them—another condition under which broker capitalism thrived.

At the time of unification in 1860, Sicily's ratio of roads to territory compared most unfavorably with that of the rest of Italy, including the Neapolitan provinces. Altogether, 177 out of about 350 communes, including 4 district capitals and 63 circuit capitals, were without carriageable roads and isolated during the winter. There were no railroads either, although rail construction had begun elsewhere in Italy. After unification, railroad and road construction proceeded on a large scale; yet, not until after World War I did hotels and inns appear in the interior. By 1960, Sicily had about 10,000 kilometers of roadway, but its ratio of roads to territory was still superior only to that of Sardinia and Lucania, and the ratio of roads to population was lower in Sicily than anywhere else in Italy (Milone 1960: 338–339).

The most striking symptom of continuity with Sicily's broker capitalist past is the structure of the island's transportation network. Primary roads connect major towns and cities on the coast. Although nine such roads cut through the interior, they rarely meet except at T-shaped intersections in the open countryside. In other words, outside Palermo the transportation network has no nodal cities or towns where several major arteries come together. Rather, settlements are linked to each other in lineal fashion by primary and secondary roads that wind incessantly in order to pass through as many communities as possible but which nonetheless fail to connect some agrotowns with their neighbors. These roads are inefficient as a means of integration, reflecting the absence of symbiotic exchange among mutually dependent population centers. If anything, pork barrel politics had more influence on the routing of roads and railroads than the requirements of a hierarchical market or state bureaucracy. Villamaura, for example, engaged in a vicious political dispute with nearby Valle Azzuro over the routing of railway lines (which meant employment) and refused to contribute to the construction of a direct road to its neighbor Montebello, ostensibly because no Villamaurese could think of any reason for going there.

Consistent with poor internal integration, the expanding national bureaucracy found no infrastructure of command through which to extend its influence in Sicily. Earlier regimes had governed Sicily without provincial capitals, which were abolished in the fifteenth century in favor of local autonomy for the baronial towns (Scaturro 1926: Vol. I, 410). They had relied upon extraordinary commissioners dispatched to the interior to deal with local rulers directly, on an ad hoc basis. The crown timidly attempted to restrict such local autonomy in the eighteenth century, but it was again fully operative during the Napoleonic wars, when England occupied Sicily. Between 1807 and 1825, England blockaded the continent and bought Sicilian wheat; English businessmen and adventurers invested capital in Sicily, and English liberalism inspired a consititution. In contrast with the constitutionalism of the Code Napoléon, which French troops were promoting at the same time in southern Italy, the Anglo-Sicilian version gave few prerogatives to the executive, vesting power rather in a parliament. It created 23 administrative districts but gave each one considerable independence from the center. Indeed, the arrangement pleased the aristocracy, which supported it. The restored Bourbon monarchy of the mid-nineteenth century bravely consolidated the 23 districts into 7 provinces, each headed by a centrally appointed prefect (trained in France).

Today, five of Sicily's nine provincial capitals are coastal cities of substantial urban development (Palermo, Messina, Catania, Syracuse,

Trapani), but the remaining four (two were created under fascism) are less distinguished. Their populations are considerably larger than the populations of other settlements, but so are their territories, suggesting that they are fed by local cultivators, rather than satellite communities. They, along with virtually every other community in western Sicily, had approximately 65–70% of their population either engaged in agriculture or unemployed, according to the 1951 census. In the agrotowns and in these provincial capitals, the remaining portion of the population was spread among various "urban" occupations. Only in the last few years have the capitals become significantly more complex and urban than the other settlements in their respective provinces. Even today, the *Carta Commerciale d'Italia* reports that in western Sicily the only true center of commercial attraction is Palermo, the hinterland of which embraces virtually all of the region (Unione Italiana 1968; Schneider and Schneider 1974). Competition from provincial capitals, their prefectures and archdioceses notwithstanding, is insignificant.

What is true of provincial capitals is even more true of district capitals. An unofficial map made in 1822, not long after their creation, shows that none of these capitals was connected by road to more than a handful of the settlements in its jurisdiction, and some were completely isolated from these settlements. In 1886, the councilors of Villamaura refused to appropriate funds for the renovation of the port of Sciacca, the district capital, because there was "no direct transitable road between Sciacca and Villamaura and no hope of there being one for 20 years." Sciacca is at least a minor coastal city, as are 10 of the 23 district capitals. More striking is the case of Bivona, an inland district capital of 6000 people. As late as 1962, at a convention of Sicilian mayors, a citizen of Bivona described the nearby towns over which his town had jurisdiction as "the centers *toward which* the interests and activities of the population of Bivona gravitate." Bivona, he added, was poorly articulated with many of these neighboring towns because of the absence or precarious condition of roads. The railroad had been abandoned, bus service was expensive, and the local telephone was "not directly linked with other centers. . . . Every phone call requires hours of waiting [Signorino 1962: 316–321; emphasis added]."

ADMINISTRATION BY PREBENDAL
CONCESSION SINCE 1860

The lacunae in Italian state formation are best portrayed by the continued practice of farming out prebends and the lax control that enables entrepreneurs to exploit them for private gain. Throughout the bossism period, entrepreneurs were able to bid for concessions to transport mail and to transport, store, and sell salt and tobacco. In communities like Villamaura, contractors ran the public funeral service, collected and distributed snow for making flavored ices, turned on the water fountains, cleaned the streets, lit the street lamps, ran the slaughterhouse, the fish house, the public bakery, and collected taxes (a property tax and a communal excise tax).

The archives of Villamaura offer many examples of abuse by concessionaires. For example, contracts were frequently let out only after two or more auctions had produced no bidders, and on terms that were considerably more favorable to the contractors than had originally been proposed. And the minutes of council deliberations lament that powerful contractors had more than once forced would-be competitors to stay away from the auctions. Furthermore, once granted contracts were often violated by the concessionaires.

In the bossism period most of the substantial contracts for tax collection, public works, and services went to *civili* and *gabellotti*: creditors of the local communes and friends of the local bosses, if not the bosses themselves. Thousands of lesser entrepreneurs, however, also won contracts and subcontracts for minor concessions and services, often with the financial support of patrons from among the gentry. In the early twentieth century, the commune of Villamaura, to promote the use of standard weights and measures, licensed no fewer than 22 "measurers and weighers" with the right to charge a fee for their services. These smaller scale entrepreneurs also showed a tendency to turn public resources to private ends. A contractor for the funeral service "allowed his carriage to decay and gravely underfed his horses." The man who contracted to run the town slaughterhouse used his position to favor one of the local butchers, to the disadvantage of the others. The contractor responsible for lighting the street lamps did so only when there was no moonlight; he sold the remaining petroleum to private parties even though the fuel had been supplied by the commune. Street cleaners gathered and sold rocks and branches. A guard hired to protect the collector of excise taxes gave protection to contrabandists. Almost every prebendal office had its built-in "fringe benefits."

Today a large number of activities once farmed out as prebends either are completely private or have been taken over completely by the state. Garbage collection, however, remains a concession in many Sicilian communities; much of the countryside is still policed by private security forces who contract with local governments for the right to exact compulsory fees from landowners; and tax collection, both national and local, is still farmed out to private entrepreneurs. Any reader of Italian newspapers in the late 1960s was aware of recent scandals in the tax collection service not only in Sicily but throughout the nation, too.

PUBLIC AND PRIVATE INTERESTS
IN POSTWAR SICILY

The imbalance between public and private interest, bureaucracy and entrepreneurs, does not require a prebendal system to survive. The immense regional and national bureaucracies which have mushroomed in the postwar period are highly privatized. Their relationship to the larger society differs from that under bossism because of the rise of political parties since the war. Yet favors continue to be exchanged for votes. Like every government office in a complex society, bureaucracies in Sicily control loans and subsidies, contracts for services, franchises, zoning variances, licenses, social welfare benefits, and, of course, employment opportunities for thousands. Often, broker capitalists mediate access to these resources, but alongside them is an army of ordinary mediators who specialize in arranging benefits for themselves and others. Most notable are the activists of the dominant political parties who, like an increasing percentage of public functionaries, come from the ranks of an underemployed intelligentsia (to be discussed in Chapter 10). Called *galloppini,* they connect their clients with appropriate patrons in return for votes. In most places the era of boss rule has ended, and the *galloppini* are not really political bosses since they lack the police power, the status, and the connections of the earlier notables, in addition to which there are many more of them jockeying for position. But the political system in western Sicily, for all its bureaucratization, seems hardly less personalistic than in the heyday of Giolitti and Crispi.

For example, parties and the secret ballot notwithstanding, there are still ways to determine whether promised votes are in fact delivered. A preferential voting system makes it possible to assign particular combinations of candidates to voters whose loyalty is in doubt and, because the election districts are small, to listen for the assigned combination when the votes are being counted. Controls of this sort are unusual in the Communist party, which is the most ideological and well disciplined of the modern parties—and which has little effective representation in Sicily and the Italian south (Tarrow 1967). In the other two major parties, the Christian Democratic and the Socialist parties, internal, policy-oriented factions control most of the patronage. We visited Villamaura's polling places after the regional election in 1968 and by recording individual voting preferences as the ballots were read off we found that virtually 100% of the people who voted Communist listed the same three candidates in the same order. From the Socialist and Christian Democratic lists, voters favored one of two or three competing clusters of candidates. While most voters listed their choices in the same order—the order publicized by the wing of the party in question—several idiosyncratic combinations also appeared, revealing the intervention of favor peddlers. That this was the case was confirmed by people active in both parties.

The *galloppini* are not alone to supplement more powerful brokers of the postwar political process in Sicily. Others, still less specialized, work at it, too. There is, for example, the petty entrepreneur who hangs around the antechambers of government offices and offers to guide the visitor through the bureaucratic labyrinth or to sell him the proper forms and tax stamps. At the other extreme is the influential citizen who leaves his hometown to take up residence in the provincial, regional, or national capital. This man almost invariably becomes a broker, as do his close friends and relatives who remain behind. One of the most spectacular careers in Villamaura is that of a former blacksmith whose cousin became a high official in the Ministry of the Interior in Rome. No longer a blacksmith except in name, this man lives very well off the monetary and political tolls he collects for access to his cousin. So varied and elusive are his activities that the town authorities have difficulty estimating his income (much of which is in kind) for tax purposes.

The complex interaction between public and private sectors, and the ambiguity of the boundary between them, cannot help but influence the operations of government. According to one source, regional administrations in postwar Sicily have risen and fallen over the allocation of offices to people, as the political parties that form the ruling coalition, and factions within these parties, do battle for control of key agencies such as the land reform agency and the Department of Public Works. Within the agencies themselves there is a strange disjuncture between the work done and the decisions made at the top. Lower level functionaries receive applications for service and follow the tortuous procedure which lies between the application and its final disposition (in the form of funds, licenses, contracts, jobs, or whatever). A completed dossier, however, does not go to the commissioner's desk for signature unless the case has been "recommended" to him by an influential friend, in which instance he might well concede the service before the file is completed. Thus, many such claims for service are archived, where they remain unless or until the applicant can muster the necessary political crunch to impress the commissioner. Of course, just prior to an election the commissioner will send his subordinates off to the archive with instructions to fish out every case that has come from his election district. He may also do this at the end of the fiscal year if there are unspent funds remaining in the agency's budget (Ciuni 1966).

THE STRUCTURE OF COMMODITY MARKETS IN POSTWAR SICILY

If the relationship between government and entrepreneurial endeavor continues to favor broker capitalism in Sicily, so does the structure of the island's most important commercial networks. For example, nodal points in the circulation of grain are flour mills, which fall into one of two basic categories: There is a "high production" type of mill licensed to purchase grain, store it, and process it for local consumption as well as export; and there is a "low production" type of mill licensed only to mill the grain that belongs to others, most often peasant producers. For this service the millers receive a portion of the flour, which they can then sell to bakers, pasta makers, or individuals. Today, virtually every town has at least one low production mill; Villamaura has three. Many of the larger high production mills are located in coastal towns and cities, but there are also a number located in the interior, and several of these are attached to pasta factories. Not all of these mills are in large towns, and there is no clear-cut relationship between the size of the mills and the size, complexity, or accessibility of the towns in which they are located. Towns with the larger commercial mills are still not true centers of commercial coordination.

Palermo is of course a central place in the circulation of grain. Two of its high capacity mills produce more than 10 times the flour of other commercial mills. For the most part these mills in Palermo process soft wheat, which they import, because today soft wheat is cheaper than Sicily's hard wheat and can be used to make bread and pasta if certain chemicals are added to the dough. Before this technological "advance" most bakers preferred to use hard wheat or a mixture of hard and soft wheats which would yield a maleable dough and high quality bread and pasta.

The big mills in Palermo are better capitalized than other mills, and they have vast storage facilities. By importing large amounts of soft wheat and by buying up large amounts of hard wheat from the interior, they can to some degree manipulate the grain market throughout western Sicily. But they do not as yet dominate the commerce of grain in the interior, partly because they specialize in grinding soft wheat for the Palermo market and partly because the smaller mills of the interior (including the low production mills) can, with their connections, successfully compete for local grain production. Indeed, the grain merchants of the interior take their grain wherever they think they can find the highest price, and this is most often not Palermo. There is no administered pricing in the sense of a regional monopoly on the market, and opportunities vary from day to day and place to place.

A grain merchant may set out for a distant town having already arranged by telephone to sell at a specific price, or he may set out with a truckload of grain and several alternative destinations in mind, hoping to pick up useful leads from friends along the way, until he finds an acceptable market (called a *piazza*). He may indeed start out for Trapani only to learn en route that there is a higher *piazza* in Castelvetrano. A merchant who has privileged access to market information forms a coalition with one or a few other merchants, a miller, and a banker so that they can jointly protect and exploit that information. The merchant's task is to raise capital, buy up grain, and sell it before others become aware of the special possibilities as, for example, when a large mill is offering an especially favorable price. Of course, a given merchant's unusual activity will arouse his competitors' suspicions, and at times the commerce of grain appears to be a game of spy and counterspy. One of our informants, a merchant, heard that a miller in Campobello needed grain and was offering a good price. The informant began buying up grain (some from other merchants) and trucking it to Campobello as fast as he could. One day, as he was trucking a load to Campobello, he noticed that he was being followed by a Fiat 500 carrying two nuns and a priest from Villamaura and driven by another Villamaurese, a close relative of a competing local grain merchant. Since their car slowed and then stopped when he pulled his truck into the mill at Campobello, he concluded that the driver was spying on him with the clergypersons along as camouflage. He was able to salvage his advantage, however, by prevailing on his friend, the miller of Campobello, to refuse the grain of other merchants from Villamaura at least during the following week. It is easy to see that this man's network of friends is a resource critical to his ability to organize such an ad hoc monopoly.

Personal networks are equally important to the commerce of meat, even though this commerce has changed considerably since the war. Many more families today consume meat than in the past. Before World War II the butchers of Villamaura together slaughtered one steer per week and shared that animal with the butchers of a neighboring town. Today Villamaura slaughters four or five steers weekly, plus sheep, goats, and pigs (according to season). Because of the radical decline of Sicily's animal patrimony, this rising demand for meat is largely met by imports. Beef steers are imported live from northern Italy, Holland, France, and Yugoslavia. The importers are not only big-city people and foreigners—many are rural townsmen whose networks extend into continental Italy. Indeed, the largest dealers of Palermo import meat for that city and its immediate surroundings but not for the agrotowns of the interior. The animals that are imported for consumption in the interior are not concentrated at intermediate markets in Palermo but are likely to go directly to local animal fairs, where they are sold to a wide range of speculators: butchers, meat dealers, "ranchers," and middle peasants, each of whom will fatten a few animals for market. Even an artisan or schoolteacher may invest in a steer and consign it to a peasant or shepherd for fattening, dividing the profits with him after the animal is slaughtered. Some local butchers purchase a few animals for stall-feeding, whether to supply their own shops or those of other butchers. Many butchers have become small-scale dealers on the side. They take great pride in their knowledge of animals and in their ability to judge by eye the weight and value of an animal. They are also proud of their acquaintance with the *massaria,* of their friendships with the *massariotti,* and they like to reminisce about the old days when buying an animal meant traveling into the countryside and spending a few days as the honored guest of the men who lived there.

Most of western Sicily's beef steers, however, are imported and distributed by fewer than a dozen dealers, each of whom covers a substantial territory. Again, their bases of operation are not market towns, but simply the places where they live and from which radiate their splendid networks of friends. The butchers of Villamaura formed an informal cooperative to purchase livestock for the entire group. At the time we were living in the town, they purchased most of their steers from a dealer in Solera, a mountain town smaller than

Villamaura. Solera has a rail head, but it is hardly more commercially specialized than Villamaura, except for this traffic in cattle. (According to the 1961 census, 1.5% of the employed population in Solera was engaged in transport and 3% in commerce. The figures for Villamaura were, respectively, 1% and 2.2%.) The Solera dealer plans to construct a modern abattoir, complete with facilities for aging and refrigerating meat, and buy refrigerated trucks to transport quarters of beef to butchers in his commercial network. It is interesting that Solera will remain his base of operations. As was the case with the grain merchants, this man's commercial domain is defined by his personal network of friends, not by the commercial hegemony of a central place.

TRICKS OF THE TRADE

The circulation of animals and grain in the west Sicilian interior tells us that, like the growing state presence, technological advances in transportation and processing were everywhere filtered by rural entrepreneurs. Roads and railroads, the telegraph and later telephones, the shift from water driven mills in the countryside to steam, then electric, powered mills in the towns, and the use of refrigerated cells have all enhanced broker capitalism without changing the structure of markets. As one of our informants put it, the telephone simply enlarges the field of friends. Little wonder that merchants continue to live by their wits, profiting from a wide range of informal and extralegal activities.

Many of our informants were proud of their ability to outwit their clients and agents of the state. Grain merchants described in some detail the ways in which they cheated the peasants from whom they purchased grain, and peasant producers ruefully confirmed many of the details. Grain is measured both by weight and volume. The experienced merchant can manipulate the scales as well as the counting bucket to carry away more grain than he pays for. Once the grain is in his storehouse, he may dampen it so as to increase its weight and volume before it is sold to a mill. At the mill, soft wheat flour may be introduced into the milling process in order to increase the miller's yield.

At a commercial mill in a town near Villamaura, employees pointed out the places where three different groups of past owners attempted to deal with the threat of bankruptcy by burning the mill down to collect insurance. Deep indebtedness is common among rural entrepreneurs because with their good connections credit is easy to come by. Several merchants told us about one miller who built a false wall in his storehouse. He filled the small space between the wall and the door with grain so that when the door was opened it appeared as if the storehouse were filled to overflowing. He used this "storehouse full of grain" as collateral to obtain loans. Finally, there are the ubiquitous stories of tax evasion. Some merchants and mill owners keep two sets of books—one to run the business and the other to present to visiting tax officials. One merchant boasted of the elaborate precautions he and his partners took to keep the "real" books from the wrong eyes—a desk with a false front and false-bottomed drawers. Once, however, when caught by a surprise visit from the Guardia della Finanza (treasury agents), they managed to save the day by suggesting that the agents seal the books in a gunny sack so that they could accept an invitation to dinner at a local restaurant. As the agents ate and drank, the partners' accountant and a local tailor opened the sack along the bottom seam, replaced the incriminating ledgers with the false ledgers, and resewed the seam to restore the sack's untampered appearance. What better evidence could we have that broker capitalism still survives in western Sicily?

BROKER CAPITALISM AND
THE EXPORT OF LABOR

A geographer, Rolf Monheim, conducted research on the west Sicilian settlement pattern around 1970 which reveals that even now contacts and exchanges between neighboring settlements are weak. He distinguished three types of settlement in Sicily—the village, rural city (our agrotown), and city—and he noted that the "rural city" is still preeminent in the latifundist region of the island. Here he found pronounced local isolation and *campanilismo* (parochialism). Interior settlements are oriented toward the distant cities of Palermo or Catania, rather than toward intermediary cities in their midst, according to Monheim. Meanwhile, these "rural cities are increasingly transformed into satellites of the great metropolitan centers of northern Italy and central Europe, with which they are tied through the migration of labor [Monheim 1971: 671–674]."

In the past, the absence of integration between settlements in western Sicily betrayed the region's role as a producer of surplus wheat for export to great metropolies. The persistence of the pattern suggests persistence of dependency, except that now the exported primary product is manpower rather than wheat. Significantly, the Italian nation and the industrial bourgeoisie of northern Italy have claimed proportionately little Sicilian labor, compared with the United States and western Europe. Similarly, the Spanish Empire and later the Neapolitan Bourbons were not the principal importers of Sicilian wheat: Most of it went to northern Italy and elsewhere in Europe. In each case—pre- and post-industrial—political and economic institutions of the metropolitan core were undermined by forces that drew the island into a world-system that transcended any state.

The Fascist period was an interesting, but temporary, exception. Fascism outlawed emigration and invested more heavily than previous regimes in roads, police, prefectures, and fairs in Sicily. It aimed at the exploitation of Sicilian resources and Sicilian labor by Italians. In the postwar period, however, West Germany and not northern Italy became the biggest importer of workers from the south. The strong ties that today bind Sicily to the West German and European economy continue to impede integration of the region.

In a way this situation minimizes the role of entrepreneurs and of the *civile* class in the survival of broker capitalism in Sicily. It suggests that exogenous "forces," rather than internal vested interests, were ultimately responsible for the path of change. Yet rural entrepreneurs were powerful enough to modify new technologies and institutions, to appropriate peasant land, and, through the combined use of coercion and patronage, to wreck a peasant movement for change, in the process preempting the formation of a leadership group committed to an independent course of regional development. Had it been successful, such an independent course would not only have promoted alternatives to the export of labor, it would also have furthered integration of the regional society.

Once a society's role in past world-systems becomes an important consideration in analyzing the present, comparison becomes harder to pursue. Unlike the old generalizations about traditional society, such an approach makes past divergences relevant. Historically there were many specialized adaptations—even if fewer than now—and each had its own economic regime, political structure, social groups, and cultural codes. There were, in other words, many different "traditions."

Yet there were also points of convergence, one of which had to do with broker capitalism. Apart from southern Italy, the closest parallels to Sicily seem to lie in *caciquismo*—the boss-type politics of many regions in Mexico, Brazil, Venezuela, and other Latin American countries. Comparative examination suggests that *caciquismo,* like its Sicilian counterpart, arose because in the consolidation of nation-states after 1870 various broker capitalist elements struck bargains favorable to themselves. The viability of these elements there, as in Sicily, derived from the manipulable and weakly organized dominance of the Spanish period. In these regions, too, private entrepreneurs manipulate networks of friends and contacts, organize short-term coalitions, and circumvent the law for profit (see, for example, Leeds 1964).

chapter 9

Mafia

The tenacity of broker capitalist structures in the nineteenth and twentieth centuries did more than bolster the interests and power of the *civile* class; it also favored rural entrepreneurs and herdsmen, who, although they held their own in the face of new, postindustrial pressures, had increasingly to resort to activities that depended upon violence, intimidation, and other illegalities. Mafia arose out of this set of conditions. Our understanding of this institution emphasizes three features: a range of enterprises that involved extortion; an organizational and ideological apparatus aimed at influencing the police and judiciary; and a protective political shield, provided at first by the *civile* bosses and later by party politicians. Clearly these features are related. A political shield and a neutral or impotent police–judiciary combined to guarantee immunity from prosecution or imprisonment.

Mafia is a creature of florescent broker capitalism. As such it shares much with social forms found in other broker capitalist societies. Mafia also resembles a host of familiar commensalistic groups which organize voluntary (often fraternal) associations to defend and expand the economic interests of their members. At the same time, however, mafia is a specifically west Sicilian institution which originated in the nineteenth century as latifundism was undermined. Because the *massaria* schooled mafiosi in the use of *prepotenza* and violence, their resistance to displacement built upon these skills. Viewing mafia as a violent and parasitic "businessman's fraternity," this chapter attempts a description of its origins, structure, and cultural codes.[1] Throughout the discussion it should be clear that we are not describing a single west Sicilian establishment "the Mafia," as it is so often described in the press, but rather a form and strategy of organization found in many Sicilian towns and cities.

THE FOUNDATION OF THE POLITICAL SHIELD

Among the many manifestations of weak state development in Sicily after 1800, two were of special relevance to the rise of mafia: the police function and the judicial–penal apparatus. In 1876, the Villamaura town council voted in vain to request that the state set up an appeals court in Sciacca because the appeals court in the provincial capital, Agrigento, was too far away. In the early twentieth century, the council agitated for the restoration of a circuit court, deed registry, and notary public in Villamaura, claiming that all three services had been stolen away from them by a well-connected land-owner in another town. This "theft" meant 16 kilometers of miserable road and insecure countryside between Villamaura and the seat of justice, and it increased the "rancor and dissidence which eats away at families and at the community as a whole [Villamaura municipal archive]."

Just as the judiciary was remote and inaccessible, so was the police. This was serious because, apart from dissidence and rancor, there was the threat of banditry, animal rustling, and kidnapping for ransom in western and interior Sicily, as well as a mounting class struggle between landlords and peasants. To property holders, whether large or small, the state seemed powerless to protect crops, animals, land, and people. To restrict animal theft, for example, the Bourbon government required that animals be registered and

<hr>

[1] The most important sources for this chapter are: Mosca (1949), Pantaleone (1962), Franchetti (1925), and Romano (1966), and two excellent recent works—an ethnography by Blok (1974) and an analysis of documents by Hess (1973). It is also based on our fieldwork.

licensed. Local mayors were to certify the identification papers of every animal bought and sold. But mayors authenticated false papers and rural entrepreneurs added to their incomes by acquiring these fraudulent documents for their clients (Alongi 1886: 99, 123–124; D'Alessandro 1959: 57–59; R. Prefettura 1896: 1). Nor was the Italian state much more effective after 1860; the correspondence between local and provincial levels of government that appears in the Villamaura archive endlessly debates the responsibility for policing the countryside. National officials accused the local authorities of neg-ligence, while local officials fired back angry letters which complained of inadequate resources. The state insisted that the town maintain armed and mounted guards, but the town had no funds for horses, arms, and uniforms. In the end the town council organized the guard as a prebend—a concession to collect fees from property holders in exchange for insuring their property against damage or loss.

In addition to the rural guards, companies of district police were maintained by the state, but one of their effects was to inspire bandits to interprovincial operations since a policeman could not arrest a malefactor outside his district. Franchetti's inquest of 1876 revealed that bandits received no one better than these policemen: "In the evening they [the policemen] arrive at a town, dismount at the local inn, lay down their rifles in a corner and sit down to drink with muleteers, traveling merchants . . . people of every type. They talk to everyone, know everyone. . . . Either they fear a vendetta or they share in the fruits of crime [1925: 46]."

The inadequacy of judicial and police administration left numerous gaps to be filled on behalf of law and order, and rural entrepreneurs, acquainted with the use of violence, rose to the task. Serving as private estate guards or retainers, hired on by large landholders to protect their property against theft, these men, who became known as *mafiosi,* went beyond their nominal function and protected not only property but outlaws as well. When damage or loss occurred, they were able to negotiate a settlement because they knew or could trace the person or persons involved. Retainer-type mafiosi also protected property from peasant rebels and were implicated in numerous murders of peasant and left wing leaders, especially after 1890 (Pantaleone 1962: 239–243; Romano 1966: 227–231). In lieu of a malfunctioning law and order apparatus, they defended the lati-fundium as vigilantes.

Mafiosi further functioned as private avengers and judges, being men of respect by reputation who "instinctively knew good from bad . . . [Romano 1966: 52]." In this role they served not landlords so much as artisans, herdsmen, and peasants, by "adjusting things when they got too complicated [Hess 1973: 101]." Popular descriptions of these services focus on a mafioso seated in his "office" (which could be a bar in the piazza), receiving clients who begged his intervention in boundary disputes, quarrels over grazing rights, damages from trespass, and so on. After 1800, the intensification of conflict between herdsmen and cultivators multiplied work for these *pacieri,* the peace-making mafiosi of the rural towns.

The vigilante and peacemaking roles of mafiosi should have become less necessary as state institutions penetrated further into Sicily. Broker capitalist traditions of the past, however, impeded this penetration. In addition, the *civile* landholders were for a long time satisfied to leave the protection of their property in private hands, even though they were paying fees or taxes to the state for such pro-tection. The private protectors were a known quantity, the public forces unknown, and mafia protection was easier to arrange. Mafiosi were more effective than were the police in dealing with bandits and offered a more reliable buffer against peasant claims since the state was at least nominally committed to land reform. Similar considera-tions decided those seeking the intervention of mafiosi in private disputes and quarrels. Even today, when nearly everyone with a cause would readily enter litigation, a mafioso's intervention is often thought to be faster and more expedient than a court battle.

Through the peacemaking role, mafiosi acquired hundreds of clients, which in turn gave them leverage with the *civile* class. People often asked their mafia "advisors" how they should vote (Hess 1973: 101). Additional leverage derived from their role as vigilante henchmen of *civile* on their large estates. Grand electors of parlia-mentary deputies, *civile* landowners were influential in government circles, and because they were indebted to their henchmen they used their political influence to protect them. They even procured licenses for their mafioso guards to carry weapons. Mafiosi, in other words, were richly endowed with patronage and protection which they obtained from the state through their *civile* patrons. The resulting political shield was an essential ingredient in mafia's evolution.

RECRUITMENT TO MAFIA

The role of vigilante and the role of *paciere* were pronounced in some periods, less so in others, never involving all mafiosi and even rejected by some. Both roles helped to legitimate mafiosi in the eyes of the larger society; both helped to win them favors from the powerful; finally, both were critical to the maintenance of the political shield. Yet neither role defined the mafioso because the state's police and judiciary, if they were poorly articulated in the nineteenth century, were nevertheless much stronger than they had been before. For the first time in Sicilian history, officers of the state could arrest malefactors and force them to stand trial. Although the means for so doing were inadequate, and easily manipulated by the malefactors themselves, the very existence of these means provoked a response. As Anton Blok argued in his recent book, mafia was an adaptation to expanding, not absent, state power (1974).

A good indication is that, when asked, a Sicilian is inclined to identify the mafiosi in his town by reference to their *fatti provi*—proven accomplishments. This term means their proven capacity to flaunt the law, to promote their own interests through violence or the threat of violence, and to do so with impunity. The most obvious sign of *fatti provi* is a long history of arrests which never culminate in conviction, in which the defendant before the bar is absolved "for lack of proof." (This may be one of the few occasions in the history of logic when the best proof is the lack of proof.) Such a record means of course that the mafioso is well enough connected and widely enough feared that he can corrupt the officers of justice, or intimidate witnesses, or both. Thus, Vito Cascio Ferro, one of the most famous Sicilian mafiosi of the early 1900s, was imputed and absolved 69 times during his life. Although few have so exemplary a record as Don Vito, a prepotent man who affects the style of a mafioso but can claim no *fatti provi* is likely to be considered an "empty sack." On the other hand, someone with such a record may be considered a mafioso even when people know little else about him (Hess 1973: 77).

People who can claim to be mafiosi on the basis of their *fatti provi* are not drawn at random from all strata of the population. Historically, two groups contributed disproportionately to the ranks of local mafias. They are herdsmen, discussed subsequently, and rural entrepreneurs connected to the *massaria* complex: *gabellotti,* overseers, estate guards, head shepherds, muleteers and carters, butchers, meat dealers, and brigands. A number of these specialists, the *gabellotti* in particular, also moved up to form the backbone of the *civile* class. Indeed, the distinction between this class and mafia is complicated. Often, participants in mafia were upwardly mobile and acquired land and status for their progeny, if not for themselves. With time, therefore, mafiosi and kinsmen of mafiosi appeared among *civile* landowners, doctors, lawyers, veterinarians, surveyors, town councilors, and mayors. By the same token the *civile* bosses, dependent on mafia to protect their property against theft and the land reform movement, verged on being mafiosi themselves, and some were. Yet most mafiosi were not *civili,* and most *civili* were not mafiosi.

Civili and mafiosi also related differently to the state. Except during the Crispian era, when the Italian government protected wheat and sent troops into Sicily against the *fasci,* the *civile* class of the island had little influence over national legislation. Its members nevertheless shaped the law by corrupting its administration. Mafiosi fell in at a lower level. They did not exert influence on legislation—they were two steps removed from that process—and not so much on the administrative arm of the state, although certainly they participated in corruption. Their greatest efforts were directed at the point of arrest and trial, where they specialized in keeping evidence out of the courtroom. In this regard we have found it useful to separate legislative–executive aspects of political integration from judicial and penal processes. Because of their particular business interests, which often led to arrest, mafiosi focused their organizational energies on the latter, leaving the former for the *civile* class. At the heart of mafia were strategies to avoid conviction and to avoid implicating others when arrested.

The second major group to contribute to mafia was herdsmen. Their careers were less distinguished than those of the rural entrepreneurs, yet they, too, were often upwardly mobile in a lifetime. Starting out as "*picciotti,*" or "boys," in the employ of other mafiosi, herdsmen frequently graduated to become "employers" themselves. Careers of this sort were also open to ambitious peasants and landless laborers, but these groups gave proportionately fewer members to mafia than did herdsmen.

As we know from Chapter 7, herdsmen frequently became rustlers and bandits. Mafia's relationship to banditry was hardly less complicated than its relationship to the *civile* class. Early mafiosi, like bandits, were much involved with the theft of animals, and mafia profited from the atmosphere of violence which banditry created. Yet mafia activity differed from banditry in important ways. The bandit was an outlaw; the mafioso, a criminal. The success of the bandit lay in his ability to live outside normal society, away from other people and away from the space that could effectively be controlled by the police. The mafioso, however, lived the life of a citizen, not lawfully, but within legal society. His success lay in his ability to avoid the constraints of law and influence its adjudication.

Costume symbolized this situation. Mafiosi dispensed with the extravagant dress, the swagger, and élan of bandits. *Picciotti* and poorer mafiosi dressed much like peasants and shepherds, while established mafiosi looked like businessmen (Hess 1973: 99). The very word *mafia* also conveyed refusal on the part of mafiosi to see themselves as different, or in a different legal status, from other citizens. In the early 1860s, Giuseppe Rizzotti, a Sicilian dramatist, produced a play called *I Mafiusi della Vicaria*. The play was about a group of prisoners in the Palermo jail (*la Vicaria*) who were treated deferentially by other prisoners and who referred to each other as *mafiusi*—men of respect. Theretofore in Sicilian dialect, *mafia* or *mafioso* was used to indicate superiority, something extraordinary, perfection. One could (and still can) describe a full and perfectly formed cabbage as "mafioso." Thereafter, the word *mafia* depicted an evolving organization, whose members' superiority was reflected in an "exaggerated sense of self," a demand for respect and deference which bordered on *prepotenza*, even when the state marked these men as criminals (Pitrè 1939: 287–293; Romano 1966: 36). In an early essay on mafia, Hobsbawm noted that in contrast to outlaw bandits, mafiosi were respectable: "*Mafia* maintained public order by private means. Bandits were broadly speaking what it protected the public from [1959: 40]."

If bandits hid from the law, mafiosi confronted it and reached an accommodation which protected more subtle kinds of theft than that which bandits committed. Characteristic mafia activities usually involved some form of extortion, the success of which depended upon manipulating, not evading, both victims and the law. In the case of banditry, power and wealth accrued to rural entrepreneurs who were sufficiently well connected to manage the clandestine sale of stolen goods. In the case of extortion this internal leadership was more specialized. Power and wealth accrued to established mafiosi who were well enough connected to influence the courts and police.

With extortion, there are no stolen goods, for a different relationship exists between delinquent and victim. Where theft presupposes no necessary connection between them, extortion is based on continuing negotiations, and the relationship is diffuse and personal even if it is mediated by a third party. Theft is a one-shot affair; you take what you can and run. Extortion leads to long-term arrangements and tribute; it leads to expanded domain, which in turn requires an ongoing investment in immunity from state interference.

THE EVOLUTION OF MAFIA DOMAIN

The earliest mafia activities grew directly out of the historical specializations of rural entrepreneurs attached to the *massaria* complex.
As the pressures of postindustrial imperialism rendered these specializations obsolete, mafiosi used violence and intimidation to perpetuate them past their time. In this regard, mafia was reminiscent of
the many historical instances in which local capitalists were powerful
enough to resist being dislodged by technologically and organiza-
tionally more advanced outsiders. Hausa cattle traders in Nigeria,
German towns in the Renaissance, and small shopkeepers in the
French Revolution are a few among many notable examples (see
Cohen 1969; Heckscher 1955: 62–73; Hobsbawm 1962: 69–70).
Franchetti, in his report, described a group of mafiosi who, by
threatening harassment, forced a steam powered mill to sell its flour at
the higher price of mills driven by water (Franchetti 1925: 126).[2]

But water-driven mills could not last forever, nor could large
estates with their pastoral substructure forever resist the growth of
peasant latifundism. The result was that mafia's earliest domain
became as vulnerable to contraction as the historical specializations of
rural entrepreneurs. Gradually but inevitably, mafiosi had to carve out
new preserves for themselves and their dependents. Using or
threatening violence, they retarded the contraction of old domains by
organizing small-scale monopolies that excluded competitors. But violence also paved the way for entry into new fields of endeavor. Typically, mafiosi encroached upon roles already occupied by others. As
Italians put it, they "intruded themselves" into arenas where they
were not needed—a strong argument against understanding mafia in
terms of the "functions" it performed for the state or society. In spite
of monopoly and violence, mafiosi were (and are) frequently in
competition with each other, for the mafioso solution to displacement
was only minimal, not optimal. Intense competition internal to mafia
was, we think, the motive force which drove some mafiosi (with their
capital) into new arenas. The following summary of activities illustrates
this point.

One of the most lucrative economic ventures in nineteenth-
century Sicily was rustling animals. Declining pastures plus rising
population made animal products more dear. As the presence of the

---

[2] Not only that. According to Franchetti (1925) the local population lodged no
complaint against the high price of flour. The basis for such compliance will be discussed later.

state increased, however, rustling assumed a form closer to extortion than to theft. Animals were stolen for restitution upon payment of a ransom (for *ricatto*). Closely related to this practice was one of the earliest characteristically mafioso activities, the organization of "protection rackets." Increasingly, in the course of the century, mafiosi forced owners of animals to pay a fee (called *u pizzu* in Sicilian) on a continuing basis to insure their property against the *possibility* of theft. If the owners refused to pay, or if they sought protection from the state, mafiosi subjected them to intimidation. Specific warnings, called *sfregi,* ranged from minor crop damage to the injury, theft, or mutilation of an animal, to the slaughter of animals, and occasionally to the kidnap, injury, or murder of people.[3] Most victims entered negotiations after one or two warnings, and rarely did one among them complain to public authorities about the threats. The threats, as a result, effectively converted the service of private police protection (long a specialty of rural entrepreneurs) into an imposition precisely as the state became involved in rural security. Private protection might have become superfluous had mafia not transformed it into a necessity by extortion.

In much the same way, nineteenth-century mafiosi preserved other domains of the past. Under pressure of intimidation, many landlords rented their estates to particular *gabellotti,* employed particular estate guards, and in general paid for more services than they would have liked. Large landholders were no less vulnerable to this pressure than were small holders (Blok 1974: 182; Franchetti 1925: 161–168). When directed against public officials, such intimidation influenced the award of public works and tax farming contracts in which rural entrepreneurs also had a stake. Competition for these perquisites was nevertheless intense, such that the level of violence among mafiosi was greater than that against outsiders (Hess 1973: 152).[4] In Blok's detailed description of a mafia in the town of Genuardo after 1870, the

---

[3] According to Hess, however, the mutilation and killing of animals was rare (1973: 153).

[4] One is reminded here of Sahlins's analysis of segmentary lineage systems among the Tiv and the Nuer (1961). He views them as instruments of expansion or predation, which is roughly the way we view mafia. The difference is that the Nuer, for example, moved against a population of Dinka whose political organization was less complex than their own; whereas mafia expansion has occurred within highly stratified, complex societies. In segmentary lineage organization, internal pressure is projected outward, while the destructive capability of weaponry increases as conflict moves farther from home. The dynamics of mafia are different. External pressure intensifies conflict among mafiosi, and the scale of violence increases the closer one gets to home. Mafiosi are under more pressure than the Nuer and move more gradually against their prey.

single most important cause of murder was competition between established and incipient mafiosi for guard posts and leases on the large estates. The homicide rate was particularly high in the periods of retrenchment which followed both world wars (1974: 160).

It seems likely that competition for positions and privileges traditionally associated with the *massaria* complex pushed rural entrepreneurs and herdsmen into sectors of the economy where previously they had played no part, sectors which were quite divorced from the latifundium. A classic example was the expanding zone of vineyards and citrus groves which surrounded Palermo. The development of this zone completely excluded the pastoral use of land and therefore upset the transhumance cycles of *massaria*-linked men in the interior. These men had a weapon, however: Irrigation works near the coast depended upon water originating in the mountains. Control over water sources gave mafiosi a new and particularly severe sanction: They could deny water to an uncooperative fruit grower.

For the mafia of the orchards we have a vivid description by Mosca, set at the turn of the century. He explained how a man would inherit a modest holding planted in fruit trees and vineyards. On early visits to his land, he would notice two or three men hanging around. One day, they would approach him, congratulate him roundly on his good fortune, welcome him to the neighborhood, and offer their services. "Sometimes you hear bad things about this zone . . . but a respected man like you need not fear. You can come and go freely at night. Your land will be watched, your wife and children can feel safe . . ." and so on. If the new landholder readily accepted the services being offered, local *picciotti* would begin to treat him deferentially. Thereafter he would take on various assistants—an additional guard to protect his crop at harvest time and ensure its safe transport to markets, day laborers to pick it, middlemen to sell it, brokers to help him when he wished to sell a portion of his land. The men who had initially approached the new owner found the personnel for these tasks and exacted a fee—*u pizzu*—for their effort. In this way, the profits of the luxury crop trade were distributed among some of those who had been displaced by it.

Suppose the new landholder were naive or recalcitrant? Suddenly he would notice a coolness toward him on the part of the local *picciotti* and, although they still greeted him with apparent respect, he would begin to suffer *sfregi*—a branch cut from a peach tree, a few lemons missing. After a while, the situation might worsen: an entire vineyard cut down; interruptions in his water supply; a threatening letter of extortion (*scrocco*); his own choice of guard threatened by a rifle shot and possibly even killed; he himself kidnapped and held for ransom. Extreme sanctions were seldom necessary, however, since a warning or two usually sufficed, and the mafiosi, eager for a new friend, would forgive the owner his original lack of good judgment. And he would forgive them. After a few days, when they claimed to have found and disciplined the lemon thieves, he would agree to offer a "gift" for these boys who did it because they were hungry (paraphrased from Mosca 1949: 233–237).

In the decades before fascism, mafia lived off the latifundia, off rustling and the clandestine sale of meat, off leases, guard positions, and the control of peasant labor. Mafiosi lived off the orchards around Palermo and off the produce market of that zone. In Palermo, mafiosi controlled all the wholesale operations of the produce market and, through their positions, received income and political credit from the distribution of retail licenses, the sale of fertilizers to growers, contracts for labor, transport and guard posts in the orchards, and the settlement of disputes. After 1900, however, mafiosi had gradually to cope with peasant latifundism. As peasant cooperatives formed in the interior, collectively renting large estates in lieu of the *gabellotto,* mafiosi responded in two ways. They opposed and menaced some cooperatives, directing *sfregi* at their leaders, a number of whom were killed, and they infiltrated others, taking them over. Mafiosi also became involved in emigration, obtaining fees as intermediaries for migrants' safe passage and eventual employment, particularly in the case of fugitives from the law (Romano 1966: 227–231).

This pattern of alternately resisting change and then moving to exploit change was repeated after the second world war. Mafiosi attacked the land reform movement and they were responsible, although rarely convicted, for many tragic deaths. When land reform appeared inevitable, they turned to capture the reform agencies and credit bureaus established by the state. Pantaleone recounted a particularly instructive example of this duplicity and how it worked. Under the law of 1950, the government created a consortium of large and small landholders in the zone around Corleone, a western interior town. Mafiosi rigged the election of the consortium's officers, with the result that the consortium blocked the construction of a dam in the mountains. This dam would have removed several hundred hectares of land from latifundist and pastoral exploitation. It would have provided water to intensify agriculture elsewhere in the interior.

It would, in short, have challenged mafiosi of the pastures and their allies in the Palermo meat trade. Finally, it would have undermined control by mafiosi over water in the orchard zone.

In Corleone in the early 1950s, there were already too many mafiosi and would-be mafiosi competing to secure a good living from rustling, lease holding, and guard posts. Established mafiosi blocked Luciano Liggio, a bright and prepotent young upstart, from marketing stolen livestock. Liggio's reputation had been made in animal theft and violence against peasant leaders. His career thus interrupted, he invested his profits from the past in two trucks and organized a transport company which obtained contracts to haul construction materials for the road building and water works program of the consortium. His interests now lay in promoting the dam, which he did in a struggle that cost the lives of several Corleone mafiosi (Liggio included) between 1956 and 1958. Liggio also became part of a major new development in Palermo. The return to Sicily after World War II of mafiosi who had escaped to America during fascism paved the way for a Sicilian role in the drug trade. Pantaleone described how mafiosi, many of them older than Liggio and some of them no doubt casualties of competition in more traditional arenas, took over the docks of Palermo, its produce market, the city's private police firms, and its garages. Such facilities, while profitable in their own right, were also instrumental to heroin traffic, and conflict over acquisition of some of them—the produce market in particular—led to a protracted vendetta. Between 1951 and 1959, there were 211 mafia-linked murders in Palermo (Pantaleone 1962: 199–211).

When we were in Sicily, between 1965 and 1967, we collected newspaper accounts of mafia arrests (not convictions). A surprising number—in fact the majority—were for such old-fashioned practices as rustling and abusive grazing, not because mafia is still "archaic and pastoral," but because mafiosi in contracting domains are probably more vulnerable to arrest than their colleagues in new fields. Under the pressure of contraction, competition becomes more intense, violence more frequent, and betrayal more likely. Arrests connected with the newer activities were interesting for the degree to which they showed continuity with the past. For example, mafiosi arrested for trafficking in drugs had in some cases belonged to cigarette smuggling networks before the war. Several arrests charged mafiosi with blowing up sand caves and quarries or blocking off their entrances. They did this to drive competitors out of the construction supply business or to force the owners to hire particular persons. A number of the accused got their start as carters, first hauling grain and then construction materials. An important series of arrests in Palermo brought to light a group that forced Palermo hotels to buy meat from certain brokers and hire certain men as guards—activities obviously reminiscent of the past. Another series focused on bus company administrators, again in some cases descendants of muleteers and carters. They were accused of using intimidation to eliminate competitors from the road. In other words, individual mafiosi, charting careers for which they had some preparation, were vehicles of mafia's movement from the old to the new.

SOME SECRETS OF MAFIA'S SUCCESS

By the last quarter of the nineteenth century, the Italian state was tough enough to contain banditry in Sicily (although not to wipe it out entirely; an endemic form of banditry coexisted with mafia into the twentieth century and broke out vigorously after both world wars). But, as the preceding review of mafia activities suggests, the state tolerated and did not contain extortion. It is now time to examine and weigh the various strategies that mafiosi employed in order to reach this accommodation with state power. One, the political shield, has already been discussed but requires elaboration. Two others, the clique, or *cosca,* and an ideology known as *omertà,* will receive detailed consideration in sections to follow.

Although the political shield which the *civile* class provided was a necessary condition for the rise of mafia, it had certain limitations when it came to extreme forms of manipulation and corruption. Protected by the *civile* bosses, and later by *galloppini* and party politicians, leading mafiosi (who generally controlled votes) could bring pressure to bear on prosecutors and judges whose careers, after all, depended on the good favor of deputies and ministers. But it was hard to go further. Occasionally, mafiosi directed warnings or *sfregi* at an investigator, a judge, or a prosecutor or—and this was extremely rare—they arranged his murder. A famous example was the 1890s homicide of an official of the Bank of Sicily, Notarbartolo, just as he was about to unravel a series of costly scandals involving the misuse of loan funds. Mosca, explaining this event to the north Italian readers of a Milan daily, pointed out that bank scandals were not unique to Sicily. They had punctuated the Crispian era of easy credit and protection for industry all over Italy. While murder was an outgrowth of the scandal in Sicily, this was not because mafia was a "great and mysterious association of *malfattori* [Mosca 1949: 253]." The explanation, wrote Mosca, was more serious because it started with the nation-state. It had to do with petty *truffatori,* or tricksters, in Rome as well as Palermo, who never knew of the plot to kill Notarbartolo, but who were already so deeply involved in giving away bank money that as this plot unfolded they could only help cover it up to save themselves.

Around this large group of *truffatori* was a still larger group of *toleranti,* people who from long experience with broker capitalism acquiesced in contempt for the law. At the highest levels of government, still another group indulged clients regardless of whether they were known to be dishonest. The result was immunity or near immunity for *truffatori* and, in this case, for assassins. For more than a decade after Notarbartolo's murder, no accusations were filed. Then Vito Cascio Ferro was tried for it, but not convicted (Mosca 1949: 249–255).

Mosca's analysis placed this spectacular murder in the context of xenophobic protectionism and easy credit under Crispi. In more normal times such an approach to the law might be too outrageous to pay dividends. Even in the old days of rampant clientelism, threats to the life of a public official entailed overwhelming political debts and stretched the political networks of mafiosi to the breaking point. As a result, mafiosi supplemented their political shield with the *cosca* and *omertà,* which were also important adaptations to state power.

THE CORE OF MAFIA ORGANIZATION: THE *COSCA*

In discussing the structure and purpose of the *cosca,* it helps to remember how fluid and changing were the economic activities associated with mafia. Like the rural entrepreneurs from whose ranks they often came, mafiosi did business in coalition with others. Their partners might have belonged to the local mafia, to the mafia of a neighboring or distant town, to mafia only indirectly through the good offices of a kinsman or friend, or to no mafia at all. Any given mafioso was likely to be involved in more than one coalition at a time. Also, like investment groups in all societies marginal to the metropolitan centers of international capitalism, the partnerships were short-lived. Quick to absorb new members and assets, but equally vulnerable to precipitous withdrawals, they experienced a considerable turnover of personnel. That mafia domains were crowded and vulnerable to contraction added to this element of instability. In an effort to counteract it, partners often tried to monopolize an activity. When viewed over time, however, most such monopolies were short-lived.

Within the context of this overall fluidity, mafiosi sought order and predictability in the local clique, or *cosca* (named for the tightly bundled leaves of an artichoke, and a much misunderstood structure).[5] In view of the dynamic picture of mafia stressed earlier, the *cosca* could not be a static association of conspirators bound to one another for life by rituals of initiation, by oath, or by blood, as some versions have it. Nor did the *cosca* as such organize economic activities. Like any group of friends who get together often—to play cards, to go hunting, to pass the time in good company—the *cosca* gave rise to instrumental coalitions but was not, as a rule, itself such an instrumental group.

Every *cosca* revolved around a nucleus of one or a few leaders.[6] At the periphery, sometimes part of its activities but often not, were the *picciotti* and other dependents, each of whom was bound to the *cosca* as a client of some particular patron in the group. Various bonds linked the members of the clique to each other and helped to maintain its solidarity. One such relationship was the tie of agnatic kinship. Because many mafiosi were *gabellotti,* they were familiar with the clan-building strategies of these large-scale operators and with their efforts to consolidate power through patrilateral parallel cousin marriages (see Chapter 4). Mafia was neither a "Sicilian clan" nor a "tribal survival," as a few romanticized accounts would have us think. Sometimes, however, patrilineal kinsmen formed the core of a local clique

[5] There are other words for *cosca,* such as "umbrella," which similarly depict a solidary group committed to secrecy.

[6] Hess (1973: 108–110, 115) has suggested that a *cosca* usually has a single leader, yet he has offered many examples to the contrary. Mosca (1949: 229) put it this way: "Turning to the mafia *cosca*, it is an extremely simple but solid organism which is neither formal nor bureaucratic. There are no presidents, no secretaries, no officers either elected or appointed, neither is there a roster of members. The association is directed and exploited almost always by three, four, or five persons who are more authoritative by virtue of their age, intelligence, social position, successful criminal actions, arrests, and above all by virtue of their experience and exceptional skill in the difficult art of unpunished delinquency. If one of these members excels the others in all of these qualities, he becomes in fact the supreme head."

whose effectiveness was enhanced by the trust and cooperation inherent in the kinship tie, at least among "ranchers."[7] The clique similarly benefited from ties of coparenthood which bound some of its members to others as fictive kin. Like kinship, the relationship of coparenthood carries a sense of mutual obligation and good will. Established by contract, it is if anything stronger than association by blood, which perhaps explains why members of a cosca—whatever their relationship—called one another compare, or "godfather," rather than frate, or "brother."

In addition to kin and fictive kin relations, the most important tie to solidify the cosca was friendship, a flexible bond which, as we know, was the key organizational element and ideological focus of the massaria complex. Mafiosi have systematically capitalized on this tie and its associated cultural code to the point that they collectively label themselves gli amici ("the friends") or amici degli amici ("friends of the friends"). "He who has money and friends has justice by the ass" is a typically mafioso expression (Alongi 1886: 76).

As far as we know, the local cosca held no formal meetings. Nevertheless, it served as a context for making contracts and generating trust over food and drink. The leader, or leaders, at least, were available to others in certain localities on a regular basis. A leader's house, a local tavern, the back room of a shop was a place where friends gathered, perhaps every evening or on Sunday afternoons. Such informal gatherings resembled a scaled down version of the banquets described in Chapter 5 in that men raised their wineglasses in toasts to friendship, and friends of the host entertained visitors with much clowning around. As at the banquets, at these gatherings decisions were made, not by the collectivity, but by various coalitions within it. Nor was the collectivity constant or clearly bounded. Regular participants brought semi-regulars and guests. Strangers who sought the intervention of a particular member came and then left. Perhaps a local cosca had as semi-regular members a nucleus of friends from a nearby town. Although the automobile has strengthened this pattern today, it was also true in the past that gatherings on the massaria were occasions for entering coalitions with individuals from other towns. The cosca placed its seal of approval, as it were, on members and their

---

[7] Chapman, describing Milocca during the Fascist period, wrote: "If evidence of cooperation [between brothers] within legitimate fields of activity is scanty, that concerning brotherly collaboration in crime is certainly not so. There was one family from which seven brothers had been taken to prison [1971: 81]."

clients, who then became known to mafiosi elsewhere as potentially reliable and trustworthy business partners.

The *cosca* supported its members in another decisive way. It helped to enforce their claims to domain vis-à-vis others, both mafiosi and non-mafiosi. It was able to deploy or threaten violence and to protect any member or *picciotto* who faced charges for illegal activities. The *cosca* leaders—older men with extensive political connections—were central to this protection for they were in a position to acquire arms for *picciotti* and to influence judicial proceedings. But all *cosca* members had a stake in keeping violence under control. Therefore the *cosca* also limited the use and threat of violence, at least during "normal" times when a local leadership was not being challenged, and there was no inter-*cosca* conflict.[8]

The *cosca* was also prepared to support any member or client who ran afoul of the law. There were two reasons for this: Such backing was just compensation for misfortune suffered in the line of duty; it also established the basis by which the *cosca* maintained its influence over members or *picciotti* if they were arrested and jailed. It was essential to the activities of all mafiosi that no one implicate another in a crime. To this end the *cosca* institutionalized the delivery of assistance in the case of arrest or conviction. In contrast to the protectors of bandits, who offered safe refuge and food, *cosca* assistance took the form of good lawyers and a "family insurance plan"— financial and other aid to the arrested man's wife and children. *Cosca* members also invented alibis, developed false testimony, and influenced public opinion as to its truth (Hess 1973: 114).

In all societies, but especially in a familist society like that of western Sicily, an important concern of a married man is the welfare of his wife and children. This automatically reduces his freedom of movement. A father of a family is reluctant to commit acts of violence that might lead to his arrest or to retaliation (see Campbell 1964: 194–196). He is tempted to cooperate with authorities, if cooperation will in turn restore him to his role as father. Many *picciotti* were young and unmarried, but many were not. To enhance their freedom, and the freedom of established mafiosi, the *cosca* was prepared to assume the burdens of fatherhood. The *cosca* did not have a fund for mutual

---

[8] Blok's detailed examples of the latter situation, as well as the vendettas described by Pantaleone for Corleone and Palermo, suggest that when rival *cosche* were in conflict, few limits were placed on the use of violence. On the contrary, the *cosche* took on a paramilitary form (see Blok 1974).

aid, no dues, bank account, or treasurer. When the need arose, however, members voluntarily contributed from their own pockets. According to Pantaleone, mafias in certain zones regularly sequestered and ransomed people in order to raise funds for legal aid and aid to the families of victims (1962: 190–192). When voluntary contributions were necessary, considerable pressure was brought to bear on those with the financial means to foot the bill. Anyone who defaulted in this obligation lost prestige and authority, acquired a bad reputation, and probably jeopardized his own future should he be arrested. There are occasional stories of imprisoned *picciotti* seeking revenge upon their release for what they considered to be abandonment by the mafia (Pantaleone 1962: 192). *Picciotti* rarely confessed, however, for this would have threatened their future protection and support. As mafiosi put it, "prison, illness and disgrace prove the hearts of friends [Alongi 1886: 76]."

The net result of *cosca* protection and mutual aid was to mitigate the effect of police arrest. By ensuring the silence of those who were caught, mafia showed itself stronger in some respects than the state, and more effective. Sometimes support to families lasted for decades and extended to the provision of a dowry for an imprisoned man's daughter. Sometimes *picciotti* voluntarily served prison sentences in exchange for the true authors of a crime, and in return for support to their families (Pantaleone 1962: 190–192).

By regulating the application of violence and by protecting members and henchmen when they got into trouble, the mafia *cosca* brought order into the struggle for domain. Sometimes, however, that struggle overwhelmed it. As a general rule, *picciotti* were loyal to patriarchs, but there were exceptions for the relationship was inherently unequal and exploitative, while few domains were secure enough that mafiosi could prevent all challenges from below. One of the cases followed by newspapers in 1966 concerned a young *picciotto* whose statement to a journalist that "mafiosi smoke me like a cigarette" led to his murder. The young man was bitter because, having planted explosives in a jewelry store under orders from a *cosca* leader, and on behalf of a rival jeweler, he received what he considered to be inadequate compensation. The newspaper accounts stressed that this situation was unusual since *picciotti* are usually constrained by fear and their own ambitions from "drunkenness and too much talk."

Yet there are also cases of younger men, like Lucciano Liggio, who are rebellious enough to form rival *cosche* (cliques). Liggio's case is especially interesting because he rode the crest of an economic shift occasioned by land reform which seriously affected the preserves of many established mafiosi. His rebellion, however, was not unique. On the contrary, it appears from Blok's evidence that *cosca* leaders advanced potentially rebellious *picciotti* in their careers more rapidly than was usual and invited them to join the more lucrative partnerships early (Blok 1974: 173–174). In this way, the leaders co-opted them.

Presumably, members of a *cosca* did not compete with each other for domain. With the exception of rustling, moreover, domain was localized. Within given geographical areas mafiosi controlled leases and guard posts, the sale of protection, construction, and markets. One would expect that any town would have had one *cosca* to protect and extend the activities of all local mafiosi. *Cosca* development, however, followed the pattern of factionalism described in Chapter 8. That is, relations between local mafiosi were inherently competitive since there were rarely enough resources to go around. Because an important resource was extralocal political protection and patronage, competition was structured by political forces at the national level. Thus, in the decades of boss politics in Sicily many towns supported rival mafia cliques, each attached to a different *civile* faction (see Blok 1974: 120–127; Hess 1973: 129). As with the *civile* bosses, protection and patronage were relatively more important than anything one could hope to gain by taking particular policy positions, so that rival *cosche* formed around patrons, not issues.

Just as single towns in western Sicily could support rival *cosche* or not, depending on the degree of local competition and the inputs from the national government, *cosche* of neighboring towns could compete or ally. Clique leaders of nearby towns were usually well connected through the tradition of banqueting, through ties of friendship, coparenthood, and sometimes through marriage. Leaders from two towns might ally to resist the expansionist tendencies of a third town's mafiosi. Mafiosi from one town might acquire domain in another. But the resulting structures were consortia and not federations. The parties to them were equal and not bound in a fixed hierarchical arrangement. Blok's fascinating description shows how members of one *cosca* encroached on domain belonging to the members of another *cosca*. When the latter group backed down, it was forced to pay tribute (1974: 161–171). Hegemony of this sort was common, but it did not transcend the borders of more than two or three towns and it did not last long. Mafia as a whole was acephalous, like so many other structures of western Sicily, including the structure of the transportation network and markets (Blok 1974: 145).

A contrary impression stems from external intervention. National level elites attempting to mobilize political support in Sicily encouraged not only the formation of rival *cosche* within towns, but *cosche* with a common focus across towns. If a national elite favored a particular *cosca* or its leaders, the head of the group might be deemed "head of the Sicilian mafia." As Mosca observed, however, this expression simply meant "he has good relations with a few *cosche*, which protect him in various activities, perhaps electoral [Mosca 1949: 232, 248]."

OMERTÀ: MAFIA AND IDEOLOGY

Mafiosi adapted to expanding state power not only through the organizational arrangements associated with the *cosca* but also by actively and self-consciously manipulating the cultural codes of western Sicily, exploiting them as ideology. In this way they were able to promote solidarity among themselves and at the same time to influence the attitudes and behavior of others (especially those who might testify against them in court). It made sense for mafiosi to become specialists in honor, friendship, and *furberia*. These codes were part of the moral lexicon of many people; they symbolized the island's distinctive qualities vis-à-vis northern Italy and the rest of Europe; and they were instrumental in competition for power.

We have already discussed the use by mafiosi of the code of friendship. It was the social glue of the *cosca*, as it was of the *massaria* complex. The codes of honor and cleverness are both represented in the famous mafia ideology of *omertà*, according to which it is a sign of weakness and cowardice to obtain satisfaction for an offense through courts of law (Mosca 1949: 228). "*Non saccio niente, ne oggi ne ieri*"—"I don't know anything about it and never did." The rule was applied with equal force in two different contexts: against outsiders who witnessed or were victims of mafia crimes and against insiders with some sort of axe to grind. Violations in either case almost automatically led to vengeance, sometimes in the form of exemplary killings in which the victim's body was symbolically mutilated to convey the reason for the murder and warn others. Only recently, and with support from north Italian publicists and fund raisers, have a few west Sicilians served as witnesses in trials of mafiosi. Previously, commitment to omertà sealed the lips of most potential witnesses, as "insufficient evidence" led to the release of countless arrested malefactors.

Obviously supported by the threat of reprisals, the ideology of omertà also struck other chords. It exploited the code of cleverness, for that code appreciates the man who has the capacity to outwit the state. Furthermore, what one does is one's own business. The rule against going to law is consistent with a general disinclination to "embroil" oneself in the affairs of others. As a friend of ours explained, "When you see two people fighting, you turn away quickly, pretending not to notice. Should you witness a theft, you do the same. Anyone who betrays a thief does it not from conscience, but to get himself embroiled with the thief or the victim." Omertà is a way of avoiding the morass of compromise and role conflict inherent in situations where people are unsure of their future relationships to the parties involved. Like breaking off ties altogether, silence before the law is a socially approved way of withdrawing from conflict without losing friends or face.

Omertà further involves a positive commitment to the idea of vendetta, according to which real men, men of honor, that is, avenge their own grievances. The linguistic root of the concept is omu, the word in the Sicilian dialect for man—uomo (Boissevain 1966b). Omu does not mean man in the abstract, but sovereign man, the kind of man whose property and dependents are respected by others because he has proven himself capable of defending them. When mafiosi proclaimed that going to law was to lose respect, people saw the logic in their argument even if they did not agree. Similarly, when local cosca leaders rushed to characterize a murder as a crime of honor, motivated by jealousy over a woman, people were well disposed to accept that interpretation since murders did sometimes occur for this reason.

As ideology, omertà helped mafiosi acquire new domains; it dulled the sharp edge of naked power and legitimated their demands. It should be noted that expansion was gradual. Rarely were non-mafiosi driven from an activity with no compensation, unless they refused to play the game. And even then, as in Mosca's example of the fruit thieves, recalcitrant victims were forgiven if they came around. Often before driving a competitor from business, mafiosi offered him the option of submitting to restrictive policies of pricing or hiring. The process of expansion was also sweetened by courteous treatment of the targets. As we noted earlier, mafiosi committed at least as many violent acts against each other as against outsiders. With regard to outsiders, in fact, emphasis was placed on making demands palatable in order to avoid excessive dependence on threats. This was done by playing on victims' and witnesses' sense of worth as men. For many it was a positive honor to be well treated by a proven mafioso, regardless of the sacrifices involved. Not only did *omertà* ensure against betrayal and confession; it assured victims that by not seeking the state's protection they, too, gained a share in respect. In this way, the expansion of mafia control, if not fully legitimate in the eyes of the population at large, was at least not repugnant to many and did not provoke widespread resentment. Mafiosi did not need overwhelming popular support to expand, but they benefited from people's sense that it was not dishonorable to refuse to cooperate with an "alien" bureaucracy. Obviously, people who gained employment through mafia—and these were not few in number—as well as people who had sought its intervention for whatever reason, gave their support.

EXPLAINING MAFIA

The problem of mafia should yield to the same analytic strategy that we utilized for cultural codes. The latter were seen to be the product of certain concrete groups in specific historical periods actively building culture in order to confront problems arising out of their historical circumstances. We emphasized that these historical circumstances were the product of Sicily's involvement in world economic systems. It was then necessary to trace the subsequent careers of these codes as well as the careers of the populations for whom the codes were, or became, relevant. To evaluate further our propositions about the conditions under which the codes originated and the conditions under which they persevered, we attempted to compare the social history of western Sicily with that of eastern Sicily as well as with other parts of the world that had been colonized by Spain.

Mafia seems clearly to have emerged in the nineteenth century, especially after 1860. The first official reference to a mafioso *cosca* appeared in the 1838 report of a Bourbon authority who noted that in the western province of Trapani many local communities supported little cliques which had powerful patrons and which deployed common funds to influence judicial proceedings. Witnesses never talked and highly placed magistrates did not want them to (Blok 1974: 95). Cliques of this sort proliferated after the unification of Italy, when for the first time and with the aid of Rizzotti's play (*I Mafiusi della Vicaria*) they became widely and publicly associated with the term *mafia*.

Clique formation was most pronounced following the overthrow of the Moderate national government in the mid-1870s. The decades of Crispi and Giolitti were crucial for the consolidation of mafia power.

Whatever forces combined in this period to encourage the proliferation of local mafia *cosche,* they were forces which affected western more than eastern Sicily. The eastern provinces—Messina, Catania, and Syracuse—are by reputation relatively clean of mafia. Newspaper accounts of mafia arrests and Rochefort's map of mafia-related murders, for example, contain virtually no cases from the east (see Map 3). Furthermore, in the orchard zone of the eastern coast, no one forces growers to hire parasitic intermediaries to protect and merchandise their crops.

What then are the circumstances which in the nineteenth century caused mafia to evolve in western Sicily? In the foregoing description we have focused on two: the threat to latifundism and to its pastoral base; and the penetration of state institutions into a broker capitalist's paradise. Neither latifundism nor broker capitalism was all that well represented in eastern Sicily, for both were consequences of a colonial dominance which had always been more pronounced in the west. In the west, moreover, both were integrated with the *massaria* complex, the institution within which rural entrepreneurs and herdsmen learned the skills which were later so relevant to mafia-style activities.

Because of its pastoral bias, arms-bearing subculture, and commitment to hospitality and friendship as instruments of commerce, the *massaria* complex is reminiscent of pastoral adaptations elsewhere. Was mafia, then, a phenomenon of pastoral displacement? In addition to our own account, several sources lend credence to the proposition that it had a pastoral undercurrent. Hess, for example, noted that mafiosi recruited shepherds whom they helped to find grazing land (1973: 113). In his early twentieth-century report, Lorenzoni wrote that goatherds would allow their animals to roam anywhere if they were not stopped by a guard's rifle. They were violent men, he said, "and often the intermediaries, executors or accomplices of mafia undertakings [1910: 142]." Barzini attributed "archaic and pastoral ways" to mafia, while Pantaleone, a Sicilian authority, suggested that control over pastures and rustling was the primary concern of mafiosi in the Sicilian interior (Barzini 1964: 263; Pantaleone 1962: 132–133). Prefect Mori, deputized by Mussolini to clean up mafia in Sicily, chose *campieri* (estate guards), carters, and herdsmen as the main targets for suppression (see Blok 1974: 182–183; D'Alessandro 1959: 106–120). We

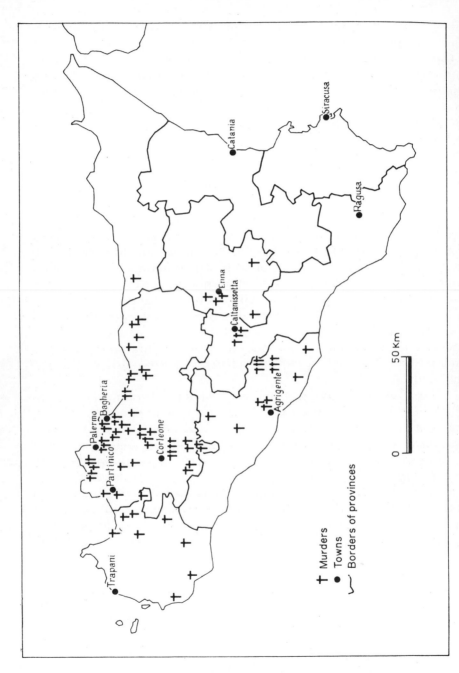

Map 3. Distribution of homicides *a Lupara* in Sicily for 10 months in 1956 and 1957 (January–May 1956 and January–May 1957). [Source: Rochefort 1961: 50; based on a report by the newspaper *L'Ora*.]

Murders †
Towns ●
Borders of provinces ⌒

Palermo
Bagheria
Partinico
Corleone
Trapani
Caltanissetta
Enna
Agrigente
Catania
Siracusa
Ragusa

0   50 Km

have already seen that during fascism, the police in Villamaura fined or arrested most of the local herdsmen, while in the community studied by Chapman shepherds "correlated highly with the criminal element [1971: 81]." Significantly, the technique most frequently associated with mafia crimes in Sicily is the *lupara,* a spray of lead fired from a shotgun, and traditionally used by shepherds to protect their flocks from wolves (*lupi*).

The close association of pastoralism with mafia raises the interesting question whether pastoralists in periods of decline elsewhere have produced mafialike institutions. Pastoral groups of northern Africa and central Asia characteristically enjoyed relationships of *"prepotenza"* with settled populations. Maintaining their mobility through the practice of transhumant or nomadic grazing, they also maintained a safe distance from political authority. A long-standing acquaintance with effective means of violence, animal theft, and the rules of self-help or vendetta encouraged them to extort resources from settled agriculturalists and from caravans passing through their territory, in exchange for protection. The "protection racket" was probably invented by ancient pastoralists.

Yet there is something amiss in the generalization that pastoralists organized mafias, because in the great majority of cases they did not have to do so. (Mafialike formations among shepherds in the mountains of northeast Sicily, in Calabria, and, more recently, in Sardinia may well be exceptions which prove the rule.) Their distance from settled peoples and from state institutions gave them all the protection they needed, and when they were subjected to pressure, as they frequently were, they attacked or moved away. Not until the mid-twentieth century have agricultural societies succeeded in the control of herdsmen, and then only because of the technological and organizational advances of two world wars, advances which leave little opportunity for the formation of mafias (Krader 1955; Lattimore 1962; Spooner 1973).

In comparing Sicilian pastoralists to pastoral groups elsewhere we must first remember that the *massaria* was more than a pastoral enterprise. An integral part of the specialized role to which Sicily was relegated by historical world-systems, the *massaria* organized the cultivation of wheat as well as pastoral husbandry. Certainly rural entrepreneurs had a stake in the pastoral economy. The most important among them, the *gabellotti,* were characteristically owners of large flocks and herds. In addition, as mafia evolved, displaced shepherds and goatherds served as a rich source of recruits with the kind of skills needed to make good *picciotti.* Rural entrepreneurs, however, engaged in both pastoral and agrarian activities and became mafiosi not only as a result of the decline of pastures but because the gamut of *massaria*-linked enterprises—from rustling to the commerce of grain—was undermined.

The close association of pastoral and agrarian uses of the land which characterized latifundism in western Sicily indicates that, unlike true pastoral conditions, the countryside of this region was not a discrete ecological niche. As compared with an uncultivated mountain range, or the arid periphery of a cultivated plain, it was neither removed from nor safe from the pressures of a world economy. On the contrary, western Sicily's virtually deserted and desertlike appearance was a consequence of these pressures since the great latifundist lords of the past had cut down forests, destroyed villages and village agriculture, abandoned roads and regional markets in order to promote a colonial mode of production.

Massarie were a detached part of a larger whole, not an independent productive enterprise. The typical *massaria* rarely housed women, children, and old people. Indeed, it was also separated from most of its labor force: The peasants who worked the land lived in town and even the shepherds and estate guards had homes and families there. When subjected to the challenges of the nineteenth century, the *massarie* were safe for a while but ultimately not far enough removed from the rest of the social order to offer long-term refuge to brigands and their entrepreneurial friends. In truly pastoral societies, mountain or desert redoubts allowed such specialists to resist state power and competing economic interests. In Sicily, *massaria*-linked men eventually had to enter the legal society, but did so with the aid of a political shield, the *cosca* and *omertà*. Mafia was in effect part of the compromise between the retention and the ruin of a pastoral-biased, rural entrepreneurial past. An endemic form of rural entrepreneurship, including banditry, survived, but only as its practitioners increased their organizational overhead.

The contrast between pastoral societies and the *massaria* suggests why, under pressure, the latter but not the former incubated an institution such as mafia. It does not, however, provide a complete explanation, for *massarie* also existed in the latifundist zones of southern Italy, but mafialike phenomena did not develop there as they did in Sicily. This brings us to the second circumstance which contributed to the rise of mafia: the articulation of new state forms with a broker capitalist past (analyzed so thoroughly by Blok 1974). This articulation was rather different in Sicily from that of the Italian south.

In southern Italy broker capitalism, although present and important, was historically less pronounced than in Sicily. At least from the time of the Bourbon administration in the eighteenth century it did not dominate the regional capital at Naples or the area around it. This area resembled eastern Sicily, the *"babbo"* part of the island, where people had civic pride and repaired their statues (see Chapter 5). Like eastern Sicily, the area around Naples was characterized by diversified agriculture and indigenous urban development since the time of the Greeks. In contrast, the area around Palermo was latifundist. There broker capitalist grain barons dominated the affairs of the capital and monopolized the island's links with the outside world. In southern Italy, the latifundist provinces of Basilicata and Apulia were geographically and socially removed from the capital, and the great grain barons of the region failed to enjoy what their Sicilian counterparts thrived on—power roughly equal to that of the crown. They were not partners in a diarchy of power, but subordinates in a hierarchy.

In southern Italy of the early nineteenth century, state institutions expanded along lines laid down by the Napoleonic code. This never happened in Sicily, where an English-style constitution failed to establish provinces or touch ecclesiastical lands and left the power of the baronage largely intact. After the unification of Italy in 1860 and the subsequent challenge of American wheat, southern Italy, no less than Sicily, experienced a brigand war. Bandits ravaged the countryside, just as in Sicily. State troops subdued them more quickly, however, because of the help they received from an indigenous bourgeoisie—small and medium landholders, artisans, shopkeepers, and professionals, some of whom constituted a kind of development elite (Molfese 1964). In Sicily this force was considerably weaker and the region's experience with state power more shallow. *Furbo* broker capitalists, with their pockets full of money, had frustrated the formation of such elements, even in the east (Graziano 1973: 10–11).

Looking back over the rise of mafia, we see that its origins as an institution and its continuity over time must derive from the fact that forces sympathetic and indebted to mafiosi controlled not only the agrotowns of the latifundist west and interior, but the island's capital, Palermo, as well. Externally generated administrative structures and structures of coercion had no way of reaching Sicilians except by this route. And when Sicilians manipulated these structures, as mafiosi did the courts and police, the existence of a broker capitalist capital in Palermo screened out interference from the state. Comparison with southern Italy suggests that without the involvement of the regional capital there would have been a less effective political shield. That shield, of course, evolved over the years, enhanced and strengthened by the obligations that national powerholders incurred with the regional elite and hence with mafiosi.

Theoretically, the hegemony of industrial powers in the nineteenth and twentieth centuries and, above all, of industrializing northern Italy, should have sent the rural entrepreneurs and shepherds of western Sicily into decline, as it rendered less useful their unique capacity to travel through the countryside, to dispense protection, and to organize communications and commerce, and as it eliminated pastures. Instead these social groups retained their integrity and their capitalist potential, partly through the use of violent means in which they were already skilled, and through the manipulation of cultural codes. This does not mean, however, that mafia can be traced to Sicilian "character" or culture. The codes of honor, friendship, and cleverness all have a wider distribution than western Sicily (for example, they are also found in southern Italy). Ultimately one must seek the reasons for mafia in the political economy of Italy in the industrial age, that is, in the political dependence of north Italian industrial interests on regional magnates throughout Italy. The particular group which dominated Sicily had many debts to rural entrepreneurs and shepherds.

MAFIA AND THE WORLD-SYSTEM

During and after the second world war, mafia became an international phenomenon. *Cosche* appeared on other continents and some mafiosi involved themselves in the long-distance shipment, refinement, and distribution of drugs. This development was linked to the great Sicilian migrations of the twentieth century, to the Allied occupation of Sicily at the end of the war, and to the strategic location of the Mediterranean islands in relation to the drug traffic. It must also have benefited from the protection of powerful figures in legitimate business and industry—from a few merchant, industrial, and finance capitalists of metropolitan core societies, especially the United States. Notwithstanding the worldwide diffusion of mafia networks, and the wealth accumulated by American mafiosi, it is doubtful that mafia has transcended a broker capitalist relationship with these metropolitan elites. Mafia domain is still acquired and kept only by diverting considerable money and energy to the classic mafia task—immunization of mafiosi from arrest and trial.

Given their expansion on an international plane, it is nevertheless an interesting question whether mafia networks have added to the capital resources of Sicily. It would seem that the opposite is true. If anything, mafiosi in Sicily helped seal the fate of the island as a source of export labor in the twentieth century, even though they themselves were capital, not labor. They did this in their vigilante role as henchmen of the *latifundisti* in a society torn by an intense struggle for land. As Blok has stressed in his work on mafia, there was a close relationship between its success and the failure of a peasant revolt (1974). In the postwar period, mafiosi maintained their repressive role, using intimidation and murder to thwart attempts to organize sharecroppers and day laborers. Failed peasant revolt meant failure of a program for bonification in western Sicily and the conversion of this region to diversified agriculture. Luxury crops have crept in, but they are poorly capitalized and poorly planned, and the "mafias of the orchards" place an additional drain on the profits derived from them. Rather than enhance the position of Sicily vis-à-vis external dominants, mafiosi have in many ways made it worse, perpetuating the latifundium beyond its time and living like a great parasite off other, more promising endeavors. The freedom of movement which mafiosi have won in relation to the outside world is largely theirs, not Sicily's.

chapter 10

Modernization without
Development

Agrarian reform was a failure in western Sicily, leaving untouched many of the essential features of the latifundist regime and landscape. And broker capitalism persisted, not only in the crystallized form of mafia, but generally throughout society. Yet, in spite of these interrelated manifestations of continuity with the preindustrial past, Sicily has changed a great deal since World War II. Because many of the changes follow upon its role as an exporter of unskilled labor, we comprehend them as a process of modernization in the absence of real development.

The distinction is important; whereas both modernization and development imply change, development alters a society's relationship to the world-system of which it is a part and as a result enhances its ability to cope with that system. Modernization, by contrast, perpetuates a relationship of inequality and exploitation between a dependent area and its metropolitan core. Changes are the consequence not of a self-initiated ordering of priorities but of diffusion from the core. Even so, the process of modernization can lead to substantial increases in employment opportunities and in the standard of living—often more quickly and dramatically than can development. This chapter describes such modifications. But, it finds in them little reason for optimism about the future. In the absence of meaningful regional autonomy, there is little to discourage a rapid degradation of resources through fragmentation. Fragmentation always existed on the land in Sicily, and it continues to do so today. But today countless other activities and assets are divided as well. The consequence is similar to what Geertz described for Indonesia in *Agricultural Involution*: "shared poverty and social elasticity" extend into urban as well as rural domains (1968). We will see that this condition perpetuates most aspects of past cultural codes.

EVIDENCE OF CHANGE

Before 1945, houses in Villamaura lacked indoor plumbing; by 1950, only 25% of the dwellings did not have these facilities; in 1960, only 2%. The number of bathtubs tripled in this period and electricity was extended to nearly every household. On our last visit, in 1971, radios, television sets, washing machines, sewing machines, and refrigerators were already following the power lines into hundreds of homes. Meanwhile there was a rise in per capita income and a marked rise in home and automobile ownership (there were some 15 automobiles in Villamaura before the war; now there must be several hundred). More than anything else, remittance money and welfarism have fostered expansion in construction and education. Everywhere returned migrants want to improve their houses or build new ones. During the decade 1950–1960, the labor force engaged in construction in Villamaura increased by 40% (from 284 to 398 persons). Most of the new houses are designed by local draftsmen–surveyors (*geometri*); there are a few architects and engineers, but they are usually in the larger cities.

The draftsmen–surveyors in the agrotowns are numerous as a result of expanding educational opportunities. A *geometra* in Villamaura recalled that 25 years ago he graduated in Palermo as 1 of a class of 50, from the only school in western Sicily that offered training in his field. Today he would be one of thousands who are graduated each year from both public and private institutions, located in rural towns as well as cities. Training schools for agronomists, accountants, and elementary schoolteachers have mushroomed in similar fashion, as better-off peasants, artisans, and returned migrants invest in their children's education. Although the resident population of Villamaura declined in the decade 1950–1960, from 8054 to 7098, the number of people with high school degrees or the equivalent increased from 125 to 171; the number of university graduates, from 36 to 60; and the number with diplomas from intermediate schools, from 136 to 295.

Expanding educational opportunities have noticeably altered the occupational structure of Sicily, contributing further to the island's quite modern aspect. In the decade under consideration, the percentage of the population employed in agriculture declined in Villamaura from 65% to 60%; for the province of Agrigento, from 61% to 50% (ISTAT 1955, 1965). In Sicily as a whole, employment increased 14.5% in industry, 23.8% in commerce, and 26.6% in transport and communication (Renda 1963: 165–166). The bureaucracies that administered the regional government and the various reform programs employed thousands of Sicilians, many with intermediary and high school degrees. At the same time, the demographic profile of Sicily changed so dramatically that it looks like that of the developed world. Both men and women marry at a later age than before the war, and their families are smaller. Four or five living children used to be considered an ideal and many families were larger; now newlywed couples hope for only two. Behind this change lies a new set of aspirations for one's children which rest on education and the acquisition of skills.

The population is also more urban. While the rural towns of the interior have lost population through migration, the cities show a net increase. Palermo grew by about 20% between 1950 and 1960. Agrigento, the capital of the province in which Villamaura is located, grew in the same period from 40,500 to 48,000. The largest growth was registered by the eastern cities of Syracuse and Catania (ISTAT 1955, 1965; Renda 1963: 115). Finally, postwar change has furthered the Italianization of Sicily, with a consequent erosion of the regional dialect and of beliefs and customs associated with the code of honor. Crucial to this erosion is the introduction of new models of behavior, propelled into the south and Sicily by mass education and television. Crucial, too, is the now vigorous and decisive penetration of state institutions into the social affairs of these regions. During the 1930s, the Fascist government increased the punishment for so-called crimes of honor, or crimes of passion, from a minimum of 18 days' imprisonment to a minimum of 3 years, and from a maximum of 3 to a maximum of 7 years. Yet the law continued to recognize the right of a citizen to take blood vengeance upon discovering adultery, rape, or seduction involving a woman in his family. Considered a concession to southern "folkways," this right is under attack in the Italian Parliament and in the national and regional press. Some Villamaurese resent north Italian intrusion into this arena and advocate reversion to the pre-Fascist penalties, but the young and especially the educated members of the community feel that "the right to kill" for whatever reason results more often in injustice than in justice. Certainly it has served as camouflage for numerous mafia crimes.

In 1966 there was a young west Sicilian woman who, with the support of her family, courageously refused to marry a *picciotto* who had kidnapped and raped her. (Ordinarily, both the young woman and her father would consent to the marriage in order to rectify the problem of honor created by the loss of her chastity.) In this case, she received moral and financial support not only from her family but also from the (national) press and some of the people of her town. According to Cronin, the people of her town petitioned the government in Rome, "asking that [her] father be made a Knight of the Italian Republic for his courage and valor [Cronin 1970: 53]." She remained steadfast in her refusal to marry the young hoodlum, supported by her position as a cause celébrè in the national press, and her "suitor" was eventually sentenced to 22 years in prison for kidnap and rape. In the wake of this event there was word that several other young men had been refused in similar circumstances and it looked as if kidnap and rape were becoming less secure strategies of courtship. Events such as this and the recent legalization of divorce in Italy cannot help but undermine some of the more stringent etiquettes associated with the honor code. Even mourning customs have begun to change as younger women, following a north Italian trend, look favorably upon the adoption of gray as a symbol of death. Older women, observing the erosion of older ways, worry that "today, the death of a kinsman means no more than the death of a dog."

MODERNIZATION AT A PRICE

One could, by emphasizing data on living standard, urbanization, education, changing sexual mores, and so on, build a case that Sicily—the absence of agricultural transformation and industrial development notwithstanding—has narrowed the gap between itself and the industrial Western societies and will, in the future, continue to narrow it still further. Social scientists in the past have often measured growth by such global indices as percentage of population employed in nonagricultural pursuits and the rate of consumption of radios and electrical appliances. What matters is not just these figures, but how they are possible and how they stack up against, and relate to, other indices of change.

In the mid-1960s, for example, Sicilian average income was half that of Italy as a whole and about one-quarter of the island's population remained illiterate (Mack Smith 1968b: 542). Moreover, the changes of the postwar period are the result of great sacrifice and unstable sources of income: emigration remittances and welfaristic investment by the state. Since the late nineteenth century, migration has been Italy's "safety valve"—a way of preserving the social order against the threat of political unrest. Upon being questioned after the war as to what plans the national government had for unemployed Sicilians, a prominent national leader said they should "learn foreign tongues." Since that time, Italy's balance of payments surplus has been entirely attributable to emigration remittances from abroad (Doty 1967).

Until recently, the great majority of postwar migrants spent only a few years in residence in the host country, bringing their saved earnings back to Sicily. Technically they were commuters, not migrants. Yet they and their families paid a big price for the increased income. Emigration removed men between the ages of 25 and 40 from their families and from the community. Many were married, but living and working in northern Europe, they were strangers to their children. They came home to visit only for a few weeks at Christmastime or during the summer. Members of a migrant worker's family were not as a rule allowed to enter the host country unless they, too, had a contract to work. Even if they were allowed to enter and reside there, the cost of living made it a difficult, if not impossible, project. The host countries did everything they could to discourage their "guest laborers" (Holland's euphemism for migrant workers) from taking up permanent residence and claiming the rights of citizenship.

Even today most wives stay home, where they remain the unhappy prisoners of the sexual code. Neighborhood gossip, still a formidable arbiter of behavior, imposes on women whose husbands are away, no less than on those with husbands in jail, virtually the same rules it imposes on widows. That these rules have been somewhat relaxed in recent years is little solace to the young wife of a migrant laborer or the young woman who cannot marry because there is a shortage of men. The migrants themselves often live in

"Emigration removed men between the ages of 25 and 40 from their families and from the community." [Photo by Nicola Scafidi.]

company barracks or rented rooms near the places where they work. Even in northern Italy, unskilled workers from the south and Sicily live in enclaves and may be the object of racist slurs. Most spend as little money as possible on themselves and work as much overtime as they can in order to invest in their families' future at home.

Perhaps one can justify such sacrifices by the material rewards they yield. Many migrants see it this way, no matter how much they dislike working in a strange country. Many others do not, for there are frequent personal tragedies associated with this way of life. In addition, migrants know that the relationship between Sicily and the rest of Europe is precarious. It depends not on the migrant's ambition and effort, but on the economic cycles, the booms and recessions of the host countries. So much does the European economy govern the economy of Sicily that rumors of cutbacks in German or Swiss factories can bring a halt to housing starts in a town like Villamaura, where new building depends almost exclusively on the credit generated by emigration remittances. Cutbacks in construction are doubly threatening for it is this sector of the Sicilian economy which absorbs the great majority of reentering migrant workers. Migrants worry that in the long run they will have little to show for their labors.

UNDEREMPLOYMENT AND FRAGMENTATION IN AGRICULTURE

The threat of impending unemployment casts a shadow on the glittering symbols of modernization—the new houses, appliances, and diplomas which remittance money buys. More symptomatic of dependency, however, is a chronic state of underemployment manifested in overcrowding and resource fragmentation regardless of economic sector. We shall begin a description of various occupations with agriculture because in many ways it serves as a model for the rest.

Fragmentation of agricultural resources has always been a problem in Sicily. Indeed, it is an endemic condition of Mediterranean agriculture and has probably been so for centuries. We discussed the reasons for this in Part I. The pressure of expanding empires on the one hand, of livestock-raising on natural pastures on the other, operated as a kind of pincer on cultivated land. Where landlordism and large estates were widespread, as in western Sicily, they intensified the pressure on peasant holdings. Here, in the aftermath of failed agrarian reform, fragmentation worsened, exacerbated not only by the breakup of holdings, but by rising population. Land redistributed but not transformed quickly lost its coherence and peasants could not escape the condition of plural occupation. Of the 8000 cadastral entries for Villamaura in 1965, 1724, or nearly one-fourth, were for less than 0.5 hectares and 3000 were for less than 1 hectare. Plural ownership held for many entries; there were 8000 entries but over 11,000 proprietors. In one extreme case, a holding of 0.8 hectares was jointly owned by four brothers and sisters (540/600), two cousins (20/600), an uncle (30/600), and another cousin (10/600). And we remember the 0.05 hectares divided in parts of 601/832 and 231/832, mentioned in Chapter 4.

To compensate for fragmented assets, peasants in Villamaura frequently supplement cultivation of the land with other activities. For example, given the proper political connections, a day laborer may find 60 days' work on a municipal construction project organized by the town and funded by the state. A sharecropper might gather palm leaves for the women of his neighborhood who weave them into brooms which he sells. A wealthier peasant (*borgese*), alone or in partnership, might speculate on wheat or purchase a steer to be fattened for market. He may also have a part interest in a truck, a grain mill, an olive press, a construction firm, or a grocery store. If he belongs to an agrarian cooperative, this will add still another fragment to his family's income (J. Schneider 1969).

Plural occupation and fragmented holdings reinforce the age-old complexities of Mediterranean agriculture. Landholdings do not give rise to integrated enterprises; rather, each head of household combines a variety of assets and activities in a loosely articulated whole, coherent because it is his. Typically he works several widely scattered plots under different annual contractual arrangements. If he keeps a few goats for their milk, he contracts with a goatherd who rents someone else's land for pasture. Meanwhile, he rents out portions of his land to a different goatherd. Today, of course, fewer cultivators keep goats. With the aid of government subsidies, many, however, have invested in agricultural machinery. The deployment of machines is much like the deployment of goats. Peasant X, for example, is part owner of a wheat harvesting combine which services the cultivators in a particular zone. Only if his wheat land happens to be in that zone will his machine harvest his wheat: Otherwise he will rent the services of someone else's machine, just as his goats feed on someone else's forage, and someone else's goats feed on his forage.

The vicissitudes of a single moderately large holding illustrate the complexity of economic life for much of the rural population. The land in question is about 50 hectares. Part of it is cultivated in wheat, the remainder is left to pasturage. In 1965, the owner contracted with a coalition of small holders and shepherds who between them owned several hundred head of sheep and a few cattle. The owner put up the land and seed; he paid for half the cost of the first plowing and half of the threshing; and he was responsible for seeking contributions from the state to support improvements on the property (a road, a fence, some trees, the construction of stalls). He also owned some animals which he added to the herds of the partnership. He was entitled to receive half of the meat and cheese which the combined herds produced and half of the wheat cultivated on the property. The partners, in addition to their own animals, owned a tractor, and according to the agreement they were responsible for half of the cost of the first plowing, all of the second and third plowings, and half of the threshing. The group also rented pasturage from other land-owners since the 50 hectares did not provide sufficient grazing land, especially when part of it was planted in wheat. And they rented out the services of their tractor by the hour to other cultivators. As is typical in western Sicily, the animals and the tractor were only partially committed to the land in question; they were bound through various short-term arrangements to other operations as well.

Although clearly indicative of change, agricultural machinery is a good example of modernization without development. Offsetting the shortage of very low cost labor (lost to emigration) machines have had little impact on production. Most people see them as small-scale capital investments for part-time speculation, not as the foundation of a new mode of production. Like virtually all industrial products used in Sicily, they are imported. Many are large "Iowa-type" harvesting combines, poorly suited to the mountainous terrain and scattered small holdings of the interior and subject to frequent breakdowns. Because of their unsuitability, the machines contribute to soil erosion and the deterioration of the land (Rochefort 1961: 147). They generate a profit to their owners largely because the government subsidizes wheat and pays up to 70% of the purchase price of the machine. Even with these supports there is intense competition among the coalitions that own farm machinery. There are simply more machines than wheat production in the area can support. In some towns mafia cliques monopolize the harvest (see Chapter 9). But whether because of mafia or unrestricted competition, many operators are forced to drive their clumsy combines long distances on the highway in order to follow the harvest from the coastal lowlands (where grain ripens early) up into the mountains of the interior. In western Sicily sophisticated machines do not create an advanced technology of production.

UNDEREMPLOYMENT AND FRAGMENTATION IN NONAGRICULTURAL SECTORS

Symptomatic of Sicily's dependent role in today's world economy, crowding and fragmentation of resources are no less true of sectors considered urban than they are of agriculture. As John Davis noted for a rural town on the south Italian mainland: "The model of the fragmented or scattered peasant holding applies with little modification to all forms of economic enterprise, from householding to metal working, from lawyering to school teaching. . . . While it is [easy] to distinguish a peasant from a schoolteacher or lawyer, their tactics for earning a competence are not very different [1969: 70]." Schoolteachers, lawyers, shopkeepers, artisans, construction workers— indeed, nearly everyone—supplement their occupations with other activities and with ownership of land where possible, just as nearly all peasant landowners supplement their livings with other, nonagricultural activities. In other words, at all social levels resources are broken into units too small to sustain integrated enterprises. In most economic sectors, there are more people than there is room for them, and new opportunities dissolve as many people attempt to exploit them.

Of course, the man who is forced to engage in a variety of disparate activities is also free to take advantage of the opportunities that come his way. His career is not overly structured, his interests are dispersed, and he can enter a new field on an ad hoc basis without committing all of his assets to any particular venture, or committing any significant asset on a long-term basis. As with rural entrepreneurs, the principal organizational device for this diversification is the coalition, which is ideally adapted to the fluid conditions of a fragmented economic domain. Also like rural entrepreneurs, only with less brilliant results, people in overcrowded occupational categories cope by wheeling and dealing.

In Villamaura today there is a plethora of artisans. In 1912, when the population reached its zenith at about 11,000 citizens, there were 5 tailors. The population had declined to fewer than 8000 by 1960, at which time there were 15 tailors. During the same period, the number of carpenters and furniture makers jumped from 14 to 27; the number of blacksmiths (now ironworkers), from 8 to 12. According to the communal records, the shoemakers declined in number from 27 to 25, but many shoemakers claim that during the 1950s they were more than 60 strong. Remittances from the earlier migration to America had, it seems, enabled many peasant families to apprentice at least one son to a local craftsman. The social geographer Rochefort, who surveyed the economic and social conditions of Sicily in the late 1950s, also found "too large a number of artisans" in settlements of the western interior: 10 shoemakers, 4 blacksmiths, and 5 barbers in the community of Roccamena, population 3200; 12 barbers in the yet smaller town of Giuliana; 25 barbers, 45 shoemakers, 30 carpenters, 30 tailors, and 25 blacksmiths for the 8300 residents of Bisacquino (Rochefort 1961: 261).

Ironically, the increased number of artisans parallels a drastic decrease in the peasant market for locally crafted items, as modern manufacturers flood western Sicily with factory made shoes, clothes, electric and safety razors, furniture, and so forth. The typical artisan engages in a number of supplementary activities. He may own a share in a wheat harvester or thresher; he may speculate in wheat; or he may be part owner of a steer, along with a shepherd who will fatten it for market. Many artisans emigrate. Others use their shops to sell a variety of commodities not necessarily related to their craft. A shoemaker, for instance, might sell (in addition to the shoes he still makes) factory-made shoes, bottled gas, turpentine, paint, insecticides, light bulbs, suitcases, razor blades, notebooks, chewing gum, and other sundries. But this puts him into the category of shopkeeper, which is equally inflated.

There is a gift store in Villamaura from which one can purchase long underwear; an appliance store that sells bottled gas and gifts; a tobacco store that sells plumbing fixtures and chandeliers; and a brick maker who markets construction materials and caskets. The town has licensed 8 yard good stores, but at least 15 shops sell yard goods; 14 sell hardware and 10 sell electrical appliances—generally as a sideline. Since overhead is relatively low, and storekeeping is not the merchant's only source of income, many of these activities can coexist in a limited market, each providing a very minimal profit for its owner. "When the sun shines, it shines on everyone," so when one man opens a coffee bar along the national highway at the edge of town and seems to be doing well, two others are likely to follow suit within 6 months. None of the three cafés can be a resounding success, given the existence of the other two, but then resounding success is not the issue. Nor is the situation very different for expensive commodities, such as major appliances and furniture. These are usually sold on consignment—the local retailer pays all or part of the wholesale price only after he has sold the item. Consequently, one can go into the retail appliance or furniture business with a minimum of investment capital. All that is required is floor space, a small amount of working capital, and the necessary contacts through friends and friends of friends to secure a license and a franchise from the manufacturer and establish a clientele. Villamaura has 15 licensed outlets for furniture and appliances.

The construction trades (23 stores sell construction materials), nominally an "industrial" sector of the west Sicilian economy, also reflect a chronic fragmentation of assets, to which people adapt by making short-term arrangements. In Villamaura, apart from public works (roads, sewers, public buildings), construction is confined to single houses, renovations or additions to houses, and summer houses, or *villini* (little villas). The latter are built in the mountains to the north of the town, many of them with state subsidies under the fiction that they are farm buildings. Construction is thus small scale, although five "high-rise" (five or six storey) apartment buildings were up or under construction when we left. Four leading construction firms, three of them organized by skilled masons who are sons or grandsons of master craftsmen, employ other master builders and 10–30 unskilled (and seriously underpaid) day laborers, depending on seasonal demand. Over a dozen former employees have become masters and gone into business for themselves, making a total of 18 licensed firms by 1971. Each firm is a somewhat shaky operation requiring the input of many outsiders. The firms, for example, do not own much of the construction equipment they use; rather, they rent trucks, lifting devices, cement mixers, and even storage space from other people who are not themselves builders but who have invested in the construction trades. Indeed, their most important assets are their reputation for competence in their trade and their network of friends and contacts, especially in the various levels of government that regulate construction.

Such arrangements are, if anything, more pronounced in large urban centers. Much useful information came to light after the infamous "collapse of Agrigento" on July 19, 1966. On that day, a quarter of this provincial capital was evacuated as an earth slide of major proportions destroyed four large buildings and so severely damaged many others that an entire section of the city was declared uninhabitable. The slide was caused by a combination of factors: the subsoil composition, underground water flowing unregulated from springs, leaking aquaducts and sewers, and the enormous weight of large buildings that had been constructed without proper foundations on the crest and sides of the hill on which the city stands. The earthslide was the culmination of more than 10 years of intensive activity in building construction, spurred by migration into the city, increased incomes, easy credit, and the cavalier attitude of local, provincial, and regional authorities toward building codes and regulations.

During this period of construction boom, almost anyone could become a contractor, and many did; among 176 construction firms in Agrigento, only 6 could be considered large-scale and stable operations. The others were "dilettantes, improvised builders, ex-peasants, ex-laborers, petit bourgeois, lawyers, elementary schoolteachers, professors of philosophy, bureaucrats. A bank functionary who has a stipend of 140,000 lire [$235] per month constructed a 100 million lire building [Jannuzzi and Viola 1966: 6]."

The "improvised" builders were handicapped by the lack of "any sensibility, tradition, technical capacity or professional experience [Martuscelli 1966: vii]." Moreover, they were seriously undercapitalized. A firm could own a minimum of construction equipment and—as in Villamaura—arrange with others for the use of much necessary machinery. A builder and his associates rarely bought land on which to build; they acquired it under a contract of exchange (permuta): The original owner of the land had proprietary rights to some of the apartments in the new building, and the builder took title to the land and the air rights on it. This space served as collateral for bank loans and ensured credit from firms that supplied construction materials even before it was utilized for construction. Thus most of the "improvised" builders were constantly skating on thin ice—they had to sell unbuilt apartments in order to meet payments on loans and supplies. More than a few went bankrupt, but enough survived long enough to build the city that came tumbling down. Each building that was constructed required a coalition of landowner, builder, lawyers, engineers, officials at various levels of government, and others—various suppliers, bankers, and mediators. Perhaps needless to say, mafiosi played a role at all levels—indeed, the very fragmentation of resources in the construction field has increased its vulnerability to mafia expansion. Each building, as long as it stood, was testimony (in reinforced concrete) to the efficacy of noncorporate strategies of entrepreneurship in western Sicily.

Minor deviations from building codes—a structure taller than the prescribed limit, personal use of public property, a house built too close to the street, a toilet or stairway improperly placed—are a matter of routine in most communities, easily arranged through friendship ties and often necessary. They become problematic only when challenged by unhappy neighbors, whose resentment may be motivated by some other, unrelated issue. One would have to argue that the local officials of Villamaura exercised considerable restraint in the interest of public safety and equity. Not so in Agrigento, where the private use of public domain was carried to unparalleled extremes and was a factor in the city's collapse. For two decades prior to the disaster, local officials collaborated in the violation of height limits, obstruction of panoramic views, illegal uses of public space, and faulty construction techniques. Characteristically, a first license would be issued to approve a structure of 29 meters, already 4 meters above the maximum. The builder then applied for and received a second license permitting him to build to 32 meters. By the time this new license had been issued, he had finished construction to 40 meters, for which the city would issue a third license, ex post facto. According to two observers, "large sectors of the local population lived for years from the commerce of [building] permits. . . . It was the most lucrative commerce of the city. Just as there is a [state] monopoly of salt and tobacco, in Agrigento there was a monopoly on 'exceptions' for building construction [Jannuzzi and Viola 1966: 7]."

EDUCATIONAL INVOLUTION

As crowded as are commerce and construction is the rapidly growing field of education. We will here concentrate on the teacher-training schools and the fate of their graduates who attempt to find a secure tenure against overwhelming odds. There are two kinds of training institution (*scuola magistrale*) for prospective elementary schoolteachers: public, state-run schools; and private schools accredited by the state. The former have the reputation of being somewhat more serious, more demanding of their students, while many of the latter are known to be "diploma mills." A private school in Montebello attracts students from all over western Sicily, many of whom have not been able to meet the requirements of the more rigorous state institutions. Two college graduates from a distant town, Sant'Antonio, founded this school, which enrolls about 200 students. One of the founders was active in the Republican party, which then controlled the regional commission of public instruction, and there is little doubt that he used his political connections to promote the new school. It was a business venture, inspired by the observation that many young people from Montebello and surrounding towns were traveling to Sant'Antonio to attend the *scuola magistrale* there. The two founders, supported by their contacts in the Republican party, formed a coalition with the then mayor of Montebello (who later became secretary of the school) and with the mother superior of the local orphanage, who arranged for the school to rent the first floor of that establishment (built with funds most of which had been donated by Montebellesi living in America). The founders then hired teachers from the ranks of unemployed college and *magistrale* graduates, some of whom were from Montebello.

Their strategy made sense. Any school being established in a community like Montebello must enlist the support of local interests by selectively hiring local personnel. A "chain" of agrarian institutes attempting to found a branch in this town in 1966 was unsuccessful for this reason: Having been staffed entirely with outsiders it got so little cooperation from the local administration, and met so much hostility from local teachers, that its directors finally moved it to another town.

The *magistrale* of Montebello is accredited by the national Ministry of Public Instruction, which also administers the final comprehensive examination for teacher certification. The major stumbling block for students who would like to qualify themselves to compete for teaching positions is this examination, in which they are at the mercy of an examining commission consisting of six outsiders (appointed by the ministry) and one local member, usually the principal of the school. Virtually every father whose son or daughter is about to take this certifying exam goes to considerable effort to have his child "recommended" to one or more of the examination commissioners. It would of course be best if the recommendation came from a close friend of the commissioner or from some powerful figure in the commissioner's home area or political party, but this is no easy task to arrange.

The names (but not the addresses) of the examiners are published in the newspapers 2 weeks prior to the examination. The first step, therefore, is to locate the target commissioners in geographic and social space. Where do they live, and whom do they know (or who knows them)? One of the commissioners may, of course, already be known to people in town, but this is unlikely. The problem is solvable because surnames in Sicily are highly correlated with places (reflecting a strong pattern of community endogamy in the past). If you know that Professore Di Rosa probably comes from, or has kin in, a particular town, you can then search the telephone directories of that area for his name. Once he has been located in space, it becomes a matter of following a chain of interpersonal contacts—many of them *galloppini* or political brokers—until he can be reached. A father from Villamaura (near the western coast) sought a recommendation to a commissioner of Alessandria but knew no one there. He went to a friend who was close to an important doctor in Gela (on the southeastern coast). The father, his friend, and the doctor from Gela went to the provincial health officer in Agrigento, who introduced them to his friend, a doctor from Alessandria, who in turn introduced them to the commissioner's brother (also see Boissevain 1966a). In another case, three fathers from Villamaura, together with the local Socialist party secretary, drove through the night to the northeast corner of Sicily to encounter the Socialist mayor of Messina, whom they hoped would introduce them to a commission member known to be a party activist. Sometimes the pathways leading to an examiner wind into continental Italy and require a considerable outlay for train fares and hotels. Rarely, however, is money the quid pro quo for a recommendation, or a key introduction leading to a recommendation. The currency involved is not cash but reciprocal obligation, and if a gift is made it is given as a token of respect, not as payment for services rendered. Reciprocity is often achieved through political loyalty and activity on behalf of a designated candidate at the next election.

A commissioner who accepts a recommendation can influence the candidate's prospects for success by treating him or her gently during the oral part of the examination, by grading the written part leniently, and by arguing the candidate's case before the other commissioners. One problem faced by both students and examiners, however, is the ever growing number of students who come to the examinations "recommended." Of course, some recommendations are more influential than others—that of a mafioso or an important political figure is worth more than a recommendation from one of the sisters at the orphanage where the commissioners stay. Nevertheless, there is widespread awareness that the recommendation as a strategy is losing effectiveness by becoming too common. Preference cannot be granted on the basis of a resource which virtually everyone has.[1]

---

[1] "Here is a letter of recommendation. It is signed by a parliamentary deputy . . . mimeographed, written in bureaucratic language certainly, but also familiar, paternal, good-natured. Several years ago the same deputy recommended five out of seven competitors for a single available post, with an identical letter. Now, out of 204 applications of functionaries who aspire to five available posts in a certain ministry, 182 are accompanied by one or more letters of recommendation. . . . Naturally, the one who is most recommended, or rather the 'ward' of the most influential patron will get the job [Lugato 1966]."

Students in the *magistrale* never place all their hope in the recommendation. They prepare for the examination, not only with the hope of passing it, but to avoid embarrassing their protector by making a poor showing. Those who traffic in recommendations (and they are numerous) agree that it is awkward to support a hopelessly ill-prepared student. So, students study for their exams. But they also pursue other strategies designed to increase their chances of success. An important part of the examination is a written theme on a topic assigned by the national Ministry of Education. The topic is mailed from Rome to arrive the day before the examination, wrapped in three envelopes, each bearing the seal of the ministry. The packet is given an additional seal and then locked in the school safe in the presence of several witnesses (students, faculty members, and members of the examination commission); it is removed from the safe the next day in the presence of the same witnesses, who inspect the seals to be sure that the envelopes have not been disturbed during the night. This ritual is designed to frustrate potential cheaters and also to sanctify the proceedings.

During the examination, students inside and confederates outside the school go through a variety of maneuvers, the aim of which is to get the examination question out, and a well-researched answer back in again, before the allotted 5-hour time period ends. In each succeeding year in recent history, the state has increased its security measures, while the students' countermeasures have become more ingenious. The year that we were in Sicily, the state went all out to make the schools secure. In Montebello, the school's windows were sealed shut, doors locked; the nuns who lived in the orphanage above the school were not allowed access to the ground floor, nor were they allowed to accept a bread delivery that morning; and the school's custodian was told not to report to work. Two carabinieri patrolled the perimeter of the building to be sure that no unauthorized persons or objects entered or left. In spite of these measures, the question was out of the building after about an hour (from a nearby building a telescope had been trained on the blackboard on which the question was written). Unfortunately, it took so long to get the answer back in that most of the students for whom it was intended did not have sufficient time to copy it.

Women students, certain that none of the examiners would search their persons, invented another approach. Under their clothing they wore a specially contrived belt that contained literally hundreds of themes copied from the books of literary essays published to prepare students for examinations. They hoped that somewhere in the belt they would have a theme that would fit the topic assigned by the ministry. Months went into the preparation of this device. With the aid of kinfolk and friends each theme had been copied onto a long strip of paper which was then folded accordianlike and stuffed into a pocket on the belt. In the first pocket was an index to the contents of the other pockets, which in some cases contained over 200 themes.

In truth, the chances of having an "accordian" which exactly coincides with the assigned topic are extremely slim; nor does a theme written by the town's leading intellectual often reenter the sealed schoolroom in time to help the candidates. All of these tactics, like the recommendations, are analogous to the unrelated, part-time, and temporary activities of the head of a family. One puts together as many different strategies as possible, in the hope that one or a few of them will pay off. One does not trust to luck or the fair play of others. Students do not organize collectively to oppose the state, the "establishment," or the school. Rather, they nibble away at the authority of these discredited institutions in ways which are truly ingenious, but ultimately ineffective.[2]

The nonobligatory secondary schools now absorb an ever increasing number of young people, especially as emigration remittances improve the life chances of small holders, day laborers, and artisans. But with few exceptions, the educational institutions do not funnel students into promising careers. Except for the state and regional bureaucracies, no sector of the economy in Sicily has grown sufficiently to accommodate more than a tiny proportion of those who are professionally trained. A closer look at the graduates of the teacher-training institutes will illustrate the problem.

To find employment in the public schools, a prospective teacher must accumulate roughly 140–160 points. Up to 10 points are given for a *magistrale* diploma, depending on the candidate's performance on the final examination; up to 40 points can be earned by taking special courses (most of which require little more than registration and payment of fees); 1 point can be earned for every 16 days of substitute teaching; and points can be earned if the candidate can secure a temporary teaching position. Finally, all candidates must take the national certification examination which is administered to tens of thousands every year in selected cities. The certification examination is given in

---

[2] Students see their plight as a common one, however, and readily share information about strategies for manipulating the educational system. They plan and execute these strategies individually or in small coalitions, but it is unusual for one student to withhold results from another. A theme entering a classroom from the outside, for example, goes first to the student or students who planned the maneuver, but then it circulates among as many other students as might have time to copy it.

two stages: Those who pass the written examination are admitted to the oral. Up to 100 points can be earned by taking this examination. Once a candidate has accumulated a certain number of points (depending on the number of jobs available nationally), he or she is placed on the national teachers' roll, which means one is *eligible* for a teaching position somewhere in Italy. No one is actually employed until there is a vacancy or until one can round up the necessary connections and recommendations to have a vacancy created. There are 10–20 times as many eligible competitors as there are positions.

Would-be teachers who are waiting for the next certification exam or, having passed the exam and been placed on the roll, are waiting for assignment, will attempt to accumulate more points and earn some money by substitute teaching in their hometowns. Regular teachers are allowed a total of 2½ months leave each year; 1 month for illness with no special justification necessary; 1 month for illness with permission; and 15 days for "personal affairs." Unemployed teachers place considerable pressure on their employed friends to take full advantage of their leave time, so that the former can earn points and money in their place. Those who do not have close friends among employed teachers will ask others to intercede for them with teachers who still have sick leave to use up. One year, in a neighboring town, an accommodating public health official "created" an epidemic of German measles among the children of regular teachers in order to justify additional sick leave, thus providing more vacancies for the substitutes.

Some teachers in search of employment also find occasional work in a state-run program that offers supplementary instruction to elementary schoolchildren. A few manage to organize a rural classroom, ostensibly giving instruction to a dozen or so shepherds' children in the countryside. Sometimes these classes are filled with children who exist only on paper. Such jobs are usually controlled by the local section of whichever political party has captured the regional office of public instruction, and they are dispensed as patronage against the promise of votes and party militancy.

The plight of the schoolteachers is shared by virtually all the professionally trained. On the occasion of one national certification exam for elementary schoolteachers held in January 1967, 135,000 candidates competed for 6000 positions. In the same month a national agency for social security examined 90,000 applicants for 700 positions. These figures reflect the crush of unemployment and underemployment at the middle levels of the social order, always worse in the south and in Sicily than in the north. Here, professionally trained people frequently seek positions for which they are overqualified. Three of Villamaura's young graduates in law from the University of Palermo were teaching French in Sardinian elementary schools; a fourth taught French at the local *magistrale*; and a fifth was a traffic policeman employed by the city of Palermo. In fact, also in 1967, there were 800 men with law degrees among the 2500 applicants for 135 positions on the force of the Palermo police department.

For most of those with professional training, emigration is difficult since they do not have the language skills necessary to compete for white-collar jobs, and their status, defined by the diploma, precludes manual labor. Many are left in limbo, unable to assume mature adult roles and quite dependent on their fathers well past the age when, in earlier times, they would have married. Some manage to combine unconnected sources of income to make a go of it. Many, however, feel frustrated by, and angry at, the rising costs of the standard of living they aspire to, and by their inability to begin making a living at all.

The combination of expanding educational opportunities and a shortage of jobs for the educated creates pressure on the public sector—its agencies and offices are grossly overstaffed. The regional government, for example, employed some 7000 people in 1966, up from 1500 just after the war. At its zenith, ERAS, the first postwar land reform agency, employed one functionary for every 30 hectares of land which it distributed and spent about one-third of its budget on administration (Rochefort 1961: 113). According to local informants, some 400 out of perhaps 1700 ERAS employees had law degrees, another 200 were schoolteachers, and there were several pharmacists. Perhaps half had some commitment to land reform; the rest looked upon the agency primarily as a sinecure. The cooperatives and industrial development agencies have similar reputations as likely places for political figures to *sistemare clienti*—to place their followers. Imagine how many more Sicilians might be gainfully employed in the countryside if these various agencies had actually transformed agriculture.

MODERNIZATION AND CULTURAL CODES

The foregoing description of life in modern Sicily contains evidence of cultural continuity with the past. Certainly the code of cleverness—*furberia*—still plays an important role: Recall the ingenious maneuvers of students and would-be teachers in response to severe overcrowding in the professions; and the contemporary myths (mentioned in Chapter 5) that contractors who spray DDT dilute it with water, while soft drink manufacturers extract juice from oranges with a hypodermic syringe. The code of friendship—*amicizia*—is also well represented, for most business partnerships, even when they are technically incorporated as joint stock associations, still fall into the category of noncorporate groups or coalitions so characteristic of broker, as opposed to industrial, capitalism. Insofar as these coalitions are unstable and vulnerable to the unilateral decisions of their members, friendship serves to reinforce trust and commitment. The celebration of friendship is still most elaborate among rural entrepreneurs—grain merchants, animal dealers, butchers, and *massariotti*. Among mafiosi it takes the form of an ideology. But while these "friends of the friends" regularly enlarge their friendship networks through lavish hospitality and feasting, eating and drinking in company is not confined to them: We also encountered this practice among local government officials and other businessmen and professionals.

There is continuity, too, in attitudes toward honor—*onore*—since many of the conditions that intensified rivalry between nuclear families in the past persist today, even if in a new form. Squeezed by inadequate opportunities, yet simultaneously encouraged by their society's chronic dependency to define their worth and status through conspicuous consumption, Sicilians are easily caught up in a web of tension, in status competition which recapitulates some themes of the past. The traditional focus on women as symbols of family honor has begun to change as young people especially reject the "right" to commit murder in defense of family honor. Similarly, disputes of all kinds now regularly end up in the courts. Nevertheless, families still jockey for position and continue to cope with rivalry and envy in the name of honor. Being *sciariatti*, or not on speaking terms, still is typical of many relationships in western Sicily.

In the countryside, for example, the age-old quarrels over boundary lines, abusive grazing, water rights, and the like occur less frequently and with less vigor, since the land itself has declined in value as a critical resource. Yet these incidents have not disappeared. During our residence in Villamaura several disputes arose from the introduction of agricultural machinery on holdings that had previously been cultivated by mule and manpower. The trucks, tractors, and harvesting machines require wider access paths, and their use often causes damage to land and crops. Quarrels broke out over rights of passage and the amount of liability created by the damage. One man was very bitter at being offered only $24 for damages caused by a neighbor's truck. He felt humiliated by the offer, which he called "mere charity"; yet he feared he could not bring the issue to court to vindicate his honor, without being criticized for squandering money. He was also deterred by the fact that he was still technically violating his neighbor's property rights to gain access to a storehouse they shared. He knew that if he pursued the issue of damages further, his neighbor would prosecute him for this infraction although it had never before been an issue between them.

In a sense, the heat which was taken off the countryside shifted to the town with the boom in construction. Some of the new construction in Villamaura is located at the edge of the town in an area recently rezoned for housing, but most of it is concentrated where people have always lived. Old buildings are demolished and replaced with new ones and existing structures are renovated and extended vertically. The town is growing up as much as out, thus retaining its high population density and compactness. Its architectural structure remains the same: Courtyard and street are extensions of the inhabitants' living spaces, not just places through which one passes on the way to home or work. They are areas where, in and near doorways, women gossip and do their household tasks while children play. The houses, all attached, were constructed piecemeal over centuries with the result that neighbors share common walls and sometimes common entrances, stairwells, and roofs. Although there are many fewer mules and goats, they are still housed in town, and one family's bedroom may well stand over another family's stall. Similarly, the rooms of one house may be contiguous to the second storey and roof of another, while the owner of a third has a window looking out on that roof. The owner of the first house needs permission from the owner of the second to erect a TV antenna, and the owner of the second is constrained from building upward if his neighbor's window has existed for longer than 20 years. For a family to install plumbing, the sewage and water conduits have to be embedded in the wall of someone else's dwelling. If people no longer want to enter their house through the stall, they may have to build a staircase from the courtyard or street to the second storey, usurping communal space over which others also have a claim. One woman in Villamaura was furious with her neighbor for attaching a three-quarter-inch water pipe to the outside wall of his house, "narrowing the courtyard" as she put it.

"The houses, all attached, were constructed piecemeal over centuries with the result that neighbors share common walls and sometimes common entrances, stairwells, and roofs."

A water pipe does not always provoke a quarrel. In fact, in spite of the ambiguity of property lines in town, most neighbors seem quite tolerant of each other. A man watching his neighbor add a new floor to his house has to think twice about whether this will restrict his own right to build or whether it will violate his rights to a terrace and a view. Only if he resents or envies his neighbor will he make an issue of the construction, though of course some people are more litigious than others.

A carpenter did not respect his neighbor, an upwardly mobile storekeeper whose ancestors had been poor day laborers. When this neighbor—having made good in spite of his family's past—decided to install a bathtub, the carpenter denied him permission to run a pipe through the common wall which separated their houses, on the ground that water gushing through the pipe would disturb his family. The neighbor apparently accepted this excuse and found another way to improve his bathroom. But when the carpenter had a minor operation a few months later, the neighbor did not come to visit him. When the neighbor's brother died, the carpenter returned the snub by not attending the funeral. The carpenter also made insulting remarks about his neighbor to a third party within earshot of the storekeeper. Subsequently, the carpenter put his house up for sale but refused to sell it to the storekeeper, who wanted it for his engaged daughter. When a mafioso was brought in to mediate the transaction, the carpenter took the house off the market altogether. In retaliation, the neighbor brought suit against the carpenter for having built an oven, many years earlier, in violation of the building code. The oven heated one wall of the neighbor's house but this inconvenience had always been ignored: It was suddenly intolerable. The carpenter conceded to damages out of court, but came away angry over the attorney's and surveyor's fees he had to pay. Neither he nor his wife and children will greet the storekeeper or his family on the street. Clearly, although certain aspects of the honor code have changed in the postwar period, ideas about personal honor and dignity and the vendetta cycle of reciprocal offenses still persist.

chapter 11

Culture and
Underdevelopment

The continuity of culture in postwar western Sicily has led some observers to the hypothesis that the island's lack of economic development is a consequence of its cultural codes. Often cited are the inability of Sicilians to organize collectively for the common good, to invest their earnings in projects that require long-term, stable commitments, to trust each other, and to relinquish the uncertain devices of coalition formation, wheeling and dealing, and corruption. Edward Banfield elevated these observations to a theory of cultural determinism when he applied the concept "amoral familism" to south Italians and, by implication, to Sicilians (1958). For centuries, foreigners and Sicilians alike have remarked on the "mutual distrust" of the island people and on their "inability to take collective action [Mack Smith 1968b: 475–478]." Such judgments permeated the record of the sixteenth-century Spanish administration of Sicily (Koenigsberger 1969), and they also were pronounced in the observations of European visitors to the island in the late eighteenth century. A government commissioner of the late nineteenth century lamented "the stupidity which thinks only of today, never of tomorrow, and the lack of common services which can be obtained only by association [quoted in Mack Smith 1968b: 478]." At one point in his recent two-volume history of Sicily, Mack Smith attributed the island's underdevelopment to certain characteristically Sicilian attitudes. He listed as serious burdens on the economy "the conviction that only short-term gains were worth considering, . . . the individualistic unwillingness of people to cooperate with each other, let alone assist government projects for reform, . . . the dislike of appearing to work hard, . . . the instinctive protective preference for monopoly and restriction . . . inherited from the high summer of mercantilism [1968b: 395]."

Mack Smith might have had in mind a coalition that was formed in Villamaura in 1960 to raise chinchillas. Responding to an article in the *Reader's Digest,* the members jointly purchased a dozen animals and the appropriate cages, vitamins, and feed from a firm in Milan. Cages were set up in what had been a stall in a member's house. But three of the five members were reluctant to invest additional capital in treatments to prevent disease. Some of the animals died, a quarrel ensued, and that was the end of the partnership.

Although one could find countless examples of this sort, the chapters of our book point to a different conclusion about the role of culture in underdevelopment. Culture does not determine a society's place in a world-system, held together by unequal relationships of dominance and subordination; rather, it reflects the various roles which the society has played in world-systems of the past. Because these roles also had to do with problems of unequal power, continuity of cultural codes is to be sought in continuity of roles. Nor does culture boil down to superstructure—a mere representation of more fundamental processes of economic production and exchange. It is, on the contrary, an integral part of these processes, insofar as they are organized and carried out by classes and interest groups. For culture assists particular groups to claim particular domains. Not being superstructure, culture cannot be said to "lag" and in this way to constitute an impediment to change. When a code appears to contradict an ongoing process of change, it is because certain interest groups have a stake in resisting that change and are, in addition, manipulating the code to do so.

That Sicily has not developed economically has nothing to do directly with its culture. It has fundamentally to do with the resources and potentialities of its own environment and with those parts of the world that claim and have claimed these resources—with northern

Italy, the North Atlantic, the United States. Unlike many un-derdeveloped regions and nations, Sicily does not challenge the hegemony of these places in an effort to utilize its own resources at home because the experience of dominance by Spain left it with an entrenched structure of dependency strong enough within the region to prevent a development elite from ever forming. Very much products of that structure, upwardly mobile rural entrepreneurs have over the years actively perpetuated past cultural codes, for the codes serve well to shore up their regional power. Sicily is a dependency of today's industrial metropolitan centers, used to benefiting—as well as suffering—if not always "legally" from the tie. This is precisely the relationship which it bore to Spain and northern Italy in the days of exported wheat. If traditional codes persist it is because, nurtured by dominance in the past, they still respond to dominance today.

ALTERNATIVE CULTURAL CODES

When confronting the cultural determinism implicit in the work of Banfield and others, it helps to ask about the origins and meanings of the alternative cultural codes which, they imply, accompany development. These alternative codes, clustered together at the modern pole of a traditional–modern continuum, include the follow-ing: (1) universalistic values that stress fairness and impartiality in interpersonal relations and support impersonal bureaucratic and cor-porate organization; (2) liberation of individuals from local com-munity and kin groups such that obligations to members of these groups do not stand in the way of work and achievement or lead to nepotism and corruption; (3) self-discipline, thought necessary for long-range investment and commitment to corporate organization; and (4) an ideology of merit, said to allocate positions in society according to criteria of talent and performance. Note that merit attaches to individuals and not families. Earning it often means the sacrifice of personal ties or, as Marx observed, the transformation of these ties into a cash nexus. Thus, in a merit-oriented society, it is distasteful to demonstrate excessive loyalty to one's family. One suf-fers the death of a close relative in silence, stoically in control of oneself and aware that "emotional outbursts" of rage or grief will only prove embarrassing to others. This is in direct contrast to the rules of mourning in Mediterranean societies.

The impersonal, bureaucratic work-oriented codes are closely tied to other cherished values such as individual freedom, parliamentary democracy, and the rule of law. They are assumed to be the inevitable corollaries of industrialization. They have tended, therefore, to serve as standards against which the relevant codes of other societies are measured and compared. In the process, however, we miss the relationship of the bureaucratic codes to power and stratification. For although they go hand in hand with freedom and democracy, they have also reinforced exploitation. They are, in short, codes of aggression, rather than defense.

First, let us consider what it takes to "succeed" and fulfill oneself in an industrial society. Apart from extensive education or training, which is denied to a very large sector of the population, there is a considerable amount of preschool and early school coaching—internalization of models and acquisition of skills—that only mothers not burdened with too many pregnancies, and liberated by servants (or appliances) from household chores, have been able to provide—often at some cost to themselves. In short, only a minority, primarily although not exclusively of middle-class background, enter the race. Of this minority, some are handicapped by "personal problems," by time- and energy-consuming crises in their families. These crises, however, are irrelevant to their work. Of supreme relevance is performance, but this has to be evaluated by others. Presumably these evaluations are made according to fair and impartial criteria but reality can only approximate this ideal. In the real world, evaluations of performance are in effect procedures by which some people affect the life chances of others less powerful than themselves. Insofar as those being judged are committed to the ideology of merit, they do not question negative evaluations, which insulates the powerful from experiencing their unhappiness. Instead they blame themselves, having learned since childhood that to do otherwise is to appear childish and maladjusted. Societies based on merit must be the only secular societies in the world where grossly unequal hierarchies exist without giving rise to constant and overt manifestations of resentment and envy. (Resentment and envy were self-consciously eliminated as legitimate human sentiments in a historical process—the witch trials of seventeenth-century England; see MacFarlane 1970.) In the merit-oriented societies of northern Europe and North America, secular hierarchies are at least as oppressive as the religious hierarchies which they replaced. Sacred societies of the past comforted the powerless with patronage and charity and with the doctrine that their station in life was ordained by God. One of the cultural codes of a merit society is that people should neither expect to be comforted, nor feel obliged to comfort others, since one's station in life is a reflection of one's work and performance.

Notwithstanding the coldness implicit in this code, the merit ideology found a place for itself in the revolutionary conditions of seventeenth-century England and the Low Countries, and it has flourished in industrial metropolitan centers of the West ever since. What, besides coercion, might explain this? Rather than ask the well-worn question whether these metropolitan centers could have developed without the Protestant Ethic, let us pose a different question: Could the Protestant Ethic have survived as an ideology in the absence of constant economic expansion, predicated on the world-wide imperialist hegemony of Europe and the United States? The "legal–rational" codes enumerated above contributed to this incredible growth by freeing individuals to invent, compete, invest, seek change and adventure; but growth could not have occurred on the basis of these codes alone. Originally, neither the codes nor their proponents were the unique products of North Atlantic culture. Ascetic codes, for example, existed in Africa and Asia, as well as in Europe. Through a process of diffusion and selection, and by the actual migration of people, this and related codes became a pre-dominant force in the north of Europe because this was where geopolitical and ecological factors most favored autonomous development on a revolutionary scale. One of the factors involved was physical distance from the Mediterranean, which, until the North Atlantic revolution, was Europe's metropolitan center and source of dominance. Another, and we think the most decisive, factor was the ecological condition which permitted the rise of a woolen cloth industry without the sacrifice of too much agricultural land. Precisely because it could not be raised in most environments without jeopardizing food supplies—the Mediterranean is a case in point—wool was a valuable export commodity, particularly in manufactured form. From the very beginning, woolen cloth found rapidly expanding export markets to the great advantage of those who produced it (Bloch 1962: 70; Carus-Wilson 1950; Power 1965).

Economic growth means expanding opportunities, an expanding middle class, and expanding numbers of people who get the chance to succeed in life despite their lowly origins. Even with population growth, it means enough self-made men to reinforce belief in this ideal, notwithstanding the fact that most people are "made by others." Constant growth must also have influenced evaluations of performance, for such evaluations made in the context of expansion are quite different in meaning from those made in contexts of stagnation or contraction. This is true from the standpoint of the judges as well as that of the judged. Where available positions are miniscule in proportion to the number of aspirants, the exercise of power inherent in the process of evaluating performance is difficult, if not impossible, to legitimate. Under such conditions many "judges" give up, while their more tough-minded colleagues and superiors bewail the "erosion of standards."

Over 300 years of almost uninterrupted expansion must also have contributed immeasurably to the stability of investment groups in Euro-American society and to the acceptance of codes that advocate long-run commitment and planning. For what is a corporate group but a legally chartered collectivity that controls property vested in the group, as opposed to its individual members. Corporate groups have a life of their own; they antedate and survive any particular set of members. Such groups are well known in primitive societies, where they are usually based on kinship, but they do not characterize all such societies by any means. In the primitive world, corporate landholding by lineages or clans seems intimately related to a given measure of stability and predictability in access to domain. Thus, primitive societies under pressure from the commercial world are as likely as western Sicily to be socially "atomized"—to have no corporate groups (see Sahlins 1968: 44–47). The same distinction applies to complex societies and to sectors within them. Here corporate organization is based on the legal protection and enforcement offered by state institutions, rather than on kinship, but it is no less dependent for its continuity on long-term, predictable access to domain. In northern portions of Europe and the United States, economic expansion guaranteed this access and people were encouraged by repeated and real payoffs in a period of over 300 years to tie up earnings and savings in such groups.

It is finally possible that constant expansion (expansion as a way of life) helped competitors to pay at least lip service to the rules of the game. Adam Smith noted that "in the race for wealth and honor and preferment, each may run as hard as he can and strain every nerve and every muscle in order to outstrip all his competitors, but if he should justle [sic] or throw down any of them, the indulgence of the spectators is entirely at an end [quoted in Neuman 1963: 257]." Competition should not kill competition, but lead to growth for all. We know that in England and America, competition is dead in a number of economic sectors. But in societies that lacked the prerequisites for constant growth, it never became what Adam Smith thought it should be—"the basic device for the continuous reproduction of society on an ever higher level [Neuman 1963: 257]." It became instead a mere "right of the entrepreneur," who destroyed his competitors by various means in the process of creating monopolies (Neuman 1963: 257). This explains the "instinctive, protective preference for monopoly" attributed to Sicilians by Mack Smith.

We are suggesting by these arguments that in a strange and unsettling way, the rest of the world paid dearly for the values that citizens of industrial societies cherish, since these values have depended for their efficacy and credibility on an expropriation of the world's resources over several centuries. Viewed in this light, the cultural codes of western Sicily become less objects of opprobrium than understandable means of resisting the further stratification and centralization of the world economy. Sicily is no empire and most likely will never be. For Sicilians to commit themselves to the merit ideology and all its associated codes would be for them to lose what little maneuverability they have in the world. In dependencies, to "delay gratification" in favor of long-range commitments is to run the risk of no gratification at all because colonies, by definition, produce for markets that they do not control. Even the chinchilla raisers operated in a putting out system, in which the only outlet for their animals was the same firm in Milan from which they bought them. Needless to say, their profits were miserable. Noncorporate partnerships, cemented by friendship but basically short-lived and unstable, are better adapted than corporate groups to this situation. Unlike the less flexible groups of advanced industrial societies, they are able to absorb the shocks of market instability and eroding domains. Their members, because they make limited commitments, experience only limited loss.

Similarly, were Sicilians to give up their shrewd tactics they would lose, not gain. Without recommendations and hanky-panky, without various forms of "negative reciprocity," many fewer would be employed by the national government, fewer would live off the orchards, and fewer would live off the schools. Yet it is doubtful that the island could muster the resources necessary to resist north Italian hegemony on "honest" terms. This is Alessandro Pizzorno's point in his criticism of Banfield. South Italians (and Sicilians) have a better chance of improving their lives through the acquisition of patronage than they do by making sacrifices for some ill-defined future common good. This being the case, they would be foolish to take collective action (Pizzorno 1966).

The code of honor is probably the most difficult to interpret in these terms since it would seem on the surface to inflame interpersonal conflict and ill feeling. As ethnographers in the field, we were able to appreciate the ingenuity and byzantine grace of programmed deception, and we were the grateful recipients of the constant and genuine hospitality occasioned by the code of friendship; but like our friends in Villamaura we had difficulty coming to terms with the demands of honor. The code of honor leads to touchiness in interpersonal relations such that most people will go out of their way to avoid giving cause for offense. Quite apart from encroaching on the property of others—hardly a temptation for most—one does not arbitrarily decline offers of hospitality, refuse favors, or neglect to make token demonstrations of respect according to customary etiquettes, as described in Chapter 5.

But think of all these obligations in terms of stratification and power. Sensitivity, and propensity to take offense, are psychological weapons that people use in relation to those of roughly similar social standing, who might move up the status ladder at their expense. For, in a society characterized by contraction or stagnation it is in fact true that A's gain is likely to be B's loss.[1] Under these conditions, people are permitted—indeed expected—to envy the upwardly mobile and to blame their own immobility on the misdeeds of others. If someone advances himself, you resent it, and mobilize your allies to share and act on your rancor. Those near the bottom of the status hierarchy may have little leeway in these matters. For them to take revenge for an insult is to run the risk of being criticized for stupidity. The peasant who thought that $24 compensation for his damages was mere charity falls into this category. Nevertheless, his withdrawal from the dispute was not gracious and he served warning that he would retaliate at the first opportunity. In a guilt-oriented society like our own, there is pressure to turn the wish for revenge against the self. This makes people other-directed, and perhaps easy to get along with; and it also ensures that losers will be "good sports." Why should a people whose dependency in world markets inevitably produces more defeats than victories have opted for what is clearly a winner's ideology?

In Part I, we examined the relationship between cultural codes and dominance. Honor, we suggested, helped preserve the family as an enclave—a political unit with autonomous domain—in a society subject to outsiders' claims on its resources and its women. The family

---

[1] One might object that the zero-sum game, or limited good economy implied by this statement, is inconsistent with the expanding opportunities opened up through modernization in the construction trades and retail commerce. Growth in areas such as these, however, is offset by population growth, by displacement in the agricultural sector, and by rising expectations.

has lost much of its integrity as a political unit in western Sicily today, but—as attention to rituals of family solidarity tells us—it has done so reluctantly and under protest. The role of "good father of the family" is as much a prerequisite as ever for entry into the status game. To improve the standing of one's family in the community is what life's work is about—not "the continuous reproduction of society on an ever higher level."

This attachment to the family and family goals might strike one as a fetter on the individuals involved, for regardless of their talents and sensibilities they are trapped in a morass of time-consuming commitments and emotional obligations. Women, in particular, have little freedom. Yet how can we be sure that a significant number of people would find an opportunity to maximize their talents in creative and rewarding ways if the family as an enclave were completely undercut? Would not economic contraction or stagnation lead western Sicily to scorn and ignore the talents of its liberated youth? It is hard to know the answer to this question (although we in the United States may soon find out firsthand).

As we lived in Villamaura it became apparent that many young people are angry and unhappy. Influenced by the status symbols of industrial societies, carried to them through the media and tourism, Sicilian youth are at a loss as to how to acquire these symbols and what to do with their lives. In conclusion, though, it seems to us that this feeling of frustration is new, that unlike pressured peoples in other, more tragic situations, west Sicilians have retained their sense of humor and self-respect. There is in Sicily virtually no evidence of severe social malaise, no drug addiction, very little alcoholism, no marked personal derangement. Wine consumption supports the tradition of hospitality and feasting, through which people form coalitions to get things done; it is anything but a symptom of despair.[2]

A LOOK TO THE FUTURE

Since Sicily's culture is not the cause of its underdevelopment but is, on the contrary, a consequence, and a means of adapting to it,

[2] The relationship between alcohol and imperialism goes way back. Gordon Childe tells us that in the early Iron Age "the wily Greeks found a key to unlock barbarian wealth—wine ... [Childe 1967: 212]." One is led to speculate on the role of Islamic restrictions on alcohol in mediating the relationship of Islamic peoples to wine-producing Mediterranean empires. In Sicily, drinking is not taboo, but drunkenness is. The *furbo,* or clever man, never loses control of himself and would be considered *fesso* if he did.

we need not conclude our book with a prediction of more of the same. But neither can we take the sanguine position, once popular in the social sciences, that change is essentially unilineal, unidirectional, and continuous. We cannot take the position that all societies will eventually resemble the industrial metropolitan centers of the West, if not in their productive systems then at least in their political institutions and culture. The framework that has guided our analysis treats unilineal evolution—movement through successive stages from simple to complex—as only one of two major types of change. The other derives from the interplay of imperialist pressures and responses to them. Territorially defined societies—nations and regions—go through phases as well as stages: phases of invasion and colonization, of withdrawal and defense against outsiders, of reentry into the international marketplace, of erosion and renewed pressure. Even the most complex societies such as the United States experience phases in which their political systems and cultures take on characteristics appropriate not only to stage but to phase. In the future these societies might "de-develop" one another through the multinational corporations they have spawned. As a result, the context of Sicilian underdevelopment would change.

Meanwhile, the process of modernization piles new problems on old ones in western Sicily. Under the impact of emigration remittances and welfaristic reforms, certain sectors of the economy—most notably house construction and education—have expanded rapidly with consequences for social stratification. In the construction trades, young boys were once apprenticed as unskilled laborers to the master masons. Although they worked long hard hours, earned little money, and enjoyed no "fringe benefits," they could look forward to becoming masters themselves after a period of apprenticeship. Now, in Villamaura, 18 construction "firms" employ roughly 400 laborers, few of whom can expect to become masters or impresarios in their own right. For many, their relationship to their employer is still paternalistic (their mothers would be furious if they went on strike), and construction is still an artisan activity rather than an industry, but the rudimentary outlines of a town-based proletariat now exist, as these young men begin to protest their long working days, back-breaking labor, low salaries (higher than they would receive as agricultural laborers, however), and lack of unemployment compensation and medical benefits.

In the field of education, the issues are different but the tensions are related. As in our own society, in Sicily education once guaranteed upward social mobility, so much so that *civile* families secured their landholdings against fragmentation only by educating one or more of their sons. Today education, although much more widely available, guarantees nothing except disdain on the part of the educated for manual labor (or, in the case of women, disdain for marriage to a laborer). Overqualified and untrained for manual occupations either at home or abroad, unprepared for white-collar jobs abroad, and unable to find such positions in Italy or Sicily, the new intelligentsia has much to protest. Moreover, in a manner typical of people everywhere who have recently climbed out of the laboring classes, an ever growing number of underemployed *diplomati* see workers and peasants as a class enemy, as potentially organized and powerful competitors for scarce resources. This problem is all too familiar in complex societies, where more than once it has proved the foundation for a fascist-type mobilization. In Sicily it simmers below the surface as continued migration keeps the pot from boiling. But watchdogs of the Italian political scene alert us to the growing attraction of the neo-Fascist MSI party among Sicilian and south Italian voters.

Fascism, however, is not a regional phenomenon, although certain regions of a nation contribute disproportionately to its rank and file. Following Franz Neuman's analysis of Nazi Germany, and thinking in terms of our model, we might characterize fascism as a phase of development associated with already industrial societies which, however, lag behind other societies or have been overtaken ("de-developed") by them. As a strategy for catching up (or overtaking), the affected industrial elite pursues an aggressive foreign policy, more or less hostile to other industrial powers and imperialistic in design. It also restructures society, reducing the size of its middle class, lowering its standard of living, and above all cheapening the labor force by systematically smashing labor organizations and the left wing press. Intellectuals who speak for internationalism and peace, for organized labor, and worst of all for both are targets, too, as are representatives of industrial and agricultural sectors which depend on free trade. The latter, however, may be coaxed along by the lure of special protection and by their dependence for protection of property on the coercive arm of the state.

To accomplish its aims, an industrial elite launching into fascism needs popular support which is gained through a mass mobilization (see Neuman 1963: 202–210). Fascist mobilization has some particular features, best identified through comparison with socialism. A socialist phase of development characterizes largely preindustrial societies whose first-order problem is to exclude from the national economy predatory foreign interests and foreign capital. Allies of foreign capital, mainly in the form of an indigenous landed class, must also be removed as agents and symbols of the dependent past. Thus the foreign enemies and the class enemies of the revolution overlap; eliminating both is a task of class action.

Occurring in already developed societies, fascism is more complex. It divides the society along lines that crosscut class. Some members of the business elite, though perhaps a minority, would prefer to stay with an open, peaceful economy. Segments of the middle class might also be torn, and stand to lose. Even the working class splits, as portions of it "actively support, or at least tolerate, . . . expansion in order to share in the material benefits that might possibly be derived from it [Neuman 1963: 211]." Whereas socialism produces the righteous myth of solidarity among the oppressed against their oppressors, a fascist mobilization conquers by dividing the oppressed. As with mobilization under bossism, but with even more *odio* or *rancore* and fewer scruples, fascism intensifies and capitalizes on bitterness between onetime equals or near equals and between people who, in a preceding era of upward mobility and expanding opportunities, were having to tolerate one another against their will.

At the present time, the Fascist votes of southern Italy and Sicily are "protest votes" cast by the would-be upwardly mobile against higher taxes and against such "leftist" measures as a recent land reform bill which favors those who work the land over those whose holdings, however small, are sharecropped by others. To turn these votes into fascism presupposes a national level mobilization, called for and paid for by a national industrial elite. Whether such a phenomenon could happen again in Italy, whether a socialist-type revolution would come first, depends upon that nation's relationships to other industrial and industrializing societies—relationships which would obviously be strained were the labor markets in Germany and Switzerland to close. The future of these markets, and of the industrial powers, is beyond the scope of our study. And yet, as we have tried to show, the world is too small to overlook its interconnections. To ask about Sicily's future, we must ask about our own.

References

Alavi, H.
1965 Peasants and revolution. In *The socialist register,* edited by R. Miliband and J. Saville. London: Merlin Press.

Alfonso-Spagna, F.
1870 Monografia sui prati artificiali in Sicilia. In *Memorie scientifiche premiate per concorso dal Congresso Agraria di Girgenti nel 1869.* Palermo: Stamperia di Giovanni Lorsnaider.

Alongi, G.
1886 *La Maffia nei suoi fattori e nelle sue manifestazioni: Studio sulle classi pericolose della Sicilia.* Turin: Fratelli Bocca Editori.

Amery, J.
1948 *Sons of the eagle: A study in guerilla war.* London: Macmillan.

Anonymous
1879 *I Masnadieri Guilianesi: Ultimo avanzo del brigantaggio in Sicilia.* Palermo: Tipografia del Giornale di Sicilia.

Arnolfini, G. A.
1962 *Giornale di viaggio e quesiti sull'economia siciliana* (1768). Rome: Salvatore Sciascia Editore.

Aymard, M.
1973 L'agriculture dans l'Italie moderne. *Annales. Economies Sociétés Civilisations* **29:** 475–499.

239

Balsamo, P.
1803 *Memorie economiche e agrarie riguardante il Regno di Sicilia.* Palermo: dalla Reale Stamperia.
Banfield, E. C.
1958 *The moral basis of a backward society.* New York: The Free Press.
Barth, F.
1961 *Nomads of south Persia: The Basseri Tribe of the Khamseh confederacy.* Boston: Little, Brown.
Barzini, L.
1964 *The Italians.* London: Hamish Hamilton.
Bautier, R.-H.
1971 *The economic development of medieval Europe.* London: Thames and Hudson.
Bernabei, L. A.
1972 Why are peasants so unorganized? Unpublished thesis. Radcliffe College.
Bloch, M.
1962 *Feudal society,* translated by L. A. Manyon. London: Routledge & Kegan Paul.
Blok, A.
1966 Land reform in a west Sicilian latifondo village: The persistence of a feudal structure. *Anthropological Quarterly* 39: 1–16.
1969a South Italian agro-towns. *Comparative Studies in Society and History* 11: 121–135.
1969b Variations in patronage. *Sociologische Gids* 16: 365–378.
1969c Mafia and peasant rebellion as contrasting factors in Sicilian latifundism. *Archives Européennes de Sociologie* 10: 95–116.
1972 The peasant and the brigand: Social banditry reconsidered. *Comparative Studies in Society and History* 14: 495–504.
1974 *The Mafia of a Sicilian village, 1860–1960: A study of violent peasant entrepreneurs.* Oxford: Basil Blackwell.
Boissevain, J.
1966a Patronage in Sicily. *Man* 1: 18–33.
1966b Poverty and politics in a Sicilian agro-town. *International Archives of Ethnography* 50: 198–236.
Borruso, V.
1966 *Pratiche abortive e controllo delle nascite in Sicilia.* Palermo: Edizioni Libri Siciliani.
Boyd, C. E.
1952 *Tithes and parishes in medieval Italy: The historical roots of a modern problem.* Ithaca, New York: Cornell Univ. Press.
Brancato, F.
1946 Il commercio dei grani in settecento in Sicilia. *Archivio storico Siciliano,* 3d. ser., 1.
Braudel, F.
1966 *La Méditerranée et le monde méditerranéen à l'époque de Philippe II,* 2d ed. 2 vols. Paris: Librairie Armand Colin.
Cameron, R. E.
1961 *France and the economic development of Europe.* Princeton: Princeton Univ. Press.
Campbell, J. K.
1964 *Honour, family and patronage: A study of institutions and moral values in a Greek mountain community.* Oxford: Clarendon Press.

Caracciolo, D.
  1785 Riflessioni su l'economia e l'estrazione dei frumenti della Sicilia: Fatte in occasione della carestia dell'indizione terza, 1784 e 1785. Palermo: dalla Reale Stamperia.
Carus-Wilson, E. M.
  1950 Trends in the export of English woolens in the fourteenth century. Economic History Review, 2d ser., 3: 162–180.
Cavalieri, E.
  1925 Prefazione alla II edizione. In Condizioni politiche e amministrative della Sicilia, by L. Franchetti. Florence: Vallecchi Editore. Pp. ix–lxiii.
Chapman, C. G.
  1971 Milocca, a Sicilian village. Cambridge, Massachusetts: Schenkman.
Chicoli, N.
  1870 L'allevatore degli animali domestici in Sicilia. Palermo: Stamperia Giovanni Lorsnaider.
Chilanti, F.
  1959 Chi é questo Milazzo, mezzo barone e mezzo villano? Florence: Parenti Editore.
Childe, V. G.
  1967 What happened in history. Middlesex, England: Penguin Books.
Chisholm, M.
  1962 Rural settlement and land use: An essay in location. New York: Wiley.
Chiva, I.
  1963 Social organization, traditional economy and customary law in Corsica: Outline of a plan of analysis. In Mediterranean countrymen: Essays in the social anthropology of the Mediterranean, edited by J. Pitt-Rivers. Paris: Mouton.
Ciaccio, M.
  1900 Sciacca: Notizie storiche e documenti. Vol. 1. Sciacca: Tipografia Bodoniana (dei Fratelli Bojuso).
Citarella, A. O.
  1967 The relations of Amalfi with the Arab world before the Crusades. Speculum, a Journal of Medieval Studies 42: 299–312.
Ciuni, S. R.
  1966 La Regione, una torre di Babele. Giornale di Sicilia, 2 Dec.
Cohen, A.
  1969 Custom and politics in urban Africa: A study of Hausa migrants in Yoruba towns. Berkeley, California: Univ. of California Press.
Colonna, N. T.
  1852 L'industria pastorale nel territorio di Palermo. Palermo: Sta. Tipografico Virzi.
Corleo, S.
  1871 Storia della enfiteusi dei terreni ecclesiastici di Sicilia. Palermo: Stabilimento Tipografico Lao.
Cronin, C.
  1970 The sting of change: Sicilians in Sicily and Australia. Chicago: Univ. of Chicago Press.
Cunnison, I.
  1966 Baggara Arabs: Power and the lineage in a Sudanese nomad tribe. Oxford: Oxford Univ. Press.
D'Alessandro, E.
  1959 Brigantaggio e mafia in Sicilia. Florence: Casa Editrice G. D'Anna.

Davis, J.
   1969   Honour and politics in Pisticci. *Proceedings of the Royal Anthropological Institute of Great Britain and Ireland.* Pp. 69–81.
   1973   *Land and family in Pisticci.* London: The Athlone Press, Univ. of London.
De Planhol, X.
   1959   *The world of Islam.* Ithaca, New York: Cornell Univ. Press.
De Welz, G.
   1964   *Saggio su i mezzi da moltiplicare prontamente le ricchezze della Sicilia.* Rome: Salvatore Sciascia Editore.
Di Cristina, L. N.
   1965   *La città-paese di Sicilia: Forma e linguaggio dell'habitat contadino.* Palermo: Facoltà di Architettura dell'Università di Palermo Quaderno No. 7.
Di Salvo, V.
   1894   *Vicende storiche della proprietà fondiaria in Sicilia dalla caduta della dominazione romana alla costituzione generale dei feudi.* Palermo: Tipografia F. Barravecchia e Figlio.
Dore, G.
   1964   *La democrazia italiana e l'emigrazione in America.* Brescia: Morcelliana.
Doty, R. C.
   1967   Flow of workers from southern Europe to the North is halted. *New York Times,* international ed., 27 Feb.
Elliot, J. H.
   1967   The decline of Spain. In *Crisis in Europe, 1560–1660,* edited by T. Aston. New York: Anchor Books. Pp. 177–206.
   1968   *Europe divided, 1559–1598.* New York: Harper Torchbooks.
Fagone, V.
   1966   *Arte popolare e artigianato in Sicilia: Repertorio dell'artigianato siciliano.* Unione delle Camere di Commercio Industria ed Agricoltura della Regione Siciliana. Rome: Salvatore Sciascia Editore.
Finley, M. I.
   1968   *A history of Sicily: Ancient Sicily to the Arab conquest.* London: Chatto and Windus.
Fisher, A. G. B., and H. J. Fisher
   1972   *Slavery and Muslim society in Africa.* Garden City, New York: Doubleday.
Foerster, R. F.
   1969   *The Italian emigration of our times.* New York: Arno Press.
Franchetti, L.
   1925   *Condizioni politiche e amministrative della Sicilia.* Florence: Stabilimenti Grafici di A. Vallecchi.
Frank, A. G.
   1969   *Capitalism and underdevelopment in Latin America: Historical studies of Chile and Brazil.* New York: Monthly Review Press.
Franke, R. W.
   1974   The ecology bomb. *Reviews in Anthropology* 1: 157–166.
Franklin, S. H.
   1969   *The European peasantry: The final phase.* London: Methuen.
Friedl, E.
   1967   Dowry and inheritance in modern Greece. In *Peasant society: A reader,* edited by J. M. Potter, M. N. Diaz, and G. N. Foster. Boston: Little, Brown. Pp. 57–63.

Friedrich, P.
  1968   The legitimacy of a cacique. In *Local level politics: Social and cultural perspectives* edited by M. J. Swartz. Chicago: Aldine.
Garufi, C. A.
  1946–1947   Patti agrari e comuni feudali di nuova fondazione in Sicilia dallo scorcio del secolo XI agli albori del settecento. Studi storico-diplomatico. *Archivio Storico Siciliano*, 3d. ser., **1:** 31–111 and **2:** 7–131.
Geertz, C.
  1968   *Agricultural involution: The process of ecological change in Indonesia.* Berkeley, California: Univ. of California Press.
Genuardi, L.
  1911   *Terre comuni ed usi civici in Sicilia prima dell'abolizione della feudalità: Studi e documenti.* Palermo: Scuola Tip. "Boccone del Povero."
Gerschenkron, A.
  1955   Notes on the rate of industrial growth in Italy, 1881–1913. *Journal of Economic History* **15:** 360–376.
Goitein, S. D.
  1967   *A Mediterranean society: The Jewish communities of the Arab world as portrayed in the documents of the Cairo Geniza.* Vol. I: *Economic foundations.* Berkeley, California: Univ. of California Press.
Goubert, P.
  1967   The French peasantry of the 17th century: A regional example. In *Crisis in Europe 1560–1660,* edited by T. Aston. New York: Anchor Books.
Gramsci, A.
  1949   *Il risorgimento.* Turin: Giulio Einaudi.
Graziano, L.
  1973   Patron–client relationships in southern Italy. *European Journal of Political Research* **1:** 3–34.
Heckscher, E. F.
  1955   *Mercantilism,* rev. ed., edited by E. F. Soderlund. London: George Allen and Unwin, Ltd., New York: Macmillan.
Hess, H.
  1973   *Mafia.* Rome: Giuseppe Laterza e Figli.
Hobsbawm, E. J.
  1959   *Primitive rebels: Studies in archaic forms of social movement in the 19th and 20th centuries.* New York: Praeger.
  1962   *The age of revolution, 1789–1848.* New York: The World Publishing Co.
  1972   Social bandits: A comment. *Comparative Studies in Society and History* **14:** 504–507.
Houston, J. M.
  1964   *The western Mediterranean world: An introduction to its regional landscapes.* London: Longmans.
INEA (Istituto Nazionale di Economia Agraria)
  1947   *La distribuzione della proprietà fondiaria in Italia. Tavole statistiche, Sicilia.* Rome: Edizioni Italiane.
ISTAT (Istituto Centrale di Statistica)
  1955   *IX censimento generale della popolazione, 4 novembre 1951.* Vol. I: *Dati sommari per comune.* Rome.
  1965   *X censimento generale della popolazione, 15 ottobre 1961.* Vol. III: *Dati sommari per comune.* Rome.

Jannuzzi, L., and S. Viola
  1966   Chi comanda in Sicilia. *L'Espresso,* 14 Aug. Pp. 6–7.
Jones, P.
  1966   Medieval agrarian society in its prime—Italy. In *The Cambridge economic history of Europe.* Vol. I: *The agrarian life of the Middle Ages,* edited by M. M. Postan. Cambridge: Cambridge Univ. Press.
Keyfitz, N.
  1965   Political–economic aspects of urbanization in south and southeast Asia. In *The study of urbanization,* edited by P. M. Hauser and L. F. Schnore. New York: Wiley.
Koenigsberger, H. G.
  1969   *The practice of empire.* Emended ed. of *The government of Sicily under Philip II of Spain.* Ithaca, New York: Cornell Univ. Press.
  1971   *Estates and revolutions: Essays in early modern European history.* Ithaca, New York: Cornell Univ. Press.
Krader, L.
  1955   Ecology of central Asian pastoralism. *Southwestern Journal of Anthropology* **12:** 301–326.
Lampedusa, G.
  1961   *The leopard,* translated by A. Colquhoun. New York: Signet Books.
  1962   Places of my infancy. In *Two stories and a memory.* London: Collins & Harvill Press.
Lane, F. C.
  1944   Family partnerships and joint ventures in the Venetian republic. *Journal of Economic History* **4:** 178–196.
Lattimore, O.
  1962   *Inner Asian frontiers of China.* Boston: Beacon Press.
Lea, H. C.
  1907   *History of sacerdotal celibacy in the Christian church,* 3d. ed. London: Oxford Univ. Press.
Leeds, A.
  1964   Brazilian careers and social structure. *American Anthropologist* **66:** 1321–1347.
Loncao, E.
  1899   *Genesis del latifondo in Sicilia: L'espropriazione delle popolazioni rurali.* Palermo: Tipografia "La Commerciale."
  1900   *Considerazione sulla genesis della borghesia in Sicilia: Saggio di storia economica e giuridica.* Palermo: Tipografia Cooperativa fra gli Operai.
Lopez, R. S., and I. W. Raymond
  1955   *Medieval trade in the Mediterranean world.* New York: Columbia Univ. Press.
Lorenzoni, G.
  1910   *Inchiesta parlamentare sulle condizioni dei contadini nelle provincie meridionali e nella Sicilia.* Vol. VI. Rome: Tipografia Nazionale di Giovanni Bertero.
Lugato, G.
  1966   La difficile strada delle promozioni. *Giornale di Sicilia,* 16 Jan.
MacFarlane, A.
  1970   *Witchcraft in Tudor and Stuart England.* New York: Harper & Row.
Mack Smith, D.
  1959   *Italy: A modern history.* Ann Arbor, Michigan: Univ. of Michigan Press.

1968a *A history of Sicily: Medieval Sicily, 800 to 1713.* London: Chatto and Windus.
1968b *A history of Sicily: Modern Sicily after 1713.* London: Chatto and Windus.

Magagnini, F.
1966 Storie dell'Italia che cerca lavoro: La Sicilia. *L'Unità,* 1 Mar.

Maggiore-Perni, Fr.
1897 *La popolazione di Sicilia e di Palermo nel secolo XIX.* Palermo: Stabilimento Tipografico Virzì.

Majoranna, F.
1855 Sulla statistica agraria per la Sicilia. *Giornale della commessione d'agricultura e pastorizia in Sicilia* 3: 73–110.

Maranelli, C.
1946 *Considerazioni geografiche sulla questione meridionale.* Bari: Giuseppe Laterza e Figli.

Martuscelli, M.,
1966 Inchiesta ministeriale sull'Agrigento. *L'Ora,* 14–15 Oct.

Milone, F.
1959 *Memoria illustrativa della carta della utilizzazione del suolo della Sicilia* (fogli 21, 22 e 23 della *Carta della utilizzazione del suolo d'Italia*). Rome: Consiglio Nazionale delle Ricerche.
1960 *Sicilia, la natura e l'uomo.* Turin: Paolo Boringhieri.

Mintz, S. W., and E. R. Wolf
1967 An analysis of ritual co-parenthood (*compadrazgo*). In *Peasant society: A reader,* edited by J. M. Potter, M. N. Diaz, and G. M. Foster. Boston: Little, Brown.

Misbach, H. L.
1972 The balanced economic growth of Carolingian Europe: Suggestions for a new interpretation. *Journal of Interdisciplinary History* 3: 261–275.

Molè, G.
1929 *Studio-inchiesta sui latifondi siciliani.* Rome: Tipografia del Senato del Dott. G. Bardi.

Molfese, F.
1964 *Storia del brigantaggio dopo l'unità.* Milan: Feltrinelli Editore.

Monheim, R.
1971 La struttura degli insediamenti nella Sicilia centrale come retaggio storico e problema attuale. *Bollettino della Società Geografica Italiana* 10–12: 667–683.

Morici, F.
1940 *Aspetti e risultati technici-economici di imprese pastorali siciliane.* Rome: INEA Studi e Monografie, Ser. I, No. 2.

Morse, R. M.
1962 Latin American cities: Aspects of function and structure. *Comparative Studies in Society and History* 4: 473–493.

Mosca, G.
1949 *Partiti e sindacati nella crisi del regime parlamentare.* Bari: Giuseppe Laterza e Figli.

Musio, G.
1969 *La cultura solitaria: Tradizione e acculturazione nella Sardegna archaica.* Bologna: Società Editrice Il Mulino.

Navarro della Miraglia, E.
1963 *La nana.* Rocca San Casciano: Cappelli Editore.

Neufeld, M. F.
  1961 *Italy: school for awakening countries: The Italian labor movement in its political, social, and economic setting from 1800 to 1960.* Ithaca, New York: Cornell Univ. Press.
Neuman, F.
  1963 *Behemoth: The structure and practice of national socialism, 1933-1944.* New York: Octagon Books.
Nicastro, S.
  1913 *Dal quarantotto al sessanta: Contributo alla storia economica, sociale e politica della Sicilia nel secolo XIX.* Rome: Società Editrice Dante Alighieri.
Nicholas, R. W.
  1965 Factions: A comparative analysis. In *Political systems and the distribution of power* edited by M. Banton. *ASA Monograph* No. 2. London: Tavistock Publications.
Nitti, F. S.
  1958 *Scritti sulla questione meridionale.* Vol. I: *Saggi sulla storia del mezzogiorno, emigrazione e lavoro.* Bari: Giuseppe Laterza e Figli.
Orlando, D.
  1847 *Il feudalismo in Sicilia: Storia e dritto publico.* Palermo: Tipografia di Francesco Lao.
Pantaleone, M.
  1962 *Mafia e politica, 1943-1962.* Turin: Einaudi.
Parca, G.
  1965 Il comportamento del maschio italiano. *L'Europeo,* 10, 14, 21 Oct.
Parisi, G.
  1966 *Note sullo sviluppo dell'agricoltura siciliana dal 1947 al 1964.* Palermo: Quaderni del Comitato Regionale Siciliano del PCI No. 1.
Parry, J. H.
  1967 Transport and trade routes. In *The Cambridge economic history of Europe.* Vol. IV: *The economy of expanding Europe in the sixteenth and seventeenth centuries,* edited by E. E. Rich and C. H. Wilson. Cambridge: Cambridge Univ. Press.
Peristiany, J. G.
  1965 Honour and shame in a Cypriot highland village. In *Honour and shame: The values of Mediterranean society,* edited by J. G. Peristiany. London: Weidenfeld and Nicolson.
Peters, E. L.
  1963 Aspects of rank and status among Muslims in a Lebanese village. In *Mediterranean Countrymen: Essays in the social anthropology of the Mediterranean,* edited by J. Pitt-Rivers. The Hague: Mouton.
  1970 The proliferation of segments in the lineage of the Bedouin of Cyrenaica (Lybia). In *Peoples and cultures of the Middle East: An anthropological reader,* edited by L. E. Sweet. Vol. I.: *Cultural depth and diversity.* New York: Natural History Press.
Petino, A.
  1946 *La questione del commercio dei grani in Sicilia nel settecento: Studi e ricerche di storia economica.* Catania: Azienda Poligrafica Editoriale.
  1946-1947 Aspetti del commercio marittimo della Sicilia nell'età Aragonese. *Bollettino Storico Catanese* (formerly *Archivio Storico per la Sicilia Orientale*) **11** and **12:** 64-75.

Pi Sunyer, O.
1967 Zamora: A regional economy in Mexico. *Middle American Research Institute Publication* No. 29. Tulane University, New Orleans.
Pitkin, D. S.
1963 Mediterranean Europe. *Anthropological Quarterly* **36:** 120–129.
Pitrè, G.
1939 *Usi e costumi, credenze e pregiudizi del popolo siciliano.* Vol. II. Florence: G. Barbera Editore.
1944 *La vita in Palermo cento e più anni fa.* 2 vols. Florence: G. Barbera Editore (Edizione Nazionale delle Opere di Giuseppe Pitrè).
Pitt-Rivers, J. A.
1961 *The people of the Sierra.* Chicago: Phoenix Books.
1963 *Mediterranean countrymen: Essays in the social anthropology of the Mediterranean.* The Hague: Mouton.
1965 Honour and social status. In *Honour and shame: The values of Mediterranean society,* edited by J. G. Peristiany. London: Weidenfeld and Nicolson.
Pizzorno, A.
1966 Amoral familism and historical marginality. *International Review of Community Development* **15–16:** 55–66.
Platzer, F., and C. Schifani
1963 L'azienda pastorale della Sicilia. *Tecnica agricola* **15:** 3–20.
Pontieri, E.
1933 *Il tramonto del baronaggio siciliano.* Palermo: Scuola Tip. "Boccone del Povero."
1961 *Il riformismo borbonico della Sicilia del sette e dell'ottocento: Saggi storici,* 2d ed. Naples: Edizioni Scientifiche Italiane.
Postan, M. M.
1966 Medieval agrarian society in its prime—England. In *The Cambridge economic history of Europe.* Vol. I: *The agrarian life of the Middle Ages,* edited by M. M. Postan. Cambridge: Cambridge Univ. Press.
Power, E.
1965 *The wool trade in English medieval history.* London: Oxford Univ. Press.
Pupillo-Baresi, A.
1903 *Gli usi civici in Sicilia: Ricerche di storia del diritto.* Catania: Niccolò Giannotta Editore.
Pulgram, E.
1958 *The tongues of Italy: Prehistory and history.* Cambridge, Massachusetts: Harvard Univ. Press.
R. Prefettura di Girgenti
1896 Provvedimenti contro l'abigeato. Sezione Publica Sicurezza No. 154. Communication from the prefect, Maccaferri, to the mayors of the province.
Renda, F.
1963 *L'emigrazione in Sicilia.* Palermo: Edizione "Sicilia al Lavoro."
Rochefort, R.
1961 *Le travail en Sicile: Etude de géographie sociale.* Paris: Presses Universitaires de France.
Romano, S. F.
1964 *Breve storia della Sicilia: Momenti e problemi della civiltà siciliana.* Turin: Edizioni RAI Radio-televisione Italiana.
1966 *Storia della mafia.* Verona: Arnoldo Mondadori Editore.

Romeo, R.
  1959   *Risorgimento e capitalismo.* Bari: Giuseppe Laterza e Figli.
Sahlins, M. D.
  1961   The segmentary lineage: An organization of predatory expansion. *American Anthropologist* **63:** 322–345.
  1968   *Tribesmen.* Englewood Cliffs, New Jersey: Prentice-Hall.
Sahlins, M. D., and E. R. Service
  1960   *Evolution and culture.* Ann Arbor, Michigan: Univ. of Michigan Press.
Salomone, A. W.
  1945   *Italy in the Giolittian era: Italian democracy in the making, 1900–1914.* Philadelphia: Univ. of Pennsylvania Press.
Sansone, V., and G. Ingrasci
  1950   *Sei anni di banditismo in Sicilia.* Milan: Edizioni Sociali.
Scaturro, I.
  1926   *Storia della città di Sciacca e dei comuni della contrada saccense fra il Belice e il Platani.* 2 vols. Naples: Gennaro Majo Editore.
Schneider, J.
  1969   Family patrimonies and economic behavior in western Sicily. *Anthropological Quarterly* **42:** 109–129.
  1971   Of vigilance and virgins: Honor, shame and access to resources in Mediterranean societies. *Ethnology* **10:** 1–24.
Schneider, J., and P. Schneider
  1974   Urbanization in Sicily: Two contrasting models. In *City and peasant: A study in sociocultural dynamics,* edited by A. L. LaRuffa, R. S. Freed, L. W. Saunders, E. C. Hansen, and S. Benet. New York: New York Academy of Sciences.
  1976   Economic dependency and the failure of cooperatives in western Sicily. In *Popular participation in social change,* edited by J. Nash, J. Dandler, and N. S. Hopkins. Amsterdam: Mouton.
Schneider, P.
  1969   Honor and conflict in a Sicilian town. *Anthropological Quarterly* **42:** 130–155.
  1972   Coalition formation and colonialism in western Sicily. *Archives Européennes de Sociologie* **13:** 255–267.
Schneider, P., J. Schneider, and E. C. Hansen
  1972   Modernization and development: The role of regional elites and non-corporate groups in the European Mediterranean. *Comparative Studies in Society and History* **14:** 328–350.
Sciascia, L.
  1964   *Mafia vendetta.* New York: Knopf.
  1965   *Feste religiose in Sicilia.* Florence: Casa Editrice G. D'Anna.
Scott, J. C.
  1969   The analysis of corruption in developing nations. *Comparative Studies in Society and History* **11:** 315–341.
Scrofani, S.
  1962   *Sicilia: Utilizzazione del suolo nella storia, nei rediti e nelle prospettive.* Palermo: Editori Stampatori Associati.
Seers, D.
  1970   The stages of economic growth of a primary producer in the middle of the twentieth century. In *Imperialism and underdevelopment: A reader,* edited by R. I. Rhodes. New York: Monthly Review Press.

Sergio, V. E., and G. Perez
    1962   *Un secolo di politica stradale in Sicilia.* Rome: Salvatore Sciascia Editore.
Signorino, A. (Ed.)
    1962   *Libro bianco sulla Sicilia: Atti del convegno dei sindaci Siciliani organizzato dalla Famiglia Siciliana di Milano a Castoreale Terme (Messina),* Feb.–Mar. 1962, No. 5. Milan: Edizioni Famiglia Siciliana.
Silverman, S.
    1968   Agricultural organization, social structure, and values in Italy: Amoral familism reconsidered. *American Anthropologist* **70:** 1–20.
Slicher Van Bath, B. H.
    1963   *The agrarian history of western Europe A.D. 500–1850,* translated by Olive Ordish. London: E. Arnold.
Sonnino, S.
    1925   *I contadini in Sicilia.* Florence: Vallecchi Editore.
Spooner, B.
    1973   The cultural ecology of pastoral nomads. *Addison-Wesley Module in Anthropology* No. 45.
Stavenhagen, R.
    1967   Seven fallacies about Latin America, translated by Otto Feinstein. *New University Thought* **4:** 25–37.
Stein, S., and B. Stein
    1970   *The colonial heritage of Latin America: Essays on economic dependence in perspective.* New York: Oxford Univ. Press.
Tarrow, S. G.
    1967   *Peasant communism in southern Italy.* New Haven, Connecticut: Yale Univ. Press.
Thirsk, J.
    1967   The farming regions of England. In *The Agrarian History of England and Wales,* Vol. IV, 1500–1640, edited by J. Thirsk. London: Cambridge Univ. Press. Pp. 1–112.
Tilly, C.
    1974   Foreword to *The mafia of a Sicilian village, 1860–1960: A study of violent peasant entrepreneurs,* by A. Blok. Oxford: Basil Blackwell. Pp. xiii–xxiv.
Touring Club Italiano
    1953   *Sicilia.* Milan: Touring Club Italiano.
Traina, A.
    1868   *Nuovo vocabolario siciliano-italiano.* Palermo: Giuseppe Pedone Lauriel Editore.
Trasselli, C.
    1962   Introduzione. In *Un secolo di politica stradale in Sicilia,* by V. E. Sergio and G. Perez. Rome: Salvatore Sciascia Editore. Pp. iii–xxii.
    1973   Du fait divers à l'histoire sociale: Criminalité et moralité en Sicile au début de l'epoque moderne. *Annales Economies Sociétés Civilisations* **28:** 226–247.
Unione Italiana delle Camere di Commercio Industria Artigianato e Agricoltura
    1968   *La carta commerciale d'Italia.* Varese: Dott. A. Giuffrè Editore.
Vaussard, M.
    1963   *Daily life in eighteenth century Italy,* translated by M. Heron. New York: Macmillan.
Verlinden, C.
    1970   *The beginnings of modern colonization.* Ithaca, New York: Cornell Univ. Press.

Vicens Vives, J.
    1969   *An economic history of Spain.* Princeton: Princeton Univ. Press.
Vilar, P.
    1962   *La Catalogne dans l'Espagne moderne: Recherches sur les fondements économiques des structures nationales,* Vol. I. Paris: Bibliothéque Générale de l'Ecole Pratique des Hautes Etudes.
Vinogradov, A., and J. Waterbury
    1971   Situations of contested legitimacy in Morocco: An alternative framework. *Comparative Studies in Society and History* **13:** 32–59.
Wallerstein, I.
    1974   *The modern world-system: Capitalist agriculture and the origins of the European world-economy in the sixteenth century.* New York: Academic Press.
Weber, M.
    1968   *The religion of China: Confucianism and Taoism,* translated by H. G. Gerth. New York: The Free Press.
Whitaker, I.
    1968   Tribal structure and national politics in Albania, 1910–1950. In *History and social anthropology,* edited by I. M. Lewis. *ASA Monograph* No. 7. London: Tavistock Publications.
Winspeare, D.
    1883   *Storia degli abusi feudali.* Bologna: Forni Editore.
Wittfogel, K. A.
    1957   *Oriental despotism: A comparative study of total power.* New Haven, Connecticut: Yale Univ. Press.
Wolf, E. R.
    1966a Kinship, friendship and patron–client relations in complex societies. In *The social anthropology of complex societies,* edited by M. Banton. *ASA Monograph* No. 4. London: Tavistock Publications.
    1966b *Peasants.* Englewood Cliffs, New Jersey: Prentice-Hall.
    1969   *Peasant wars of the twentieth century.* New York: Harper & Row.
Wolf, E. R., and E. C. Hansen
    1967   Caudillo politics: A structural analysis. *Comparative Studies in Society and History* **9:** 168–179.
Ziino, N.
    1911   *Latifondo e latifondismo: Studio di economia rurale.* Palermo: Orazio Fiorenza Editore.

Index

DATE DUE

MAY 13 '01			
			PRINTED IN U.S.A
GAYLORD			